The Psychology of Screenwriting

The Psychology of Screenwriting

Theory and practice

JASON LEE

BLOOMSBURY

LONDON • NEW DELHI • NEW YORK • SYDNEY

Bloomsbury Academic

An imprint of Bloomsbury Publishing Plc

1385 Broadway	50 Bedford Square
New York	London
NY 10018	WC1B 3DP
USA	UK

www.bloomsbury.com

First published 2013

Library of Congress Cataloging-in-Publication Data
Lee, C. J. P. (Charles Jason Peter)
The psychology of screenwriting : theory and practice / by Jason Lee.
pages cm
Includes bibliographical references and index.
ISBN 978-1-4411-2847-8 (pbk. : alk. paper)– ISBN 978-1-4411-0498-4 (hardcover : alk. paper) 1. Motion picture authorship. 2. Motion picture authorship–Psychological aspects.
I. Title.
PN1996.L3855 2013
808.2'3–dc23
2013004540

ISBN: HB: 978-1-4411-0498-4
PB: 978-1-4411-2847-8
e-pdf: 978-1-6235-6251-9
e-pub: 978-1-6235-6473-5

Typeset by Fakenham Prepress Solutions, Fakenham, Norfolk NR21 8NN
Printed and bound in the United States of America

Contents

Acknowledgements

I began teaching screenwriting at Barnet College in North London in the mid–1990s when I was doing my doctorate on film at the University of Sussex, so I would like to thank those at the college for that excellent opportunity. Growing up in Elstree, over the bridge from Borehamwood and the film and television studios, meant I lived and breathed cinema. I want to thank my family and friends for all their kindness. Specifically, once again, Rebecca Griffith has been really generous with her time in assisting with the final stages of this text, as has M. M. Lee. Thank you to Ben Richards and Sian James. A lot of the material here, especially concerning rewriting, I gathered from working closely with Colin Dyter at the University of Derby and I am more than grateful for this. Professors Neil Campbell and Paul Bridges, also at the University of Derby, have been very supportive, backing my applications for funding which enabled me to work on this book. Anne Wales, Head of the School of Humanities and Assistant Dean at the University of Derby, has also been very supportive. Working with students at the University of Derby has been stimulating and fun and I especially thank them. I would particularly like to thank Katie Gallof at Bloomsbury for her support over the time of this project.

006

Half of everything is luck, James.

007

And the other half?

006

Fate

GoldenEye
(directed by Martin Campbell and written by
Jeffrey Caine and Bruce Feirstein, 1995)

1

The psychology of identity

Introduction

The major thesis of this book is that all writing needs to appear as if it was meant to be, that is, predestined. The symbiotic relationship between written narratives and life is analysed and a plethora of paradoxes examined and extrapolated. The best screenwriting asks open-ended questions about the human situation. Mediated Fate, the final part of this book, lays bare the central paradoxes of the human situation. Through an exploration of the psychology of screenwriting, including theory and practice drawn from a wide variety of cognate disciplines, there is a focus on meaning and identity. An eclectic range of thinkers are utilized, from Friedrich Nietzsche to Erich Fromm and Gilles Deleuze, amongst others. Overall, this book should be of use for readers reflecting on screenwriting psychologically and philosophically, for the writing of screenplays, people interested in the psychology of narratives in general, and those who want to understand the human situation. I understand screenwriting as a discipline to be: a growing and diverse body of knowledge that can be studied as an entity in and of itself; plus a practice, a craft, that hopefully produces new and original screenplays.

Chapter 1 explores practically and philosophically whether a script is actually necessary and examines the historical development of film, psychology and writing. Chapter 2 focuses on the fundamental practices of screenwriting. Chapter 3 concerns the important area of character in relation to psychology, utilizing the Enneagram along with other tools such as myth. Chapter 4 is on writing good dialogue. Chapter 5 – Individuation – brings together important elements in the psychology of screenwriting. The term individuation is used in analytical psychology and, in this sense, the screenplay achieves its goal when, like the psyche, all important elements are individuated. Chapter 6, the conclusions, while incorporating essential practical elements on rewriting includes the wider philosophical analysis, summed up in the final part, Mediated Fate.

There is theory about the craft of writing and theory that is more philosophical and reflective, that is often called Theory with a capital, and various branches have their zealots. Students can be turned off by theory because it can be challenging, which is a good way to put it given it should challenge traditional thinking. Those outside academia, or who may have a myopic view of reality, have a tendency to dismiss it as mere 'mumbo-jumbo'.[1] Good theory enables us to question our thinking. While I do have running themes that I hope will be useful, I do not claim to have one indisputable theory or take and recognize with Gilles Deleuze that all theory should open up discourse rather than shut it down. With this in mind, screenwriting studies is combined here with more general writing studies, philosophy, film and literary studies, enhancing reflective creative thinking and practice.

The examples utilized are American, European and British which has its limitation and benefits. In an age of globalisation, where funding streams for films may stem from a variety of places and artists from a plethora of nations, these divisions can be contested. But I hope this Western film bias is in some ways compensated by an engagement with Eastern thought. And what are these examples exactly? Can we see films and fictional characters as actors, a type of aesthetic idealism, or would this make us fall into 'the abyss of a retrograde religion of art'.[2] Has the theorizing, practice or the product of art become a religion, the unholy or even holy trinity?

Along with the missionary zeal concerning theory, figures such as Jacques Derrida and Jean Baudrillard since the 1980s have been high-priests of literary and cultural theory, with Christopher Vogler and Robert McKee being the gurus of practical theory. Similarly, it is hard for those writing about the actual practice of art, in any form, not to take a missionary zeal and claim that art is about changing the world or our humanity in some form. This then makes the endeavour worthy, with a capital W, as if the art cannot exist for its own sake. Humanity must be improved by art to make it worthy, goes the dictum.

Defining what humanity actually is in the first place is a difficult task, although it is easier to speak of the 'human condition' today than it was in 1500 due to globalisation.[3] We may not agree on one definition of what it is to be human, but to see fictional forms as dynamic actors might not be so far-fetched. Thinking about scripts as dynamic actors as well enhances both the critical engagement and theorizing of them, their development and final product.

Creativity concerns breaking boundaries, stepping outside normal restrictive frameworks, transgressing established boundaries. For originality the rules need to be turned on their head. The problem with some books on screenwriting is that they offer the established framework, the rules, perhaps a step-by-step guide which can be useful, but that is it. Hopefully this book offers something more philosophical, reflecting on psychology and its relationship with on-going issues connected to choice, free will, ideology and elements of theology. Some of these areas might seem less important than others, particularly in such a relatively recent discipline such as screenwriting, more relevant to the Middle Ages than the contemporary world. Despite this, numerous popular feature films contain what can be termed salvation narratives, where a character who is psychologically wounded gains some form of wholeness. Through the stages of the narrative they come to be aware of their wound or, dare I say it, their 'sinfulness' and this may instigate heroic action, as in ages-old myths. The notion of a metaphysical wound is complex, but it concerns what alienates us from our deepest nature and stories can re-engage us with this.

There is a need to transgress to create, so it is easy to see the necessity of transgression. 'Sinfulness' can be interpreted to mean transgresson of a divine law. But when it is acknowledged this divine law is actually just the authority of society the question arises why conform to this. As Thomas Aquinas put it, 'God can never be insulted by us, except we act against our own well-being'.[4] The classic, anonymously written, fourteenth-century text *The Cloud of Unknowing* claimed that while initially nobody can meditate without looking on their sinfulness (woundedness), the key was to 'submerge meditation under the cloud of forgetting if he is ever to pierce that cloud of unknowing between himself and God'.[5]

Psychotherapist and philosopher Erich Fromm explained true hell is absolute separateness and this is overcome momentarily 'by submission or by domination or by trying to silence reason and awareness'.[6] Long term, however, this does not work, for overcoming is only reached through moving from egocentricity to oneness with the world. Only through psychological awareness can this movement take place. This is the situation all of us face. All of us are simultaneously in the world and yet alienated from it. Whenever there is a screenplay that concerns characters, and inevitably popular screenplays do in some form, then there will be a concern with psychology and identity. These are in turn concerned with moral choices, and these choices will concern oneness or separateness. This desire for unity can, of course, itself be seen as an illusion.

Thinking and doing are often separated in many cultures, viewed intrinsically as binary opposites. It is as if a separate mind does the former (thinking), with the body doing the latter (doing). This can be viewed as a hangover from the philosopher Descartes, although there are multifarious spin-offs. Some belief systems separate the mind from the body and also, mysteriously, position a soul in there, somewhere. Questioning these systems can be difficult, as they are innately tied up with the way people see themselves, their fundamental ontological essence. Often these apparently separate identities are difficult to define.

Once these zones are questioned the errors in this way of thinking are obvious. Even the body can now be extended out from a physical human form through technology and virtual means, so nothing is clear-cut. In the Western world the mind and body are continually thought of as Janus-faced, conflicting heads on diverse coins, as if one does not thoroughly involve and integrate with the other. Merely analysing what 'thinking' is leads to the conclusion that this might not be a purely mental process and binary oppositions need to be avoided between body and mind. As the Roman poet and philosopher Lucretius put it:

> In fact, we often see people collapse in consequence of the mind's terror. It is a simple matter for anyone to infer from this that the spirit is intimately linked with the mind, and that the spirit, once shaken by the mind's force, in its turn strikes the body and sets it in motion.[7]

This division is ultimately unhealthy. There are some other unhealthy divisions, such as in theory practice follows theory and in practice theory follows practice. In other words, you think about doing something then do it, which is the theory model. Or, you do something and think about what you have done, which is the practice model. Intuitively, deep down, it is easy to realize these two behaviours do not merely relate but co-exist and are entwined. Practice can be a form of theorizing just as theorizing can be a practice.

This book should be useful to those who want to write a screen 'play', as well as those who want to think about screenplays in a theoretical and philosophical sense as a work of literature and art in its wider context. I have used inverted commas above around the word 'play' as I want to emphasize this idea of play. I am not saying that the screenplay composed in images in your head appears magically without any effort whatsoever, or that large-scale filmmaking is not an industrial process full of hard work. But without imaginative play screenwriting becomes writing by numbers, devoid of creativity.

Both work and play have been thought of as activities that set us free. Free from *what* exactly is an interesting question. As Douglas Kellner has explained, Jürgen Habermas utilized Husserl's phenomenology to come up with the term 'life-world'. This consists of culture, society and personality, which are intruded upon by the 'system'. That the detrimental wielding of power will have an impact on psychology is not just an ideological or political position, but an empirical fact.[8] How art tackles this disruption is important for its deeper success. These themes are not new. Tolstoy tackled them in *Anna Karenina*, published in instalments from 1873 to 1877 in *The Russian Messenger*.

This story concerns the damaging impact of power and money, as the 2012 film version (directed by Joe Wright and written by Tom Stoppard), also shows. A bold assertion is to maintain that within the psychology of screenwriting, writers need to counteract psychopathologies. Societies and the conception of the arts and culture have metamorphosed since Theodor Adorno condemned the culture industry outright for promoting the ideas of purity and chastity, as if it was the same as religion. Adorno was here primarily referring to television, but with the popularity today of television channels such as Sky Movies, the World Cinema Channel, and so on, the separation between cinema and television is less clear-cut, not to mention the myriad of mobile devices for viewing films.

For Adorno, mass media's aim is to achieve 'integration' but he admits this is nothing new because conformity and conventionalism were elemental to early popular novels. What is new is that, 'these ideals have been translated into rather clear-cut prescriptions of what to do and what not to do'; and this moral framework is anathema because society always wins the battle between society and individual, and the 'outcome of conflicts is pre-established, and all conflicts are mere sham'.[9] Adorno made this point first in 1954, in *The Quarterly of Film, Radio and Television 8*, and was referring to an especially American form of mass media.[10] American film has been the most commercially successful globally. Centrality, as Edward Said called it in the early 1990s, still reigns supreme.[11] This virtually blocks any marginal discourse, with any difference in the mainstream political and media elite being spurious.

In the seven decades since Adorno was writing, while dominance in general is still there, so is more diversity and the society does not always win. Certain filmmakers and screenwriters have formulated an approach more akin to liberation. Even prior to the release of *JFK* (directed by Oliver Stone and co-written with Zachary Sklar, 1992), about the assassination of president Kennedy, the director Oliver Stone was attacked for altering 'reality'.[12] The fact that people think some fiction films are documentaries is disturbing. As T. S. Eliot put it in the poem *Burnt Norton*, 'human kind cannot bear very much reality'. Surely 'reality' is not scripted, and any script will be false?

Is a screenplay necessary at all, or is it part of our psychology to always stick to a script, a believable narrative, for the sake of continuity, to develop a self out of many divided selves? This may seem like an absurd question, but it is certainly not ridiculous to ask if there is a need for a screenplay as it is traditionally known, given their restriction to and on artistic experimentation. Behind the psychology of screenwriting is a basic human need to tell stories, to fantasize, but it can be easily argued that more honest fantasizing can go on when nothing is written down. What this is also really addressing is the power of the unconscious, an area we shall be exploring in more detail.

Ban the script?

The classic Mod film *Quadrophenia* (directed by Frank Rodam and co-written with Pete Townshend, Martin Stellman, and Dave Humphries, 1979, based on the rock opera, 1973) did not have a traditional script written prior to casting. This is partly why the film seems so authentic, the writing taking place organically, there being a dynamic two-way process of development between the actors and their characters as they grew. Even blockbusters such as *Minority Report* (directed by Steven Spielberg and written by Scott Frank and Jon Cohen, 2002, from a short story by Philip K. Dick, 1956) allow for improvisation and experimentation in the making of the film.

Early films did not have scripts and there have been many attempts by filmmakers to get back to what could be termed 'real' or 'authentic' filmmaking. One was the Dogme movement, founded in Denmark in 1995, which attempted to work against the grain of the 'pre-formed, the premeditated, and the commodified'.[13] Even with unscripted work, a larger philosophical question is whether it is ever possible to move away from the premeditated, something that *Minority Report* tackles and predictably confirms. This is a major Hollywood message – there is always a choice.

The Dogme movement aimed to take people back to the 'core', and 'back to the essence of our existence'.[14] This was an explicitly psychological aim as if somehow audiences had all been duped by the very medium they used to seek to take them back to this essence. Part of the idea was that film and television 'reality' had become so manipulated by editors, directors, and technicians, and this had to be subverted. Much of the new Dogme code was grounded in a sense of openness, of splitting open the illusion that surrounds the subversion of disbelief. Importantly, however, it was in the area of script-writing that there appeared a large conflict within the movement and nothing dogmatic.

There is nothing explicit about losing the script in the official manifesto and many Dogme films follow a clear-cut script. But for Lars von Trier, one of the movement's four founder members who swore an allegiance to a 'vow of chastity, the philosophy was initially to get totally away from the script'.[15] A set script that is religiously adhered to may thwart some of the spontaneity, but if the writer is of the quality of say David Mamet then there should not be a problem. A good writer can step out of their writing, and make it seem as if it is spontaneous and directly from the mouths, brains, and bodies, of the actors. Surely that is the point.

Mike Leigh is another filmmaker always mentioned in this context. Leigh works with the actors, the director and actor developing characters and scenarios, *Naked* (directed and written by Leigh, 1993) being a powerful example. In many ways *Naked* breaks the rules of screenwriting and becomes significant art, especially when David Thewlis' character Johnny goes on a rant about the apocalypse. As with many film directors and writers, Leigh began his life in the theatre and this monologue seems very stagey and unfilmic, breaking 'the rules'. His monologue does not really move the action forward, as it should in traditional screenwriting, it exists in and of itself as a poetic piece. The power of it is that it still is extremely authentic.

Films could be and are made minus a screenplay in the traditional sense but some form of screenwriting would still occur, whether this was merely in the process of the shooting of the film, or in the heads of all those involved. An interesting way of bringing about spontaneity is none of the actors knowing the overall story. Even if the film was without dialogue, somewhere there would be a blueprint as to how the film was going to be made. When those writers who became the directors of the new wave were writing, 'they were not writing about cinema, they were not making a theory out of it, it was already their way of making films'.[16]

Our traditional idea of what a script or film is needs to be re-assessed. Looking back, the high age of theory was the 1980s, as well-satirized in the novels of David Lodge. Then in the 1990s the questions became 'what's left of theory?' or, more importantly, what is the use of theory. This had been debated vociferously in the previous decade. Back then the idea was that critical and cultural theory would resurrect philosophy, which was seen to be in a dead end, and the 'practice' in this context was the practice of political engagement.[17] Theory is a form of 'cognitive estrangement', meaning, the point of theory is to try and separate the 'us' from 'our' thoughts, so eventually it is seen that the origin of our thoughts is not ourselves, and furthermore, it 'robs us of the vain notion that we exist in the form we think we do'.[18] Theory attacks this popular lived script that the self and thought exist in the manner that is commonly accepted.

In this instance then, part of the game in the practice of theory is to demystify and unveil. But in all honesty how many people have read theorists and become even more mystified, seeing it as the serpent chasing its tail? Maybe that is part of the game, so the practice of theory has a certain pleasure, adding more and more layers of mystification. Professor Stanley Fish, who apparently was the model for Professor Zap in David Lodge's novel *Changing Places* (1975), commented that theory 'relieves me of the obligation to be right ... and demands only that I be interesting'.[19]

Derrida is demonized as the man who demolished meaning and truth. The reality is, however, that when one narrative is not necessarily privileged over another we are moving towards equality and this needs celebrating not denigrating. For Derrida every form of presence, such as logocentricism and foundationalism, is rejected just as Buddhism attacks Vedantic thought.[20] After contesting the notion that there is a need to get away from theory and back to people, the answer to the question of what is left of theory may be gained from, or at least addressed to, popular culture itself.[21] In this sense the film is the theory, or the screenplay is the theory of the film or the screenplay is the theory, regardless of any reference to any film. But if the screenplay is exemplary it dissects its essence, in the process of its unveiling, theorizing and criticising itself seamlessly.

The twentieth century can be viewed as the century of psychology and film and their nineteenth-century origins are symbiotic. The heavyweight philosopher of the latter half of the nineteenth century, Friedrich Nietzsche, had called for an art form similar to dream that was all-encompassing.

> *Dream and responsibility.* – You are willing to assume responsibility for everything! Except, that is, for your dreams! What miserable weakness, what lack of consistent courage! Nothing is *more* your own than your dreams! Nothing *more* your own work! Content, form duration, performer, spectator – in these comedies you are all of this yourself![22]

Free will, responsibility and choice are all components of this discourse 'the wise Oedipus was right, that we really are not responsible for our dreams – but just as little for our waking life, and that the doctrine of freedom of will has human pride and feeling of power for its father and mother?'[23] This is of interest to screenwriting because films that seem as if they had to be, that they were predestined if you will, have the most impact. Despite his belief that unity is impossible film fulfils Nietzsche's desire that the subject and the object can be traversed; paradoxically for him the whole knowledge of art is illusory.[24]

Nietzsche the philosopher saw himself as a psychologist and suggested that an art form akin to film was the way of redeeming the world via illusion. This new art form was then functioning as a type of mass psychologist. What this means is that there is an illness for which the philosopher-psychologist is offering to provide a cure. Emotion and memory are central areas in psychology of course but, paradoxically, the fact that details are not remembered accurately is beneficial. Anything else would make life intolerable, as the story 'Funes the Memorious' by Jorge Luis Borges makes clear. In the story, Ireno is paralysed in a riding accident but it also makes his memory infallible. This is a nightmare because the ability to think comes from our ability to generalize.[25]

The way memory functions can be equated with the process of film but it does not take an invocation of anti-Oedipus theory to see that to define desire as that which is natural is limiting. It is limiting for both desire and the natural. There is the comic and despairing mantra that other than desire what else is there. But if it is 'the other' that we desire to capture then, again paradoxically, we can only hope this is unreachable, for if we reached it then there would be nothing.

In some senses the morality of screenwriting is the psychology of screenwriting but this does not mean, as Adorno maintained, that all popular culture is just moving the individual to agree with the status quo. Sometimes attacks on society and the way individuals live can be slipped in. This is not the same as saying the psychology of screenwriting is the morality of the screenwriter. Pulitzer Prize winner Wallace Stegner disagreed with Oscar Wilde's notion that if someone is a poisoner it has no impact on their writing. He maintained most artists to be flawed but they should make an effort not to be.[26] As novelist Anita Brookner explained, for a novel to remain pure it has to project a moral puzzle, and anything else is not really substantial, it is just fooling around.[27] There is nothing quintessentially wrong with playfulness of course, for this is paramount to experimentation and creation. But as writers of screenplays and watchers of films there is a need for deeper questions to be raised. What does this tell us about the human situation?

Writing for popular narrative film, for better or for worse, is primarily concerned with character. Having stars attached to a film can be negative as well as positive. Writing 'for' an actor can also have both negative and positive elements. Fundamentally, the essence of producing good writing is understanding psychology, your own and that of others, the two being indivisible. Otherwise the writer produces flat caricatures that are just moving through films, without any depth, unbelievable to an audience. This tells us nothing about the human condition and is destructive. You may have seen at least a few films that do just that. Think of a few now.

Character is plot and plot character. When someone is spoken of as being a 'character' in real life it is meant they have something about them that is different, larger than life, or at least an edge that enables us to question what it means to be human. Certain types of dull characters can be interesting in the right hands for these dull characters are 'characters', meaning they are eccentric.[28] An example of this is Ed Cran (Billy Bob Thornton) in *The Man Who Wasn't There* (directed and written by Joel and Ethan Coen, 2001). More interesting filmmakers and writers, such as David Lynch and Jim Jarmusch, play with characterization and character through enabling the film audience to question the very essence of what it is that makes us human. They transcend our traditional notions concerning human psychology.

Even in the second decade of the twenty-first century there is still the debatable idea that human identity is fixed and permanent and that characters are unchangeable. More maverick yet highly popular filmmakers, such as Lynch and Jarmusch, question this essentialism. And, with the Deleuzean idea of the 'aesthetics of the false', there is the notion of exploring 'real emotions through false images'.[29] This is not denying psychology, quite the opposite. This form of writing and filmmaking makes a form of psychological insight the very essence of a film. Again, this exploration of the human condition and what I call mediated fate is central here. Ultimately this is liberating, as with all original art works. In Lynch's films characters often merge, or transform, without any traditional signals or warnings, this being one of his main signature traits.

In *Mulholland Drive* (directed and written by David Lynch, 2001) an innocent young girl seeks fame as an actress in Los Angeles. Naomi Watts in this case is playing two people – Betty Elms/Diane Selwyn. Not surprisingly, Lynch has claimed that mystery is better than psychology, because for Lynch psychology destroys the magic.[30] In this instance the word psychology could be replaced by the words theory or criticism or thinking. Audiences watching Lynch films might be left asking what is happening, as it is not clear-cut, and the films themselves may or may not provide some sort of insight. A straightforward psychological framework for analysing anything will be limiting. In the context of psychology and psychiatry as they are commonly understood, Lynch is correct. Reducing everything to a single neurosis actually limits potential for the infinite, working against the mystery which is fundamental to storytelling, art in general, and any form of psychological development. The cure is often the illness; the illness often the cure.

Identity, history and psychology

The history of the development of cinema parallels the history of the development of psychology. For Walter Benjamin film made possible a 'heightened presence of mind' and demolished the religion of art with its high-priests and exclusivity.[31] The strange paradox of Lynch's films and those like them is that they encourage not just the psychoanalytical readings that film theorists love, but a form of questioning of psychological identity, going against the grain of any easy psychological labelling. It would be so easy for us to move in a world where everyone could be labelled a particular type and then everyone would know how to relate to them in a particular way. Realistically, many of us do this anyway, positioning people in ways that relate to gender, sexuality, class, ability or disability, ethnicity and so on. Complex psychological frameworks which I shall come onto, such as the Enneagram, should not be mistakenly used in that manner. Similarly, it would be so easy to write a screenplay following obvious archetypes for characters, for example – a form of writing by numbers. What makes the work of certain directors and screenwriters far more interesting is that they challenge the usual assumptions and break out of the model. Obviously there will be fewer films made in this mode, as they worry studio executives who want movies made in the same manner, which in this respect proves Adorno was correct.

A great example of breaking down psychology and types is the master-piece *Dead Man* (directed and written by Jim Jarmusch, 1995). Johnny Depp plays an accountant William Blake, who is mistaken for the poet William Blake by a Native American called 'Nobody' (Gary Falmer), a nomenclature he prefers over his Native American name which literally means 'he who talks loud saying nothing'. There is a paradox here as with all good storytelling. Film has led us to question the very notion of what it means to be human, along with identity and fixed notions of psychology, while at the same time re-enforcing it, with film writing exploring and not always subverting identity and psychology. There is still a great deal of misunderstanding and a lack of understanding of the unconscious. Despite continued disputes as to its nature, since Freud most people working in this area agree that the uncon-scious is 'the true psychical reality' as he put it.[32] As clinical psychologist Frank Tallis has explained, in neuroscience up until relatively recently the idea was that there was a 'central executive' in the brain. For Tallis, this is almost along the same lines as Descartes' theory of consciousness who claimed in the seventeenth century that this was situated in the pineal gland. The brain functions with numerous cells, or sub-systems but none of these are actually conscious. Tallis uses the analogy of identity being to the brain as the shape of the wave is to seawater. In this sense, for many neuroscientists ego does not really exist. The sense of self we share is an 'illusion' and we as we know ourselves 'have only a feeble claim on existence'.[33] Science actually has no need for the idea of an inner self but many would consider the idea of doing away with this notion anathema, leading to a destruction of the moral order.[34]

Literary critic Elaine Showalter has maintained that syndromes concerning misidentity, such as Capgras syndrome, have taken hold and there has been a fundamental shift in America since 9/11, with claims of multiple personality having diminished. Doctors and other experts have collaborated with patients to construct variations on this new diagnosis. This has various explanations depending on your approach, be it neurological, psychological, psychoanalytical, or sociological. In many cases delusional people believe their relative has been replaced by a machine or has taken the form of an animal, Showalter claiming this is not just the current zeitgeist but forming an epidemic. Showalter has outlined a whole cultural history of the subject in the twentieth century. The trajectory spans from the fiction of Shirley Jackson; to Jack Finney's novel *The Body Snatchers* (1956, serialized in *Colliers Magazine*, 1954), with its various versions and spin-offs; to Ira Levin's satirical novel *The Stepford Wives* (1972) and two film versions (Brian Forbes, 1975; Frank Oz, 2004); to Dennis Lehane's 2003 novel and film *Shutter Island* (Martin Scorsese, 2010); to references to the novel *Echo Maker* (Richard Powers, 2006), where a man believes his sister is an imposter, Showalter reflects on the wider political situation asking: where do you go when all your references and signposts have been wiped out after 9/11, when you know the government is lying, that there were no weapons of mass destruction? A significant number of Americans believe Barack Obama is an imposter and these discourses have replaced alien abduction stories and many other fantasies.[35]

Similarly, writer Will Self builds on our cultural history of imposters, doubles, deceivers, and invaders, most famously *The Strange Case of Dr Jekyll and Mr Hyde* (Robert Louis Stevenson, 1886), not forgetting Shakespeare's comedies, such as *Twelfth Night* (1601). In reality the question over an authentic core self stays unanswered, and is absurd to many postmodern critics, although some psychological techniques, such as psychosynthesis, see it as central to well-being. Even though Britain's most populist philosopher recognizes our tenuous hold on this authentic self, for him there is no doubt that it is there and should be sought.[36] Traditional ideas of what a human being is have been transformed and writers need to address this in their work.

For Nietzsche, 'I and the Self must be replaced by an undifferentiated abyss, but this abyss is neither an impersonal not an abstract Universal beyond individuation.'[37] Deleuze explains that this 'I and the Self' are the abstract universal; this must be replaced through individuation in the world of Dionysius but the individual is still beyond 'I and Self'. Many writers and teachers of writing have emphasized ultimately that 'the problem is we think we exist'.[38] Paradoxically, writing on and for the internet concurrently enables people to trace, track and sometimes stalk others but also is in many ways more ephemeral. Despite issues around socioeconomic deprivation and limitations, life has for many become more transient, less fixed and restricted by prescribed class, gender, sexual, religious, and physical boundaries. But, even if 'I' speak as 'I' in my writing, it is important to remember the words are not me but simply my thoughts and emotions at the time of writing. We need to remember we change every minute and to not get so wrapped up in our writing, thinking we are one with it or admiring it so much it then becomes impossible to edit.[39] Because writers need to look at the world twice, seeing everything a second time, writing can be a political act, because it concerns entering into the details of a situation, rather than being caught up in the emotions.[40]

Writers gain ideas and develop them in multifarious ways and it is up to the writer to individually establish what works best. All writers draw on a combination of their own experience and their imagination. Interestingly, the sciences and the arts are not as separate as some still believe. The English poet Coleridge, a master of the imagination, has been credited for introducing 'psychology' as a word into the English language, imported from the German.[41] The psychology of screenwriting involves in many respects the psychology of the screenwriter and characters we create are going to contain elements of ourselves. For Nietzsche we see in things only our self, so any objectivity in the writing process, or even in the final edit, might be difficult. Of course such an awareness of this will help but it needs to go further.

In a study of psychotherapy by psychiatrist Arthur Deikman, differences between the 'object self' and the 'observing self' are noted. The object self thinks it is clear that each of us is a finite biological entity that can communicate but that is essentially alone. The observing self is, 'the transparent center', aware 'prior to thought, feeling and action'.[42] As Deikman shows, it is not 'I think therefore I am', but 'I am aware therefore I am'. And if all of this is prior to thought, feeling and action, this radically subverts our notion of self.

What drives a human being, if such an entity even exists, as it is not even agreed upon what a human being is? The humble service of others, out of deep love and personal sacrifice, placing others first and being a friend to the world, what in Buddhism is termed a bodhisattva, and the desire to create meaning and purpose. The craving for power, acknowledgement from others, ambition, obsession with money, and possession by these cravings, and the need to have affirmation and fame, stemming from: feelings of inferiority and unworthiness; feelings of superiority and entitlement; a pre-programmed drive.

These are obvious drives and it can be far more complex. All of these elements can work symbiotically. Why should there be a choice or even a difference between being absorbed in the One and removing the self and being a self and ignoring the whole? The approach that sees others as equal, if not more important, that places our self out of the situation, that plays with the notion that the self is an illusion anyway, can understand character and the psychology of screenwriting deeply. Not only do we walk in other peoples' shoes through empathy but we are one with them. This, in itself, may occur in the very act of writing. Like acting, writing is playing a role, taking us out of our self and placing us more in an omniscient position, like God. The psychology of screenwriting is in many ways a non-psychology of the self. An awareness of self therefore needs to be had before this is overcome and every step in life involves elements of putting ourselves, or others, first. Seeing ourselves as one with others, there ought to be no contradictions; but only a dead man is without contradictions. Essentially it is the stuff of contradictions that makes good drama, characters and good writing.

> Humanism fails because it reduces difference to the same, thereby obliterating specific, local and contingent elements in the name of a universal principle from which humanity is said to draw its essence. The failure to live up to ideals is the *crisis* of modernity: the inability of power regimes to deliver universal values and justice, as promised by the Enlightenment and as determined in the theoretical articulations of both empirical and rationalist modes of subject formation.[43]

This obsession in the theoretical discourse of many divergent thinkers, such as Alain Badiou, Terry Eagleton and Jean Baudrillard with the same, forces us to confront our relationship with power and the status quo. Do we ever have individuality? To tell stories that are meaningful we need to go deep within what it means to be human, what makes us human. People often function in the real world as automatons and caricatures, which is part of our fear and fascination with cyborgs. While it is the uniqueness of humans we are interested in, the human concerns difference and identity. Individuality can be seen as a form of infinity.[44]

If we truly had what could be termed a postmodern position on identity – nothing fixed at all about who or what we are – then writing characters that have depth might be difficult. We can subvert our subjects and do so wittily. We see this done bluntly in the hellish film *Natural Born Killers* (directed by Oliver Stone and co-written with Dave Veloz and Richard Rutowski, 1994). Quentin Tarantino, who wrote an early version of the script, chose to have his name removed from the final version; interestingly, there was potentially something more subversive and comic in the original script.

The film plays with the notion of stereotype, of two-dimensional celebrity and fame-seeking culture, and literally moves into cartoon. The mass media in the film get blamed for glorifying violence, but the back story, the element which explains the psychology of the two central characters, is that

Mickey (Woody Harrelson) and Malory (Juliette Lewis) Knox were abused in childhood. Aetiology, cause and effect, is outlined, but we need to question this relationship given that the film was released at the exact time juries and judges were dismissing cases of child abuse.[45] Whether the film is making a mockery of trying to understand character at all is a good question. The characters do not seem to be really grappling with moral choices because they have stepped beyond that zone in a Nietzschean fashion. The unsubtle point is that in this mass-media, mass-consumption, and celebrity-driven world of the 1990s, morals are anathema. While it is an unsubtle point, it is a good one.

The moronic fans of Mickey and Mallory adore them, suggesting that there is no choice about this and there is no free will. Whether it is the Beatles or anyone else, fans can be made to love anyone or anything. There is a deeper point here. 'We obey orders that are issued from below the threshold of awareness, and we obey like automata.'[46] We do not have to be a follower of Freud to realize that behaviour is first and foremost determined by the unconscious.[47] With reference to Daniel Dennett, Tallis noted that only a theory that explains conscious events in terms of unconscious events could explain consciousness.

The killer couples' love for each other is all that matters but it is hard to know whether we are supposed to accept this or understand this as mocking this kind of obsessive romantic love, as portrayed in the Oliver Stone screenplay *A True Romance* (directed by Tony Scott, 1991). Despite capturing the zeitgeist, the themes in *Natural Born Killers* are perennial. The audience is asked to see the bad deeds of the protagonists as inevitable, the script is predetermined. However, whether the audience revel in these deeds or not is a matter of choice. Anthropologist, novelist and philosopher George Bataille has come to be known as the King of Transgression. If we consider the complexities of postmodern identity and violence it is dangerous to ignore his work. There is a difficulty with this love affair which theorists have with Bataille, given there is no escaping his own 'committed affinity for orgy, torture, and bodily suffering, as well as his obsessive insistence on eroticism understood in terms of violence and violation'.[48] Whether writing should serve an ethical purpose, such as enhancing humanity, is debatable. It is not debatable that it should provide us with a deeper understanding of the human situation.

People in real life and in fiction develop, or not, through significant choices. This is far from a linear process and can be as complex as you want it to be. Popular does not have to be dumb, or dumber, as screenwriters like Charlie Kauffman have shown. But pivotal moments in our scripts are where a character makes a choice that will change them and which offers potential and hope. Without potential and hope all dedication and talent are a waste. Even though in *Leaving Las Vegas* (directed and written by Mike Figgis, 1995, from the semi-autobiographical novel by John O'Brien, 1990), Ben Sanderson (Nicolas Cage) is on a mission to drink himself to death, which seems hopeless, the hope and potential is there with his relationship with Sera (Elisabeth Shue) the prostitute. In this manner, art is an education and the subtlety of how this is achieved marks a great script out from a mediocre one.

In *An Education* (directed by Lone Scherfig and written by popular novelist Nick Hornby, 2010), sixteen-year-old Jenny (Carey Mulligan) is academically bright and beautiful but stultified, living with atypical parents in a boring suburb of England, attending a strict school in the 1960s. Seduced by an older man, she gives up her academic education for him. When Jenny loses her virginity in Paris, the now so-called worldly educated Jenny remarks drily how strange it is that romance and love are written about so extensively yet sex is over in seconds. The Paris setting is apt, given the existentialist question: what is the point of pleasure once it is satiated? The difference between fiction and reality are unveiled. Jenny gains the knowledge of forbidden fruit, an education of sorts that makes her unripe, fallen fruit, learning that another type of knowledge contained in hard work and study offers far more sustenance. We may baulk at this traditional promotion of the Protestant work ethic, but this is a clear example of where the moral and the psychological are entwined. Through this understanding she grows up. Luckily, a teacher who has seen her potential agrees to take her on again after Jenny discovers her seducer is married and she is not allowed to return to school. The morality is emphasized. Psychology and morality are interwoven in life, as they are in screenwriting.

'Good' writing usually means writing that has an aesthetic value and this in many ways is arbitrary and depends on taste. Writing that is 'good', e.g. writing that upholds certain virtues, morals and truths, is another way of interpreting 'good'. In a theological context, it is not just actions that are judged for, according to 1 Thessalonians 5.22, it is important to, 'abstain from all appearance of evil'. Virtue then must be projected at all times and this includes through words. This concept of virtue has a smattering of didacticism about it. Nobody really wants art that lectures and true art asks more questions than it solves. Despite Nietzsche, relativism and postmodernism, the notion of goodness still exists and many films do contain this idea. Conversely, film is frequently still perceived as slightly perverse, a wicked indulgence, entertainment that is just a diversion from the so-called real world. This might be due to its concern with 'appearance', with the idea that even contemplating so-called evil deeds in artistic form has a damaging impact. Practice is theory and theory is practice, but in the academy it is still thought more rigorous to teach the criticism of writing rather than writing itself, the latter often condemned as self-indulgence or mere entertainment and not hard core. The elitism of thinking still reigns over doing.

The eighteenth-century author Dr Samuel Johnson declared the purpose of the novel was twofold: firstly, to entertain, through helping us to escape into other worlds, and secondly, to teach us how to endure being human. Writing is concerned with bringing us back to what it really means to be human, enabling us to find a higher humanity. It is easy to forget what being human is and that great art humanizes us. This divide with the novel is commonly there in film e.g. entertainment on the one hand in the American model; meaning on the other hand in the European framework. While this bifurcation is spurious, in Buddhist terms all life is suffering, all life delusion. The stories told or presented help humans deal with this illusion. Fiction is the greatest truth. Through our unrealities reality is gained, through our fictions the fictions played in reality are explored and exploded. So seeing through the game helps in playing the game. We are dealt our cards, we take a gamble every step of the way and then we deal with the illusion.

For screenwriter, critic and filmmaker Jean Luc Godard, cinema is truth, twenty-four times a second. Cinema is also closely akin with death and therefore sex. We make attachments and then we deal with losing attachments, the two inextricably linked. At its very heart all human psychology is as simple, and as complex, as that. In the viewing of a film we are creating attachments and losing them, often twenty-four times a second. Posing a primary purpose of film, such as to make us feel, is absurd, for how can we ever say there is a primary one and only purpose. But we cannot step outside the psychological. The psychological will involve all the elements that drive us and we want a film to engage us and some people want this to be at a deep level. Alternatively we may not want it to make us feel or think more deeply. During the early years of cinema people used to show up at the cinema and take a potluck approach to what they might see, the random nature revealing that it was not so much the product itself as the cinematic process, the experience. During the Golden Years of Hollywood, up until the 1950s, it was common to go to the cinema twice a week, so it did not matter so much if one film was a hit and the other a turkey, plus, all features had an accompanying film. The plethora of reviews on the internet has lowered the excitement of cinema, as if in our risk-free culture people must be prepared for anything.

Many psychotherapists use film with their patients, often to enable them to access feelings, and psychiatrists use fiction films in their training. On the other hand, repressing feelings might take place for a very good reason, and if watching a film drags up something psychologically this could cause problems. Film has been known to drive people psychotic but the psychosis must have been latent already. The first psychological laboratory was founded at Leipzig University in 1879, during the era of the birth of cinema, and there has since been a symbiotic relationship between film and psychology. Two years earlier Englishman Edward Muyerbridge developed his *Horse in Motion*, or *Sallie Gardener at a Gallop*, revealing that all the hooves of a horse leave the ground when galloping. There is no narrative in this film but we might create one around the film. Film historians usually put the birth of film decades later than this. Debates over what is a narrative continue. This really comes down to what is considered to be a story.

While there are chronological links between photography, film and psychology as disciplines, there are more nuanced relationships. With the development of the close-up, cinema enabled audiences to view the human more. The stillness of screen acting and slower pace of dialogue allowed for a closer engagement with the human than stage. Concurrently, due to conventions of narrative and genre, complexities within the human psyche were overlooked. During the 1920s sound and colour were introduced. Not only did films start to generate the reality they reflected, films also constructed the inner psychological world of their audiences, which manifested itself in outer behaviour; with the development of the cinematic society, truth became impermanent.[49] Screenwriting that dealt with this impermanence became the most profound, such as Charlie Kaufman's *Synecdoche New York* (directed and written by Kaufman, 2008).

In popular mythology some indigenous tribes find photography problematic as they have the belief that to be caught on camera steals souls. Everywhere the love affair with the camera is Janus-faced. In *Downcast Eyes* (1993) Martin Jay revealed how influential thinkers attacked occularcentrism and how film and other visual media was interpreted as being detrimental to the human. Since the 1980s it has become popular to talk about the post-human subject, as if we are in an era when the human has been surpassed due to our relationship with technology. Humans are jumping the gun, given there is a very limited understanding of the essential components of human life, such as what impacts on how the brain functions. Subverting expectations in real life is something incorporated within films constantly while audiences, paradoxically, also want their expectations confirmed. Audiences expect it, like the traditional 14-line sonnet, with the final line offering a reversal of fortunes. This screen device could be said to be part of real life, despite sometimes being denounced as a contrived happy ending.

Life itself is a complex narrative, not an either or situation, and films, along with computer games, have played a large part in developing our understanding

THE PSYCHOLOGY OF IDENTITY

of contemporary lives as narratives and as a game. From *Tron* (directed and written by Stephen Lisberger, 1982); to *Lawnmower Man* (directed and written by Brett Leonard, 1992), to *The Matrix Trilogy* (directed and written by Andy and Larry Wachowski, 1999, 2003), and numerous remakes, spin-offs and imitations, these films reflect not only on the problems of the individual in a simulated world but on the belief that all reality is a construct within the mind, that all is manufactured, and that identity itself is an illusion.

This type of thinking was partially initially informed by the existential movement of the middle of the twentieth century, which at times verges on nihilism, but goes way beyond it because even phenomenology is questioned, there being nothing that can be known, not even the self. While this may move down a route of dangerous non-meaning, where anything is permitted, it also frees the whole conceptual framework of what is known as human, which, after all, is a category itself without any agreed-on notion of what the human is. How can reality be known in such a world, and does such a thing exist, can anyone know anyone else, let alone themselves?

We will end up stepping out of a cinema or turning away from the page we are reading with the rhetorical question 'so what' unless what we see and read takes us deeper into understanding what it is to be human. It might be concluded that humans, as the subject, do not create the object but, vice versa, it is the object that creates the subject, the text creating the reader, and the film the viewer. As with any form of writing, the writer must write to find out what they are thinking about and this deepens the writer and forms them as a human being. The screenwriter does not create the screenplay, therefore, but the screenplay creates the screenwriter. If it does not create itself then it will seem false. All writing needs to appear as if it was meant to be. While the screenplay goes through many re-writes, often at the hands of numerous people, initially, even if it is an adaptation, it is an idea that is being worked on, worked out and worked through. Usually nobody knows what they are trying to say until they get it down on paper.

The screenwriter might make it their mission to show the individual as a free-willed person, who can make and take moral choices, battling against the system. This occurs in the cult 1960s television series *The Prisoner*, where a secret agent who has resigned is then kept imprisoned in a strange town, isolated from everywhere. *The Prisoner* series, remade in 2010, implies both that there could be free will and that there might not be, that the either or situation does not have to be the case, even in the same show. Both series suggest that it does not matter whether the individual has free will or not, in the bigger picture, as ultimately we are not in control. We can ask therefore can we have both free will and no choice, or is either a state of mind? In ancient belief systems, like Buddhism, an essential tenet is breaking through the illusion.

> Whatever appears to us, we perceive as existing from its own side. This is mistaken appearance. We perceive "I" and mine as existing from their own side and our mind grasps strongly at this appearance, believing it to be true – this is the mind of self-grasping ignorance.[50]

If everything is one as this suggests, and as has been referred to previously with reference to Erich Fromm, this relates to how we write. All our writing will be about us, as it is filtered through our own mind, but then it is about others, as there might be no separation. Any kind of opposition is purely in the mind which must be overcome.[51] We might gain emotional intensity from real-life events, and 'based on a true story', regardless of whether it is or not, often helps. But it is important when writing to not stick so closely to real-life events that we cannot divorce ourselves from their reality. Wordsworth famously maintained that even poetry takes its origin from emotion recollected in tranquillity, so this distance, eventually in the editing process at least, needs to be maintained.

Ideas may or may not come easily to us, bursting through like a blinding light, or a faint glimmer under a door. Some fortunate people get good ideas continually but often the trouble is that this is all they remain. Having ideas is one thing; it takes discipline to develop them or to even simply sift the wheat from the chaff. Often it is only substantial distance from the original spark of an idea and time that really shows us whether an idea is outstanding and worth putting all of our being into. We may not have the time to decipher which idea to work on and have to just begin with our desire to write. As well as our own imagination and experience, second-hand sources such as the real-world news, research into literature and other films, more objective observations in life, writing exercises, snippets of overheard dialogue and conversations, offer a constant access to interesting ideas.

So how much energy must be put into filtering these ideas and what makes a good idea for a screenplay? As with any piece of creative writing the important question to ask is 'so what' and this is linked to a number of other very powerful questions, such as, 'do we really care enough'? There needs to be an emotional shift, because without it nobody is really going to care and we are just going through the motions, the actions, rather than revealing the emotions. Where is the moral dilemma? People go to see drama, on stage or on film, to be moved. This does not have to be warp factor five and earth shattering, and always about the end of a life, country, planet, universe, although many contemporary films are. It might be very subtle, about the ending or the start of a relationship. But if your idea contains no emotional shift then you probably need to discard it. This is one way of filtering out your best ideas and beginning to work playfully, but in a disciplined manner. A lot of people want to be writers but, weirdly, they do not take the time to plan or structure their ideas, or even to write.

A writer needs to approach things for the first time, each time.[52] This is about moving away from a linear sense of time and seeing each event as unique in and of itself; this is central for the writer as this will be key for the reader, who wants to reconnect with humanity. This is more easily said than done, as it is easier to just always see things the same way. For Natalie Goldberg the best way to generate ideas is to start with what is in front of you, and then even if you do not know all the details about it, own the details. There is also the notion that our best ideas will be our obsessions. If we are obsessed with a sport, such as hockey, then why not write about it? Something only becomes a cliché if someone else could have said it. What is your own take on it? This comes from a great deal of practice and then confidence grows. For Goldberg, nobody owns capability, it is just a matter of tapping into it, and you learn through the process of writing. She quotes Katagiri Roshi, 'Capability is like a water table below the surface of the earth.'[53] With hard work the capability comes through you. Interestingly, this smashes the Western myth that people are born with talent that they alone 'possess'. This could just as easily be viewed as an Eastern and romantic myth, but at least it allows us to recognize that, whether talent and ideas come our way or not, there is no need to get possessive about the process.

There is a healthy aspect to obsession but some forms such as the novel encouraged an obsessive element in the writer, and in the reader.[54] During his period, and perhaps since, no other individual was studied so closely by psychiatrists and those interested in psychology than the writer Émile Zola. Zola himself constructed huge dossiers on his own work and there is no doubt that creative writing has given us the structure of the 'case study' as it is known today. Lennard Davis has cogently argued for the origin of the scientific case study as stemming from the novel. Science and even being human in modern life involves being obsessive in relation to everything, including work and sexuality. There is a circuitous path, 'from science to work, work to body, body to mind, and then back to science', this being 'part of the obsessional structure of the nineteenth century'.[55] This use of a case study, 'found its fulfilment in the work of Freud and Josef Breuer, having been previously developed in the laboratory of the novel'.[56] While creativity is frequently associated with chaos and openness, Zola's mania and productivity seems to stem from the opposite, a psychological obsession with control.

Film goes hand in hand with modernity and its relationship with the novel is still obsessively debated. In the nineteenth century, questions were asked by physicians and artists as to whether Zola was a great genius or a graphomaniac, along with debates over whether disease was obligatory for genius and the very foundation of modernity.[57] In the main, Freud's 'discoveries' were the reworking and systemisation of the work of others, as has been clearly documented.[58] For Zola, for Charcot, and for Freud, analysis 'revealed the fixed attention and desires of patients and characters while it disguised the position of the observer'.[59] In the academy the arts have often tried to play catch-up with the sciences, usually because of funding sources, and governmental interference in universities and institutes. Here we see the foundation of a 'science' stemming from literary sources. Indeed, one of Freud's greatest gifts, if not his greatest, was his literary prowess in his writing up of his 'case studies', working like a literary critic, analysing his characters, and drawing on a vast range of literature in the sciences and arts. Just as literary endeavour, from novel writing to screenwriting, became an obsession, so did psychology, psychiatry, and neurology.

Marketing campaigners often promote films as 'magical' and magic is a popular theme in film and the 'cult' of psychoanalysis is often equated to magic. Magic has always been a dominant factor in society and popular culture and the 'theatre' of the Roman Catholic Church, particularly in areas of Europe such as Portugal and Spain, had to absorb 'black magic' to remain popular.[60] Freud's obsession with psychoanalysis was obviously not purely scientific, the 'thinking was more or less magical', a 'glorified version of idée fixe'.[61] Because Freudian developments have dominated so much thinking in the Western world it is difficult for many to think outside of this discourse. Freud's system is based traditionally on representation rules. There is more than this, however. What we could have is an 'ontological unconscious', which is now on a plane of 'virtual memory'.[62] In practice this means that instead of representing and reproducing the past, which has a Freudian overtone, and is very predetermined, there is a movement towards new presents/futures, which is far more refreshing and creative.[63] For Deleuze the individual life moves towards a 'pure event' which is, 'freed from accidents of internal and external life, that is, from the subjectivity and objectivity of what happens'.[64] This pure event can be equated with the writing process previously explored.

Consider Erich Fromm's thesis that in the 'having mode' – the one that dominates many societies, and includes accumulating things, like possessions, even memories and so on – there is only time: the past, present and future. While a three-act screenplay will not necessarily follow a linear trajectory in this order, most contain elements of past, present and future. They therefore confirm and promote this trajectory, in a restrictive fashion. In this mode we are what we have gained in the past and we are the past. Interestingly, given that Fromm was a psychoanalyst, this is part and parcel of the cult formed by Freud. This, Fromm has argued in *To Have or To Be*, is limiting, given that even though we 'have' a future, in a similar manner it will be limited to what we 'have', and what we 'have' will have us, possess us. The present is within this limited framework, where the past and future meet. In the far deeper 'being mode', being is not outside time, but it is not governed by time. For Fromm the artist's vision transcends time and for thinkers writing happens in time but conceiving ideas is outside.

> It is the same for every manifestation of being. The experience of loving, of joy, of grasping truth does not occur in time, but in the here and now. The *here and now is eternity*, i.e. timelessness. But eternity is not, as popularly misunderstood, indefinitely prolonged time.[65]

Screenwriters like Guillermo Arriaga, Paul Haggis, David Hare, Charlie Kaufman, Bràulio Mantovani and Christopher Nolan are furthering screenwriting by pushing the boundaries of narrative, often in relation to time, having created complex scripts, such as *21 Grams* (directed by Alejandro González Iñárritu and written by Guillermo Arriaga, 2003), *Crash* (directed by Paul Haggis and co-written with Bobby Moresco, 2004), *The Hours* (directed by Stephen Daldry and written by David Hare, 2002, adapted from the novel by Michael Cunningham, 1998), *Eternal Sunshine of the Spotless Mind* (Michel Gondry, 2004), *City of God* (directed by Fernando Meirelles and Kátia Lund and written by César Charlone) and *Memento* (directed and written by Christopher Nolan, 2000).[66] But Peter Greenaway, famous as a director and writer of wonderful films, such as *The Cook, The Thief, His Wife and Her Lover* (2001) and *Prospero's Books* (1991), in 2007 announced cinema had died in 1983 with the birth of the remote control. Being deliberately provocative, he claimed the American video artist Bill Viola was worth ten Martin Scorseses who was still making the same films as D. W. Griffiths made at the start of the twentieth century.[67] Greenaway has a point.

   Mainstream film has developed very little. For Greenaway, who trained as a painter, the image rules supreme and any adaptation of a Jane Austen novel, for example, is a total waste of time. While interactivity has come about to a degree with computer games, Greenaway's claim that audiences want to be actively involved in narratives by somehow changing their course of action might be far-fetched. Throughout history the death of one art form or another has been declared and now with the plethora of interactive screen media the death of film is frequently declared. A number of different endings might be shot for a film and then pre-release audiences shown versions. While films are watched in different formats, the larger cinematic format will always be there, so to argue that this change in technology has had a revolutionary impact on screenwriting is hyperbole.

Inferiority complex

For a variety of reasons sometimes screenwriting is not considered to be a 'proper' or 'pure' form, as if the screenplay is inferior writing or not even writing at all. This is connected to the popularity of film versus the elitism of some forms of writing, particularly poetry, and the notion that the screenplay is a means to an end. Snobbery still exists, especially amongst writers. In the US television show *Californication* (2007–), starring David Duchovny, a novelist gets writer's block once his novel is turned into what he believes to be a trashy film. The New York Public Library has tried to overcome this snobbery. In 2012 it held an exhibition to celebrate their centennial which included their most important objects, such as Beethoven's manuscript in one box near Paul Schrader's annotated screenplay for *Taxi Driver* (directed by Martin Scorsese, 1976). One repeated claim is that, unlike a novel, it is impossible in a screenplay to reveal the inner life of characters. This is spurious. The opposite could just as easily be argued. The screenwriter can show the thoughts of their characters through obvious or unobvious action and dialogue, along with voiceovers, and words or diagrams appearing in the scene, as in *Pulp Fiction* (directed and written by Quentin Tarantino, 1994) when Mia Wallace draws a square outside the restaurant. We can feed this into psychological development in general.

Some therapists like to use the term breakthrough, when the patient has what is a personal eureka moment, an epiphany of awareness, which might change them. This, in itself, echoes a deep need for hopeful narratives that suggest we are not purely at the mercy of circumstance, or just predetermined from birth, like a programmed machine that cannot function in any other fashion. Concurrently, as the dialogue previously from James Bond suggests, deep down we may like the idea that all we have is luck and fate. Often characters are constructed that believe this and behave in this manner, but these are in themselves examples of people who basically deny responsibility for their own actions. These function in narratives often as examples of how not to behave. The worst thing any writer can do is preach, apparently, but this mantra is a preachy statement, and there are many exceptions. Some of the best screenplays break this 'rule', such as *Adaptation* (directed by Spike Jonze and written by Charlie and Donald Kaufman, 2002), which, ironically, is preachy about how to write. The only 'rule' should be to break the 'rule' successfully, for then you may, just may, be doing something original.

As with spiritual traditions, like Buddhism, artists like Picasso saw their work as a way of breaking through illusion and entering into a higher consciousness. Within the psychology of screenwriting, there is the need for the writer to be deeply aware of the psychology of their characters – are they convincing enough, are they charismatic, how much of a presence do they have, do we care enough about them? There's also the psychology of the audience to be aware of. Are they stimulated enough, do they stay with the film, or lose interest, how does it fit in to what they already know? And we have the psychology of those we are writing with: initial readers, fellow writers and script editors, and others, such as producers, directors, actors, carpenters and so on. Most importantly is the need to be aware of our own psychology. If not, the writing becomes some form of therapy, which makes it less easy to edit, like cutting off a limb as in *127 Hours* (directed by Danny Boyle and co-written with Simon Beaufoy, 2010). And following F. Scott Fitzgerald's remark, only speak if you have something to say, that is, if a story must be told. Fundamentally, all of the essential elements of screenwriting clearly involve personal psychology.

Versions of depth psychology use ancient systems such as the Enneagram to explain part of the complexities of human nature, an area we shall come onto. What drives us to behave in the way we do? If we can grasp this for our characters, and ourselves, for our characters are often spin-offs of ourselves, then we are really making inroads into revealing something about the workings of the inner psyche that our audiences will relate to. If we do not, then we will be producing cardboard cut-out characters. The problem with characters such as Patrick Bateman in *American Psycho* (directed by Mary Harron and co-written with Guinevere Turner, 2000, from the Bret Easton Ellis novel, 1991) is that these are the characters we are often given. Because of the apparent realism of film, and the often intrinsic veracity of photography, Harron's film in this case does lose some of the ambiguity and psychological depth of the novel. Bateman is what could be termed a posthuman being, without redemption. This is fine, but limiting, and reveals an element of the problems concerning adaptation. But Bateman is a truly filmic character, his whole personality is based around this, and it is this aspect of double observation that I propose here. The cinematic audience knows they are observing a character, played by an actor, who knows they are being observed. There is the idea that the best acting, along with the best cinematic viewing, switches off this awareness, and functions on an unconscious level. But what about the best writing; does the writer need to switch off or switch on?

The writer may imagine the scene being played out in numerous ways, as is comically portrayed in the film *Adaptation*, with the various scenes, sequences, and scenarios of the writer portrayed, based on the screenwriter Charlie Kaufman himself. Clearly, if anything interrupts this flow, this might break the imaginative capacity to see the scene to the end, and to let it play out. So who is in control here, the writer's will or the imagination? Film can be considered as functioning as an unconscious mind, always one step ahead of the conscious. While this is in many ways a false separation, many critics have considered the psychological interpretation of film, particularly equating it with dreams. This apparent dream world is not antithetical to 'reality' given that media images construct the myths we live by and often possess a value higher than truth.[68] Cinema, we have seen, led to the impermanence of truth. In discussing the classical period of history, Michel Foucault assessed their perception of madness as being the inability to distinguish the truth. This he contrasted with the nineteenth-century view of madness as the condition where no limits are known. Christian Metz and Jean-Louis Baudry are just two significant theorists in the history of psychoanalytical interpretations of film who have made an impact. Popularly, the extreme end of psychology is madness, although it can easily be argued everyone slips in and out of madness constantly, that our current construction of society is madness, and film, like dream, induces this madness.

Inability to distinguish the truth and the condition where no limits are known are inseparable, for without the ability to distinguish the truth of one's situation one may well believe one's capabilities are limitless.[69] In this sense, without a limit nothing is known. But from the belief in the self as infinite there is the possibility of the acknowledgement of the infinite beyond the self. Madness is a break or absence to Foucault and the same could be said for the experience of film as a whole. For Metz this is a form of regression, 'to perceive as real the represented and not the representer (the technological medium of representation)', film being similar to the madness of dreams.[70] Although socially accepted, cinema is a 'loophole opening on to something slightly more crazy, slightly less approved than what one does the rest of the time'.[71] This could be termed the 'triumph of madness' where, following Metz, the subject and object become one.[72] This is a position Nietzsche thought impossible but I believe it needs to be the intention of the screenwriter. Show me a sane man and I will cure him, said Carl Jung. It can easily be argued that sanity itself is insanity; as Jimmy (Phil Daniels) in *Quadrophenia* yells at his parents, 'Oh yea, what's normal then?'

When storytellers invent scenarios that break traditional patterns, a moment of chaos must be allowed to enter, a moment of madness; the 'what if' scenario. If madness is the place where no limits are known, or where, at the very least, the boundary of the limit is transgressed, if then reaffirmed, then this needs to be engaged with by writers. Creativity is a loss of control.[73] Roland Barthes has analysed how some texts, such as those written by Bataille and others, are from the centre of madness but if they want to be read they must contain a part of neurosis necessary for the seduction of the reader.[74] Some might object, absorbing the notion that a screenplay is not a piece of writing, but merely a tool for a visual art and nothing more. Practically, reason must be distanced, and madness breaks in, allowing for creativity; chaos then is essential to this. Nathanael West remarked, 'your order is meaningless, my chaos is significant'.[75] The imaginative leap, where the invention becomes reality for others, is a form of madness, for in many ways it is not real. Writers therefore must possess this sense of madness, be possessed by their characters and stories, to allow fiction and reality to blur.

But it is more than allowing characters and stories to have you, to possess you. You need to be them, in Frommian terms, to experience them, and to write them, at the deepest level. Baudry used the term fiction effect, and the reason why film can have such an impact is that the film viewer believes it is producing the film, on one level dreaming the images that appear, or as if they are projecting them onto the screen from the head. For Baudry, when we watch a film we are in a state of artificial regression, before the formation of the ego – before the separation of self and other, internal and external. In this state these divisions have not been established yet. More importantly still, there is also the inability to distinguish between perception (of an actual thing), and representation (an image that stands for it).

The viewer is in the same position as an early infant, unable to differentiate between itself and the world.[76] Freud maintained dream was a normal hallucinatory psychosis, but for Baudry in film there is an artificial psychosis, that the audience has no control over, so there is a clear difference. What makes an interesting screenplay, psychologically, will engage with these issues, often surreptitiously. The majority of Hitchcock's films, particularly films like *Rear Window* (1954) written by John Michael Hayes, are packed with playful psychoanalytical ideas, which lead the audience to question not only what it is they are seeing but the very act of perception itself and issues of identity. In doing so the individual questions their own identity, and that of others, and through this process of defamiliarization there is a rediscovering of what is important, this being the essence of what great art can achieve.

Ultimately, we want to be able to encounter the world with new eyes, as if seeing the world for the first time. This is virtually a mystical aim and highly ambitious. To make your work have any long-term worth you need to have this in mind. As Doreen Carvajal has quoted, T. S. Eliot wrote, 'And the end of all our exploring will be to arrive where we started, and know the place for the first time.' Carvajal also referred to psychiatrist Dr Dreffert who, working with savants, has concluded that their knowledge can only be there through genetic transmission.[77] Dogme style of filmmaking attempted to move away from the predetermined but, given this, perhaps the predetermined is a more authentic way of filmmaking, writing and existing. Before we start dismissing certain psychiatrists, and especially Freud, Jung and Lacan as insane, importantly, for psychoanalytic film theory, the member of the film audience is not a real flesh-and-blood person, but a construct, actually created by the cinematic process itself. This is crucial to remember.

What goes into this construction?: a state of regression is produced; a situation of belief is constructed; mechanisms of primary identification are activated; fantasy structures, such as the family romance, are put into play by the cinematic fiction; whatever marks the film with authorship must be concealed.[78] There are exceptions here, particularly with regards to the last point, when films knowingly highlight authorship. When considering the psychology of screenwriting it needs to be fully understood that the cinematic process allows the spectator to 'become' someone else, while simultaneously reinforcing the ego.[79] This is at the heart of why cinema is so enjoyable, and central to its psychological power. Of course this does depend on the type of film. Obviously, some films will enforce what can be termed ego-thinking, which re-enforces the idea of a singular self or soul, while others will acknowledge that there is no such thing as an independent ego or substantial existence.[80] It is this playing with and sometimes subverting fixed identity that needs to be examined in relation to its social, political, and moral implications.

Back to basics – ideology

The way numerous popular narratives are structured means that all of society's ills can be dealt with within the current social structures by the sole actions of individuals.[81] Popular narratives function to restrict collective responsibility, the wider focus being ignored. Capitalism fosters individualism, working to eliminate the state so it is under command of market forces, rolling back collective responsibility. This means there is no reason to change the way we live, collectively, in any core way. Even with great ethical thinkers such as Aristotle, the 'other is not primarily what brings me into being, but a potential threat to my being'.[82] Popular culture promotes the myth that happiness and a meaningful existence come through a focus on the self, as does contemporary philosophy, and it 'fails to register that there can be by definition no meaning, whether of life or anything else, which is unique to myself alone'.[83]

All drama is conflict. Systems of competitive capitalism depend on conflict, so drama is a mirror.

A society whose principles are acquisition, profit, and property produces a social character oriented around having, and once the dominant pattern is established, nobody wants to be an outsider, or indeed an outcast; in order to avoid this risk everybody adapts to the majority, who have in common only their mutual antagonism.[84]

Paradoxically, however, we have to change to stay the same. Because of the lack of a collective approach to global warming, for example, Professor Steven Hawkins in the *11th Hour* (directed and written by Leila and Nadia Connors, 2007) suggests that the earth could possibly one day turn into a planet akin to Venus, where instead of raining water it rains sulphur. The focus is not on the extinction of the planet but of the human race. However, anthropomorphizing is part of the problem. One can wonder at the logic of this individualistic approach, considering the impact of this individualism on the environment. The popular mantra: plot = character and character = plot, confirms this, although there are always exceptions. Whether conflict is indeed the true nature of being is questionable. According to Henri Bergson, biologically, nature works by bringing together many parts but a mere glance at developmental biology indicates life working in a very different way. '*Life does not proceed by association and addition of elements, but by dissociation and division* (italics in text).'[85]

Film can covertly or overtly ignore ideology by concealing it. This is the very essence of ideology. Some writers and critics denounce theory for a variety of reason. Theory can be viewed as the tail wagging the dog and it is in many respects far easier to theorize than to produce, so the question inevitably occurs why make theory necessary at all. But theory, when by theory we mean philosophy, is when you have ideas. Ideology is when ideas have you. We need the theory to test out ideas, as theory entails having ideas about ideas. All of this may sound politically correct but, put simply, are screen-writers so desperate to eat and have their writing developed that they do not care about this anyway? Surely you must feed the system that feeds you, although it is possible to challenge this system simultaneously.

Anyone who does any writing at all knows that in the main it proceeds by trial and error. Granted, some might be like Milton, who managed to compose perfect poetry in his head before dictating it to a scribe, but this was out of necessity as he was blind. Trial and error is not necessarily a bad thing, but it is in the editing we become more conscious. *The Guard* (directed and written by John Michael McDonagh, 2011) was eventually made with Irish funding, after London-based funding bodies refused the project, preferring to make many films in the same old mode, unable to accept that originality involves risk. There is for the writer and director a trial and error process.

A film can be revolutionary by not emphasizing one point of view, in the way say Jean Luc Godard's films are, because there is no absolute resolution.[86]

This takes us back to the purpose of cinema itself: is it to entertain, to inform, to challenge, all three of these, a combination of these, or other purposes, such as to blatantly make money, self-expression, to exploit others, propaganda, or to change the world? In the psychology of screenwriting do we really need to ignore all this and just think about developing our idea we are passionate about? Clearly, it is worth engaging with these debates if we want to develop our idea into something more substantial.

Many films, such as *We Need To Talk About Kevin* (directed by Lynne Ramsay and co-written with Rory Kinnear, 2011, from the Lionel Shriver novel, 2003), which concerns a mother who feels unable to love her son, and the son then turns into a murderer, manage to tackle wider social issues through a focus on the individual. They enable the audience to walk in the shoes of the central characters and deepen their understanding of the human condition, to expand their psychology, if you will. In this case perhaps, and in many others, as Voltaire put it, understanding is forgiveness. Of course, just because someone is not particularly wanted by their mother it does not mean they will go out and murder their classmates, so the film raises deeper questions than this. This is a central point. A film without this element, in some form, will probably fail. There is a deep psychological need to understand, to look for motivation. Film creates heroes and villains and then, through a good screenplay, subverts binary approaches to psychology, challenging our own simplistic assumptions and judgements. The creative thinking human brain seeks this subversion. Screenwriting poses a question about the human condition.

The importance of the creative and affective power of cinema and the writer's role in this should not be overlooked. A number of filmmakers, including Lynch and Fassbinder, contest the view that cinema is just about control and ideology. Of course, this depends on what 'type' of cinema. For Lynch, cinema can 'take emotion away from the sentimental level of the known and the ideologically sanctioned to the affective level where emotion becomes as creative and self-begetting a force as thought itself'.[87] When the power of feeling is invoked it becomes, as this suggests, only valid when it is compared to thought. Western rationality, even when allowing for feeling, can only incorporate feeling within this prescriptive framework, what can be viewed as the hierarchy of thinking. Importantly, however, while it is obvious that film has been, and still is, a supporter of ideologies, following Deleuze, it is important to remember that cinema can even invent new emotions, distinguishing 'creative works from the prefabricated emotions of commerce'.[88] So in writing a screenplay ask: what new emotions have you created and what subversions have you enabled?

Evil and knowledge

There is a deep fascination with evil, and James Bond films, for example, among many others, offer the audience a chance to engage with their dark fantasies. Discourse about evil is similar to that on ideology. Evil might be akin to chaos and conflict, but just as no man is without contradiction, no discourse on this area is either. For example, it is difficult to tell whether Jesus of Nazareth, who in the Christian tradition vanquishes all evil as the Christ, is speaking metaphorically or not and, of course, these are translated words written sometime after they were supposedly spoken. In the Gospel of Matthew he declares: 'Do not suppose that I have come to bring peace to the earth. I did not come to bring peace, but a sword' (Matthew 10.34).[89] By this he may have meant the Holy Spirit, although it suggests the necessity of so-called evil. Then later in 26.52 he comments 'all who draw the sword will die by the sword'.[90] The Holy Spirit is compared to a sword in Ephesians 6.17. Concepts such as 'falsehood', 'evil' and 'culture', are positioned in Western thought as deficient and secondary forms of other concepts, such as 'truth', 'good' and 'nature'.[91] There is no good without evil, and vice versa and the concepts of absolute evil or absolute good are difficult to swallow. Following Sausurre's findings that language is not meaningful in and of itself, 'but only as it *differs* from other elements within the system', Derrida breaks the Socratic 'metaphysics of presence'.[92] This moves us away from the absolute.

Film has long been equated with types of evil, such as making the masses ignorant, by both the left and the right. According to right-wing US commentator Rush Limbaugh, Christopher Nolan's 2012 blockbuster *The Dark Knight Rises* was an attack on the Republican presidential candidate Mitt Romney. The villain in the film, Bane (Tom Hardy), is apparently there to get Americans thinking about the dodgy company Bain Capital, which Romney founded in 1984. For Limbaugh, a 'lot of brain-dead people' are going to hear this Bane in the movie and are going to associate Bain Capital with this villain.[93] The ludicrous nature of this accusation becomes even clearer when one considers Nolan began the trilogy in 2005 and planned this part of it in 2010, so for Limbaugh to be correct he must be a prophet, with superhero powers.

In a Platonic sense the origin of evil is ignorance. Within Christianity, evil is concerned with the privation of God and loss, and in some Christian contexts knowledge itself is concerned with evil, for it is the loss of innocence. For Kant it is the failure to be consistent and radical evil is inhuman. For Arendt evil is merely banal, or thoughtlessness, and is not hatred. It is clear then that evil is at the heart of much human behaviour and can be considered benign in some circumstances and, like aesthetic taste, is open to interpretation. Often protagonists in film reach a point where they are at one with the antagonist, confronting the evil externally that is in many respects inside them. *This* is a central plot point if not the central plot point. This is not a rule for screenwriting but worth considering. In *We Need To Talk About Kevin*, mother Eva Khatchadourian (Tilda Swinton) is thoroughly aware of her own part in Kevin's (Ezra Miller) behaviour. Similarly, the audience must reach the point where they fully understand this conjunction within themselves and enter a profound level of identification. This is the revelation, not the deed, as the film is told in flashbacks. Evil then is not something separate and other but part of the self. This can be equated with individuation in a Jungian paradigm. At this point catharsis can take place and an emotional shift.

The notion that the writer must be invisible in the text is useful but not always accurate. Art frequently highlights the role of the artist in the creation of the piece and it is in many ways more genuine to not cover up the artifice. Artifice can be overcome by actually highlighting the artificial, or by at least knowing and ironically acknowledging the process. 'The best poetry will be rhetorical criticism ...' wrote Wallace Stevens in 1899.[94] This seems prophetic now given that all 'good' poetry consists of this. A masterpiece of this type of screenplay is *Synecdoche New York*, by Charlie Kaufmann, which concerns the making of a stage play, where the walls of the stage are continually being walked through into another version, highlighting the constructed nature of everything.

There are some obvious examples in films where the screenwriter plays a central role in the plot, and is highly visible. Interestingly in terms of the power of adaptation, in *Sunset Boulevard* (directed by Billy Wilder and co-written with Charles Bracket and D. M. Marshall Jr., 1950), for example, Paramount thought Wilder was following a short story *A Can of Beans*, which did not actually exist and allowed him freedom to develop the script how he wanted. There are plenty of other examples, such as *Barton Fink* (directed and written by Ethan and Joel Coen, 1991), *Leaving Las Vegas* and *Adaptation* (directed by Spike Jonze and written by Charlie and Donald Kaufman, 2002, from the non-fiction book *The Orchid Thief* by Susan Orlean, 1998). This visibility is about finding or losing power as a writer or individual, the psychology of screenwriting being central.

Freud observed his grandchild playing with a cotton reel, throwing it and imagining it was lost, then recovering it. Something is lost then recovered. This fort/da game, where the child endeavours to find compensation from its separation from its mother gained through the mastery of language, is possibly the shortest story there is.[95] If we look at a wide range of narratives from different periods, and set in different countries, we can fit all stories into this box. Two quite different examples are *The Wicker Man* (directed by

Robin Hardy and written by Anthony Shaffer, 1973), where Rowan Morrison is apparently missing, and *The Lord of the Rings* (original trilogy by J. R. Tolkien, 1954, film adaptations by Peter Jackson, 2001–3). *The Wicker Man* is also an interesting example for as well as being a quest narrative it was condemned at the time of its release for being a film that could not make its mind up about what it wanted to be. Was it a gothic horror, a comedy, a romp, or merely a bunch of fools acting a silly pagan ritual?[96] What this critic failed to realize was that the combination of these 'genres' was what made it so appealing, and that the hint of danger in the film was actually far different to the sex-comedies on offer during the same period. While for the initial pitch, and some marketing, a genre has to be agreed on, inevitably the more interesting films will transgress boundaries.

From romance, to science fiction and horror, to tales of salvation, Freud's game is central to the tale. Whether it is about restoring order overall, and re-establishing the set ideology and status quo depends on the film. In the book of Genesis, which as well as containing the creation myth, concerns Adam and Eve being ejected from the Garden of Eden due to eating of the tree of knowledge, the fall is portrayed as tasting knowledge. Ultimately, with film based on feeling rather than thinking, a screenplay inevitably advocates going back to a pre-fall state by-passing thought, which is impossible to a degree. The point is, being locked into our own perspective is what is so limiting, and inevitably screenplays that attempt subversions of this will be the most sublime. A lesser-known figure in the history of psychology and psychoanalysis who took this myth very seriously was William Reich who, unlike Erich Fromm, and along with Herbert Marcuse, believed in the significance of sexual repression in terms of political structure.[97] Interestingly, despite the joke that Freud once said sometimes a cigar is just a cigar, it is often thought Freud is a literalist, but if he is compared with Reich this is far from the truth.

While Freud believed no neurosis was unrelated to the sexual, he took sexual to mean sexual in the broadest sense. One of the achievements, or problems with Freud, depending on your position, is the level of nuance and ramification he brought to the interpretation of language. Antithetically, Reich, while acknowledging the non-genital manifestations of sexuality, believed that all problems in the individual and society came down to problems with the genitals. In *Die Funktion des Orgasmus* (*The Function of the Orgasm*, published in 1927) he claimed all else was insignificant.[98] It seems that Reich's belief is still held and promoted in many areas of popular culture and Steve McQueen's 2011 film *Shame*, co-written with Abi Morgan, is just one example. The screenplay and the film are tedious, but they too get across the banal and deadening life of a 'sex addict'.

Many think this is the case with pornography overall, pornography having a close relationship with death and boredom, but *Shame* is far from pornography. The film is about a miserable 'sex addict', Brandon Sullivan (Michael Fassbinder), who frequently masturbates in his toilet at work, something Freud might say would cause illness, is addicted to pornography and voyeurism, often has sex with hookers, sometimes more than one at a time, and seems to be denying his sexual desire for his sister Sissy (Carey Mulligan). Brandon is clearly suffering, making him an ideal protagonist. He exemplifies the Reichian figure who, while trying to prevent a sexual explosion, must constantly return to sex acts that are without communication.

The one attempt Brandon has at a meaningful relationship, with Marianne (Nicole Beharie), leaves him impotent. Their encounter is in many respects the only interesting element to the screenplay. Brandon asks Marianne where she would like to be, in the past or the future, and she replies the here and now. He calls her boring, and then she tells him to fuck off. After this failure, he resorts to fingering a woman in a bar, gets her to smell his fingers, and then is beaten up outside by her boyfriend. With the painful look on his face while he has sex, it seems that sex is always a masochistic act, despite him actually being quite 'normal' in what he desires. Importantly, sex can only be conducted if money is exchanged.

The void depicted in this film, particularly travel on the subway, is paralleled with the corruption of work and, being generous to a film that really has little new to say about the human condition, capitalism itself seems to be under investigation, if obliquely. As with buying sex, in psychoanalysis money is exchanged. In *Infinite Thought*, after pointing out that all genuine thinking is free, Alain Badiou claimed all genuine politics and science is disinterested and, despite everything, psychoanalysis is disinterested. For creative writing it is more complex. 'Because writers need to look at the world twice, seeing everything a second time, writing can be a political act, because it concerns entering into the details of a situation, rather than being caught up in the emotions.'[99]

Freud's or Lacan's goal is not only the cure of the client. 'The goal is *to think* the singularity of the human subject: the human subject confronted on the one side with language, and, on the other, with sexuality.'[100] While it is still debated how far Freud followed nineteenth-century positivism, there is no debate concerning Reich's wholehearted embracing of it, being the inventor of terms such as the 'sex economy', a kind of unification of Freud and Marx, so the libido is no longer a metaphor.[101] Reich, utilizing the story of the Tree of Knowledge, believed that self-consciousness was the core problem, for self-knowledge removes emotional and biological spontaneity and that there were two protectors from the biological, character structure internally and patriarchy externally. 'Reich, like Freud, concluded that the source of human unhappiness lay within man himself. At the same time the anti-intellectual bias implicit in all his thought finally achieved explicit formulation: man knew too much for his own good.'[102] Unfortunately for Reich what he hoped the most against, that men would unleash 'a free-for-all fucking epidemic', in many ways came true.[103]

Deep down it appears Reich was a bit of a prude himself. Ironically, as Paul Robinson has revealed, Reich tried to substitute 'sexual intercourse' with the term 'genital embrace', and died of a heart attack on 3 November 1957, having served eight months of a two-year sentence at Lewisberg, Pennsylvania. He had refused to appear in court following the Federal Food and Drug Administration's complaint against him for his 'Orgone Energy Accumulator' in 1954. The patient sat in the box and absorbed 'Orgone radiation', after character analysis and 'vegetotherapy' failed; this was a six-sided box, like a telephone booth, made of metal on the inside and wood on the outside.[104] At least the device would have a use in film writing; Woody Allen in his 1973 film *Sleeper* set in 2173 satirizes this machine with his orgasmatron.

In the book of Genesis innocence is lost, as we have seen, but a further discovery is made, as with the film *An Education* already mentioned, and this encapsulates a multitude of narratives. Adam and Eve, when they are living in accordance with God, however we interpret this, were not separate from him, but once Adam ate the apple, the inciting incident in screenplay terminology, innocence was lost. Following this simple action the quest began. This innocence could never truly be recovered, but Jesus, in the Christian story the innocent Son of God, restored it. Between the old and new testaments in the Bible action-packed sequences lead to this restoration, and examples are there in most world religions, with obvious cultural differences, which concern the deeper parts of our personal and collective psychology. There is a gap that needs to be filled. Having wholeness restored is psychological. Whether a screenplay attempts to restore this wholeness, or highlights elements around this theme, we cannot escape the psychological and spiritual implications.

Those studying literature frequently come across the idea that language constructs being. This sounds far-fetched and it might be hoped humans are more than language or a text, but if this is accepted, writing is taken much more seriously and creative work will be more profound. Nobel Prize-winning author Toni Morrison claimed that fiction is a tool that fills the gaps in history. The need for stories is immense, they are the myths we live by, enabling us to function and relate. Whether there is just a repetition of old stories in new formats is open to argument, as is whether archetypal characters and stories exist that transcend time and space, and are part of our collective unconscious. As Emerson once put it, when time and space in relation to matter have no affinity we become immortal. How to write screenplays that engage audiences on a deeper, psychological, level sounds ambitious and it might not be your aim. Your specific audience might not want to be engaged with at a deeper level. Of course entertainment is also about distraction, but it is important to remember F. Scott Fitzgerald's point: you do not write because you want to say something, you write because you have got something to say.[105]

Because there are so many stories competing for our attention the more powerful stories are multilayered, include an emotional shift, and take us deeper into the human condition and puncture our bubble of complacency. There is no common agreement on what it means to be human, so in a profound sense we want stories to help us see what we really are, might be, and what we may become. Stories are about moving the human species forward and are undeniably a part of evolution. Unfortunately, in the reporting of film events in the media, frequently the financial aspects get highlighted, such as whether the film was the largest grossing film ever, or economically a total flop. About a thousand English-speaking feature films a year get made, but only around fifty of these are totally financed by the major studios. The majority of the world is dominated by the Law of the Market, so the Market is God. These aspects are important, given film is in many respects an industry, but we also do well to remember that not all so-called flops, either critically or financially, are so-called bad films. History sometimes proves this, when films are rediscovered or gradually become classics. *Citizen Kane* (directed by Orson Welles and co- written with Herman Mankiewicz, 1941) was not understood at the time of its release and then became voted constantly as the number one film of all time.

Writing a two-hour film, with a ninety-page script, is a huge task. Starting small is true with any writing; less is more is a truism that can be used in a multitude of ways. So start with a small script, get the film made, and then you have evidence that you can do a good job. Get anything made. That is the first task for, ultimately, we learn through practice and however hard we may dream, we need to think about the concrete, not just what but how. This is about getting a track record and learning the ropes. Some people get lucky, jumping a few rungs, and it is not necessarily a linear process, but before you start thinking about an amazing blockbuster set in outer space think small. While ten million for *The King's Speech* (directed by Tom Hooper and written by David Seidler, 2010) is not a trivial amount, compared to *Avatar* (directed and written by James Cameron, 2010), it is a small-budget film.

The Museum of the Moving Image in Queens, New York, runs a workshop on soundtrack and film, with *Titanic* (directed and written by James Cameron,

1997) as an example of the excesses that throwing money at films leads to. In the scene where the ship's funnel collapses, there are eight separate recordings that make up the soundtrack. Some of these were taken from a sound bank of collective sounds that can just be lifted others involved a great deal of work. This included actually recording the sound of ice cracking in remote Canada. The collapse of the funnel was the sound of an elephant. Verisimilitude here, despite the extravagance, is not perfect given the lighting of the scene, which makes it seem false.

As with censorship that can cause artists to think more creatively about what they are producing to subvert the censors, the lack of budget can lead to even more creativity. I am not saying lose the high concept budget idea completely, but ask what you can achieve with the resources you have. The smaller the project, theoretically, the more likely it is to get made, and the more control you have. You are the boss. You may be in an environment where you can use the equipment of your institution, the knowledge of your tutors and peers, and the talent of those around you. So collaborate. There are various notions about what a script is as a document in and of itself, and what different versions of the script might be in literary terms. Basically the script you write is the blueprint, for want of a better phrase, that can then be worked with. When people say the writer has no power they are to some degree wrong. It could just as well be argued the script is everything. I touched on the Dogme 95 movement previously. Despite stories about British director Mike Leigh making it all up as he goes along, and actors doing what they want, improvising continually, without a script you get nowhere.

2

The psychology of practice

Finding your intention

While any clear division between the unconscious and the conscious would be inaccurate, in general the unconscious mind is always one step ahead of the conscious mind. This means, for the purpose of creativity and originality, any activity that manages to tap into this source will be fruitful. Is it only by acknowledging the power of the 'imaginary self' that we can begin to subvert it?[1] And why would or should we want to subvert it? Some writers and teachers of writing get hung up on developing their style and voice; it is not about finding your voice but the story's voice and the voice of your characters. For Amanda Boulter this includes three things: relinquishing the search for our own voice; working with and for the reader; welcoming the competing voices of characters.

To find our voice we must lose it in the voices of others. This fully engages with a movement in theory and in practice. Boulter is discussing fiction, such as novel writing, but this applies equally to the screenplay. It can be very difficult, psychologically, for the writer to step back from their work, as the two seem so entwined, capitalism driving the cult of the individual and originality and the cult of the art work. You are not your writing. The characters in a screenplay obviously can just be aspects of the writer, rather than real entities that go beyond the writer. To find their voice the writer must know, at whatever level of conscious or unconscious imagining, their own intentions as an artist.[2]

What then, essentially, is our intention as an artist? Can we summarize what we are doing? Often people can write tens of thousands of words, but find that writing a good premise in just 50 words is difficult. Ask the question, what is it about? Then ask it again, no, what is it really about? If we want to summarize our screenplay in 50 words it might be difficult to offer a subtext, but try. Even do it in 140 characters, like a tweet. In this way we find our true story and we stick to it. There is no problem if we write different endings to different scenes, or experiment with different ends to the whole screenplay. But zoning in on the spine of your story early on means you stay on the path and eventually nothing will be extraneous. Despite the red herrings, the twists and turns, your screenplay will then appear as if it had to be written.

Case study: A Dangerous Method

As has been referred to with reference to Freud's fort/da observation, often in a narrative something is lost and the narrative is about approaching this loss. This could be about unveiling a secret or at least approaching this secret or secrets and the tensions that result. The reader in this instance is the co-conspirator and it is important to resist the temptation to over or to under explain. One film that is conceivably guilty of the former is David Cronenberg's A Dangerous Method (2012). This might be too critical a judgement, given that not everybody knows of this story about psychiatrist Carl Jung, the founder of analytical psychology. Sometimes it is necessary to spell things out to an audience who may not know the context or subject that well. This is always the danger when covering a non-fictional world. This all depends on whether we are being taken into the past to find out something new, which is the case here. It is not exactly the exposition but the manner in which it is done, as in another biopic, Bright Star (directed and written by Jane Campion, 2009) from Andrew Motion's biography of John Keats.

Having Sigmund Freud (Viggo Mortensen) and Carl Jung (Michael Fassbinder) read out the letters the other has written to them for explanatory purposes and to set the tone, atmosphere and indicate disagreements between them, can seem too obvious. But it shows the intensity of the relationship. There is art and beauty in their composition, the letters themselves being treasured items, Freud eventually taking down his photo-graph of Jung and putting it in a special box with his letters. But it can come across as an obvious form of quite blatant exposition, without nuance, where basic ideas and differences are exposed. Tensions build in these letters, then Freud is killed off by the usurping son, who claims Freud is infantilizing those that disagree with him.

There is also didactic exposition in the film's dialogue. This does fit the style of the period piece, however, and there is a literal element that is in keeping with the subject matter. There is very little room for the audience to

interpret or misinterpret the dialogue, to read between the lines that ironically include dreams which are open to interpretation or misinterpretation.
Freud does offer his interpretation of Jung's dreams, ever paranoid of his
gifted prodigy usurper but gives nothing back. What is conveyed is a sense of
literalness in a period when the more metaphoric meaning was still becoming
more pronounced and Freud's literalness is extreme.

The film is far more interesting than merely a depiction of screenwriter
Christopher Hamilton's battle between the two men due to the focus on the
transformation of Sabina Spielrien (Keira Knightley), whose name appears
almost uncannily invented (this could be translated as smile talk). Briefly
highlighting some weaknesses shows firstly that they can also be seen as
strengths, but also suggests that a successful film can be produced even
if the screenplay might be weak in certain areas. This brief observation
goes against all the traditional thought in screenwriting theory and practice,
although numerous other films could be analysed and yet have similar blatant
weaknesses. Ultimately, a successful screenplay, like a successful theory,
will be one that opens up questions rather than shuts them down.

The clash of these two men parallels the clash in Western thought. Jung
has told Freud of a 'catalytic exterior phenomenon', perhaps the origin of his
later work on synchronicity, when in Freud's study he feels his inner stomach
go warm, just before Freud's bookcases make a cracking sound due to the
heating. Hamilton has Spielrien as the catalyst that unites and divides the
two men, which in itself is not an uncommon device, but here it goes beyond
a mere love triangle. Spielrien is a difficult case for Jung, her behaviour
appearing to both prove and contradict Freud's theories. There is a complex
set of questions the film provokes. If she could remain as a case then it would
be easier for Jung, and we have to wonder whether she would have been
cured faster, or at all, had Jung not developed a sexual relationship with her.

Both Freud and Jung have what seem to be incurable cases presented in
the film, this being an obvious narrative device, like the unsolved crime. But
Jung succeeds with his patient using Freud's technique, while it is suggested
that Freud's difficult patient Otto Gross (Vincent Cassell), another doctor,
never recovers. This is a central point, as it is Jung's faith in a cure that wins
out. A profound irony is that Spielrien goes on to train to be a doctor and
psychoanalyst who Freud refers his own patients to. Jung's personal belief
in the cure is emphasized and, with his mystical side touched upon, what
comes through in the film is the solid message: 'If you believe, you will
receive whatever you ask for in prayer' (Matthew 21.22).[3]

In *Mysterium Coniunctionis* Jung maintained events have an a priori
element of unity, and synchronicity suggests, 'an interconnection or unity
of causally unrelated events, and thus postulates a unitary aspect of being'.[4]

Whatever our own personal views on coincidence, synchronicity, or the catalytic exterior phenomenon, it is important to consider how fictional narratives can in some way manufacture fate, a powerful sense of inevitability, 'it is written', and how film functions to instigate this phenomenon.[5] This is the central factor in screenwriting, for there is the combined paradox of presenting events as original and unique but simultaneously inevitable and believable.

Spinoza's view might not be especially attractive, and Buddhist interpretations of what the self and ego are might make us nauseous if rationality is our belief system but, despite this, it is difficult to argue with Deleuze that the ego is constantly changing in time. Therefore, to rely on Descartes' 'I think, therefore I am' is inaccurate. The point being, to speak of a subject I must synthesize time, but the ego changes in time. There is therefore no subject, just points of view.[6] Furthermore, if all language is always already metaphorical then all is indirect. Nothing is pre-metaphorical or primary, and 'all meaning derives from an unstable system of figures which does not have linguistic constraints'.[7]

With reference to Agrippa and Hans Driesch, Jung refers to the idea of 'inborn knowledge', which relates to imagination.

Final causes, twist them how we will, postulate a *foreknowledge of some kind*. It is certainly not a knowledge that could be connected with the ego, and hence not a conscious knowledge as we know it, but rather a self-subsistent "unconscious" knowledge which I would prefer to call "absolute knowledge." It is not cognition but, as Leibnitz so excellently calls it, a "perceiving" which consists – or to be more cautious, seems to consist – of images, or subjectless "simulacra." These postulated images are presumably the same as my archetypes, which can be shown to be formal factors in spontaneous fantasy products. Expressed in modern language, the microcosm which contains "the images of all creation" would be the collective unconscious.[8]

A Dangerous Method touches on Jung's more original work but, while siding with Freud on many issues, Spielrien's ideas are innovative, especially from today's perspective, when sexuality is often equated with being, and seems to be the primary ontological ground of being. Her ideas develop Freud's and claim that true sexuality is actually the destruction of the ego. This movement forward by Spielrien enables Freud to equate more fully the sex drive and the death drive, the final movement in his own thinking. And, while not mentioned in the film, similarly this is central to Jung's most original work on transformation.

Freud's status, therefore, rests on the work of an originally unstable woman, who is transformed through the work of Jung. Similarly, Jung would not have succeeded if it had not been for the strength and wealth of his wife or her ideas, as she constantly talks of coincidence, which he originally does not believe in, but then transforms into his theory of synchronicity. Plus his love of Spielrien and her own work, which he developed with her and her impact on his early work, is manifestly revealed as elemental in his own success. Remarkably, he tests out free association on his wife, with the help of his mistress, without telling either who the other is, Spielrien guessing the patient in the experiment is Mrs Jung in many ways placing her own fantasies on Mrs Jung's free associations. Jung believes Spielrien has proved herself through this process, as if it is a rite of passage.

Freud can accept this development of his beliefs from a woman, a fellow Jew, and a disciple whom he obviously believes he can keep under his control. What he cannot accept is a Protestant trying to usurp him as the Father of his movement, and the film depicts an historically accurate event where Freud physically collapses at a meeting when he is challenged by Jung. The moment when Freud offers some of his patients to Spielrien can be interpreted as a brief, unwitting, moment of self-disclosure for Freud. This is as if Spielrien will really be treating part of Freud himself, as he moves towards his own death. Freud emphatically declares that Spielrien had no chance having a relationship with an Aryan, Jung, but again this may be a form of his own counter transference, as it were, for his anger appears to come from his own sadness at the end of his relationship with Jung, indicated when he holds the photograph of Jung to his breast. Jung clearly feels as deeply about their relationship as does Freud, the rupture in their relationship driving him into a serious breakdown, although both the older Freud and Jung had breakdowns at the age of 38.

In his 1910 book *Totem and Taboo* Freud explained aspects of how memories can be passed down, but Jung gave the collective and individual unconscious a more teleological aspect. For Jung the self exists, and through therapy individuation can take place; this appears to be more hopeful than Freud. While both Jung and Freud wrote about external events from time to time, the inner world was paramount, especially the unconscious. Alfred Adler, another member of the original group, and now far less well known, broke away because he believed Freud over-emphasized the unconscious, and it was the external battle between the individual and society that had more significance.[9] I explained in detail in *The Metaphysics of Mass Art* Volume II, how film functions to promote teleology. Frank Tallis has pointed out that Jung's system is not just a psychological system but a metaphysical belief system.[10]

Film theory versus screenwriting theory

The stark differences between film and screenwriting theory can be viewed as a Freudian-Jungian dichotomy. Jung was addressed by Freud as 'heir apparent' and 'Crown Prince'.[11] There was, to be sure, a clear difference between them. For Jung the unconscious was not the place of repressed and dangerous desires but, the 'repository of collective wisdom', including figures such as wizards, tricksters, and 'the cast of the world's mythology'.[12] Jung has been so appealing to creative writers and screenwriting gurus who want to access this wisdom for practical purposes and have a plethora of symbolic material to play with, but it would be a mistake to think that Jung was the first person to posit such ideas. In 1814 Gotthilf Heinrich von Schubert, had published *The Symbolism of Dreams*, arguing that dreams contain universal timeless symbols 'that can be interpreted irrespective of their temporal and geographical provenance'.[13] In 1861 Karl Albert Scherner published *The Life of the Dream*, plus there were other noteworthy publications by Marie-Jean Hervey de Saint-Denis, and the Dutch poet and psychiatrist Frederick van Eaden who invented the term lucid dreaming and, significantly, Johann Fridrich Herbart, who, writing decades before Freud, had introduced the term repression.[14]

Jung had the heavy German Romanticism that believed in this mythology united with the clout of medical science. Screenwriting gurus could then select what they wanted from this wealth of writing. On the critical side, Freud and post-Freudians, including Lacanians, and everyone else, are so appealing to critics, in my view, because they want to access the repressed in the text. Obviously, and ironically, Freud not only wanted to silence Jung, but all of his critics, this is why around 1912 Freud began to choose his own daughter Anna over any other successor. According to Mark Edmundson, Freud did so because, as a self-professed godless Jew, he was seeking immortality and she could provide the unshakeable dogma and legacy. Anna, with her best-known book *The Ego and the Mechanisms of Defence*, provided the defence mechanism 'not just for the ego that was Freud, but for his entire legacy'.[15] The complexity of Jung's relationship with Freud, his father figure as he puts it, is only one part of his psychological difficulties.

Jung is repeatedly shown to be a prophet in Cronenberg's film, predicting the blood flowing in Europe, and the hounding of the Jews in Vienna. The film is in some sense resurrecting Jung's status, given attacks on him for apparent anti-Semitism. While Jung may have the foresight that this was about to happen, he can do nothing about it, just as the analyst may understand their patient but cannot stop the symptoms. This is at the heart of the difference between the realist Freud and idealist Jung. Vision and prophecy are central to both of these important figures. The early Jung is optimistic, but Freud becomes the prophet of doom when on their journey to America he states, 'do you think they know we're bringing them the plague'. Freud virtually despairs at man's aggression in his later writings, but he dismissed the idea that he was a prophet, admitting he was guilty of providing no consolation.[16]

Whatever this kind of humility suggests, Freud saw himself as part of a tripartite revolution that involved: Copernicus, who drew attention to the fact that the earth is not the centre of the universe, Darwin who found evidence that humans evolved and were not placed on earth in a privileged position by God, and Freud, who saw most vigorously than anyone before that humans were not in control of the unconscious but the antithesis.[17] For Freud, 'human megalomania will have suffered its third and most wounding blow from the psychological research of the present time which seeks to prove to the ego that it is not even master of its own house'.[18] Given the plethora of Freudian-related theorizing that has dominated the twentieth century it would be easy to forget any empirical science. In 1884, however, when film was in its infancy, psychologists, such as Charles Peirce and Joseph Jastrow in America, were publishing work that demonstrated the intelligence of the unconscious in the laboratory.[19]

For both Jung and Freud, Spielrien is the catalyst that breaks theories and challenges the status quo. Spielrien has the preponderance for sitting on her ankle, attempting simultaneously to defecate and resisting defecation, causing herself immense pleasure. Her initial neurotic symptoms appear to be out of guilt at enjoying being spanked when she was young and not being spanked now. She embodies her theory that desire and destruction are the same, her central quest being to discover why something as pleasurable as sex should lead to so many complications, given sex is so natural. While Jung informs Freud of these activities of his new patient, who has been sent to him by Freud, the older man is not particularly impressed. Freud just situates Spielrien amongst all of the other patients who just prove his theory concerning the oral, anal, and phallic stages. However, Jung clearly shows that Spielrien does not have an anal personality, quite the opposite. And she appears to practice what she preaches. From the age of four Spielrien's father has spanked her. She enjoyed it, involving Jung in the same when he takes her on as a patient.

In the nineteenth century women visited their physicians for 'clitoral stimulation' for it was widely believed that symptoms, such as hysteria, arose from sexual repression. Freud removed the physical interaction between patient and doctor by instigating the talking cure. The film reveals Jung was the more physical of the two, but Jung is not depicted enjoying spanking Spielrien.

Jung was the son of a pastor, the archetypal Protestant, spanking his patient out of a sense of duty, this being part and parcel of the work ethic. Regardless of the veracity of the story, the narrative is traditional. Freud basically needs Jung to accept his view that we must give up on any idea of trying to cure people, for if we do not we are exchanging one delusion for another.

Hyperbolically, the film ends by claiming Jung was the greatest psychologist of the twentieth century, his vision underlying this praise. In the final scene, where he meets the successful Sabina who now is a practising psychoanalyst, he predicts the bloodshed of the First World War. The film portrays him as a man prepared to enter uncharted territory, unlike Freud, and in doing so to find the many voices of others around him. Whether it is in sexuality or writing, instead of worrying about the originality of our own voice, or how it remains the same, as in Freud's case, we must focus on the ways we encourage the reader, and ultimately the audience, to imagine. 'And so the emphasis on craft is newly stated: not in terms of *finding our own voice*, but in terms of *finding the voice of our reader*' (italics in text).[20]

A Dangerous Method confirms the concept that a good story is about what the characters want and cannot have. A good story will have obstacles in the way of the heroes which enable them to grow as a protagonist. Here we have Spielrien and Jung wanting each other and Freud stating this is impossible due to their different ethnicity, Spielrien being a Jew. Freud is in a sense his own obstacle, wanting everyone to accept his beliefs without question; this is his strength and his weakness. Importantly, it is implied that for Freud it does not necessarily matter if they are true or not, just that everyone needs to fully accept his theories without question, otherwise those outside the movement will be able to destroy it. Freud's position in this instance confirms the idea of what a 'good' story is. His desire to have everyone think the same way as him cannot come about, with his greatest disciple being eventually his greatest enemy.

The psychology of obstacles

The more interesting and varied the obstacles encountered the more profound the character development and therefore your story and screenplay will be. Science-fiction stories can be full of the most profound obstacles. This is not a definitive list but indicates areas that can be developed:

1   Gender, race, class, and sexuality – these are all obstacles characters may deal with in the sense that they might prevent characters getting what they want, given most people want equality and want to

succeed, and *A Dangerous Method* touches on all of these, hence it is a profound story.

2   People – those who think differently, as in the case of Jung v Freud.

3   External places – geography may be limiting and an obstacle, although this might be complex. In *A Dangerous Method* Vienna is the centre of the psychoanalytic movement so anyone who wants to excel in this field must be there, but Jung warns people that they should leave Vienna. They do not listen. There are plenty of other examples where it is the small-town mentality that is the obstacle the protagonist wants to overcome, as in *Billy Elliot* (directed by Lee Hall and written by Stephen Daldry, 2000) and *Billy Liar* (directed by John Schlesinger adapted from the novel by Keith Waterhouse, 1963).

4   Internal places – it could be the internal struggle a character has that underlines a major element of the obstacles in the screenplay, and this is very apparent in *A Dangerous Method*, both with Spielrien and Jung – her symptoms of 'madness' are severe, so it is this internal space that is the obstacle that must be overcome.

5   The Self – in *The Damned United* (directed by Tom Hooper, 2009, adapted by Peter Morgan, from the novel *The Damned Utd*, 2006), a story based on the experience of the football manager Brian Clough at Leeds United for 42 days, it is the hubris of the protagonist that is the main obstacle, his Self, but this is also part of his heroic nature, like Freud, so to state this is the obstacle that needs to be overcome is problematic. The point is this cannot be overcome. The adage too much is never enough is relevant here. Whatever Clough does he will never be able to beat his rivals, but he is not really competing with them but his own inner demons. This sense of being driven we can also equate with *The Hurt Locker* (directed by Kathryn Bigelow and written by Mark Boal, 2008) where, despite having a wife and child (or perhaps because of this) the protagonist goes back to Iraq to dismantle bombs, taking more and more risks. And with *Apocalypse Now* (directed by Francis Ford Coppola and co-written with John Milius, 1979, loosely based on the Joseph Conrad novella *Heart of Darkness*, first published as a three-part serial in *Blackwood's Magazine* 1899 1000th anniversary edition).

6   The Body – there could be a physical problem that is the obstacle, as in *The King's Speech* (directed by Tom Hooper and David Seidler, 2010) where the king has a speech impediment, and *The Elephant Man* (directed by David Lynch and written by Christopher De Vore

and Eric Bergen, 1980) based on the life of John Merrick, who had neurofibromastosis type 1 and Proteus syndrome. The physical obstacle may be chosen and may embody a wider political metaphoric element, as in *The Tin Drum* (directed by Volker Schlöndorff and co-written with Jean-Claude Carrière, Günter Grass and Franz Seitz, 1979, from the novel by Günter Grass, 1959) about a boy who never grows old.

7   The supernatural – there may be a major problem in this area, as in *The Exorcist* (directed by William Friedkin and written by William Blatty, 1973, from his 1971 novel) when a girl becomes possessed, but it might be too easy to specify one obstacle where there are several, such as here when complex interrelated issues around politics, sexuality, wealth and class all come into play.[21]

8   Time – the past or the future may be thwarting what the character wants and with Spielrien it is the past experiences with her father. In *Sexy Beast* (directed by Jonathan Glazer and written by Louis Mellis and David Scinto, 2000) the character's past haunts him and comes back like the return of the repressed, but it also relates to 3., where it is the small-town mentality of England that is the obstacle that needs to be overcome.

9   The Environment – *The Road* (directed by John Hillcoat and written by Joe Penhall, 2009), *Titanic* (directed by James Cameron) (which also includes 1.).

10 The Other – a colonial force can be the obstacle, a population that is in the way of 'progress', as in *Avatar* and *Apocalypse Now*, or an alien other, as in the *Alien* series (beginning with Ridley Scott's 1979 film written by Dan O'Bannon).

Multiple obstacles

In all these cases the obstacles may have literal and/or a multitude of metaphoric meanings, and most likely may not stand in isolation. Paradox is at the heart of a good story. The most profound screenplay will combine elements to contain powerful paradoxes. In *21 Grams* previously mentioned, Paul River's (Sean Penn) obstacle is not having a well-functioning heart, symbolic of his problematic relationship with his partner. The physical needs to be met by the metaphysical. Paul appears to not have his heart in the relationship; this is not just a physical obstacle. He then seeks to overcome the obstacle to his own happiness by going on a quest to find the person who donated his new heart to him. The man who accidentally killed the person from whom he has received a heart appears to be the obstacle to his new happiness with the wife of the man he has received a heart from. But without this man accidentally being a murderer Sean Penn would not be living.

The psychology of treatments

A treatment is a useful tool when writing a script and is part of the pitching process. First you need to develop a premise, which will be around 25 words. The premise asks a question, but does not answer it, encouraging the reader to want to know more. Below is an example from a second-year Bachelor of Arts student Sian James.

PREMISE

In a small town where everyone knows everyone's business a young woman is forced to confront the moral issue of right and wrong when she makes a decision that not only affects her but a trusting elderly man. Will she regret her decision and attempt to reconcile or will it be too late?

TREATMENT

15th June, 2010; Tredegar, a small working class town in South Wales. GRACE MORGAN is twenty one years old. She has a petite frame with large eyes heavily darkened by make-up. She has five piercings in her left ear and six in her right. It is 8am. Grace is in the front room of the two bedroomed terraced house she shares with her MOTHER. Her mother has muscular-dystrophy and is wheelchair bound. The front room has the curtains drawn, dirty plates are stacked upon a stained coffee table and the sofa is strewn with pillows and clothes. Grace is late for work, as she rushes around trying to meet her mother's demands she keeps glancing at the clock.

Grace leaves for work. Outside it is already warm, the edges of the sky are striped with

lilac and orange. As she walks she shrugs
her leather jacket down past her shoulders
and kicks at the small stones in her way. A
neighbour nods good morning to her and a cat
creeps across a stone wall.

Grace sits behind the counter in work. She is
an assistant manager at a Bookmakers. The shop
is small and bright with artificial lighting,
no windows and a door facing a wall. The drone
of falsely enthusiastic commentators is played
from speakers. In the shop are three customers,
all are elderly. Two sit on low blue stools and
stare at the newspapers displaying the forms of
various horses. The third stands to the left of
the counter, leafing through a pile of papers
that he has pulled from his pocket. In walks a
small man with a large build and a cap pulled
low. Tufts of white hair curl from below the
cap. He moves slowly with the aid of a walking
stick. Grace greets the customer with a smile,
sarcastically remarking that it is strange to see
him. He is BAILEY DAVIES, known as Old Bailey,
aged seventy two. He wishes Grace good morning
and takes a seat on a stool next to the counter.
He gives Grace a mint humbug and she thanks him
and slips it into her jacket pocket. Grace makes
him a coffee and they chat for a while. Old
Bailey sips his coffee as he continuously plays
games of bingo and asks Grace to check if he
has won because he struggles to see the numbers
due to bad eyesight. Old Bailey wins nothing the
first three games but on the fourth game Grace
checks and sees that he has won six pounds. She
hands him the money. Old Bailey is pleased with
his win and tells Grace to keep a pound.

A young, rugged looking man enters the shop.
He is BILLY JONES, twenty-six. He flashes Grace
a smile and walks over to the counter where he
leans on his elbows. Grace is happy to see him,
she stops talking to Old Bailey and moves over
to Billy. Billy asks her how she is and if she
had fun last night.

THE PSYCHOLOGY OF PRACTICE

Flashback to the night before, the shop is dark and the shutters are down. Grace and Billy are lying across the counter, their bodies tangled together. There is a tattoo in a Celtic design on the back of Billy's left calf.

Grace giggles awkwardly and moves away from Billy to serve another customer. As she gives the customer his change the phone rings. On the phone is her mother and Grace argues down the phone over what time she will be home. Grace finishes the conversation and puts down the phone. She sighs as she sits down. Billy asks her if she is OK, Grace replies that she 'don't give a fuck anymore.' Billy goes to the other side of the shop to study the papers. Grace serves Old Bailey again then sits with her face propped in her hands. She is deep in thought. She takes a humbug out of her pocket, starts to unwrap it then changes her mind and places it back. Grace kicks the bar of the chair upon which she is sat with her heels and runs her fingernails up and down the coin stand. Old Bailey asks for another coffee. Grace pauses before making one. As she hands him the coffee she shoves it roughly across the counter. Old Bailey fails to notice.

A horse race ends and a middle aged customer with a large stomach strides over to the counter and hands Grace a slip. He is rubbing his hands together and a grin is spread across his face. Grace drops the slip and sees there are no returns. She explains to the customer that the bet was put on too late, the race had already started and therefore the bet is void. The customer kicks off. He demands his money and curses at Grace, calling her an 'idiot'. Billy warns the customer to calm down. Eventually the customer accepts that he is not getting paid and leaves, slamming the door behind him. Grace is flustered. Old Bailey tells her not to worry.

The shop quietens down. Only Grace, Billy and
Old Bailey remain. Grace doodles pictures of
sunshine and stars on a scrap piece of paper.
Old Bailey starts singing 'love is all you
need,' to himself. Grace appears annoyed by
this. She presses down harder with the pen.
Old Bailey hands her a bingo slip and asks her
to check if he has won anything. Grace checks
the slip and sees that old Bailey has won
£500. Without thinking she pays out the slip
on the machine but turns and tells him that he
hasn't won. Grace is shocked at herself. Her
face reddens and she tries to focus on a spot
on a poster on the other side of the shop. She
notices Billy looking at her thoughtfully.

Old Bailey says goodbye and leaves the shop.
Grace paces around behind the counter. She
checks to see whether Billy is looking. He
is facing away from her playing on a games
machine. Grace picks up her bag, crouches down
and opens the safe and takes out £500. Her
hands are trembling. She quickly puts the money
in her bag then pushes the bag under the chair.
Grace stands up and sees Billy at the counter.
She jumps. Billy asks her what she is doing
and Grace stutters her words. She explains to
him what happened. Billy shakes his head and
tells her she needs to give the money back. He
reaches towards her and holds her hands in his
and tells her that he understands.

Grace takes her break when her colleague
comes into work. Outside the sun is high
in a cloudless sky. Grace walks towards Old
Bailey's house. She watches her feet as she
walks, slowly placing one foot after the
other. She nervously twirls a strand of hair
around her finger. Grace stops as she waits
to cross the road. She can see Old Bailey's
house across the street. It is the end house
in a row of terraced houses painted white with
dirt splattered up the side. Grace takes a
deep breath and looks down. Before she has a

```
chance to look up she is knocked to the floor as
someone punches her in the side of the face.

Grace lies unconscious on the floor. A handful
of sweets, mint humbugs, lie on the floor next
to her where they have spilled from her jacket
pocket. Her bag lies open a few metres away,
the money has gone. The footsteps of the mugger
fade away into the distance, due to the hot
weather he wears cut-off denim shorts, on the
back of his left calf is a tattoo in a Celtic
design.
```

Here the humbug is similar to one of Hitchcock's McGuffins. We follow this sweet, the name also meaning what it signifies – humbug, or balderdash, and believe it is some form of Chekhov's gun, discussed in pages 151–2. Clearly it takes on a heightened significance. But then it is not the actual Chekhov's gun, which is the tattoo. The names of the characters are all significant. Old Bailey is the infamous law courts in London. Billy Jones is a typical lad, perhaps more of a bad boy than usual, verging on the stereotypical. The stereotype is broken because he urges her to take the money back, but then reconfirms this stereotype, and, oversteps it, bluntly, with the punch. The tension builds, there is rhythm. Each action is foreshadowed and prefigured by a previous action. This is the secret of great writing, where the narration sequence builds. We have the conflict with the mother, suggesting desperation on the part of the daughter, the omen of the cat, the altercation in the betting shop that parallels the later violence of the punch.

Many of us love to contemplate the complexities of philosophy and enjoy films like *Inception* (Christopher Nolan, 2010). But when it comes to writing a treatment it needs to be simple, straightforward and obvious. Some might be offended by the simplicity of questions such as who is the good guy, who is the bad guy, but this is what a producer or director is going to ask, and who would play this or that part.

Typical mistakes are:

- Thinking it is a summary of what happens;
- Writing in the past tense and not writing in the present tense;
- Thinking it is a short story version of your film;

- Not stating where it is set – personally, I like this to be specific, but there might be a problem with it being too specific. E.g. for some reason your film might not be able to be shot in Manchester, so could your film just as easily be shot in some other city?

- What period is it set in? Are you assuming it is now, and if so how now is now?

- Not naming the characters or giving them an age. Sometimes this is done for a reason, to make the film more avant-garde, but be careful here;

- Having elements that cannot be seen on screen, e.g. having the thoughts of characters – we cannot feel a thought;

- Finally, ask 'so what?' at the end of everything you do.

The psychology of format

As has been explained, we may believe that life itself is scripted to a degree and that there is a set path that we are uncovering as we walk upon it, or, that everything is random. Whatever our views on any metanarrative or teleology to life itself, there is no garden without a fence. Working within a format gives us the leverage and template to position our ideas in such a manner that our writing has this kind of resonance – it was meant to be. We want this to come across, even if our screenplay is in the Dogme model or contains what appear to be random incidents that do not conform to an overarching theme or arc. The ending of *28 Days Later* ... (directed by Danny Boyle and written by Alex Garland, 2002) has such resonance, as if it is a dream coming true – that it was meant to be. Without a script being properly formatted it will not be looked at. And yet many people never properly format a script or get confused about it and leave it to the last minute.

There are plenty of software packages that can do the formatting for you and as technology advances so rapidly there is no point mentioning specific packages here. But we cannot allow machines to do everything. Saying the software does it for you may add to the mechanical, depersonalized, nature of the process of screenwriting, so we feel it is not an art form that creates something new. Psychologically, just because a machine can do the formatting for us might mean we do not think about it, or at least think about the story more. Differences and divisions between the human and the machine are not clear-cut and numerous films deal with this very subject, such as *Metropolis* (directed by Fritz Lang and written by Lang and Thea Von Harbou, 1927), *RoboCop* (directed by Paul Verhoeven and written by Edward Neumeier and Michel Miner, 1987), *Terminator* (directed by James Cameron and written by Cameron, Gale Anne Hurd and William Wisher Jr., 1984), *Blade Runner* (directed by Ridley Scott and written by David Peoples and Hampton Fancher, 1982, from the novella *Do Androids Dream of Electric Sheep?* by Philip K. Dick, 1968), and *A.I.* (directed and written by Steven Spielberg, 2001, from the Brian Aldiss short story 'Super-Toys Last All Summer Long', 1969). Frequently, these films reveal the machine to be more human than the human, or the nightmare that all humans are stereotypes, a mere copy of a copy, as in *Moon* (directed by Duncan Jones and co-written with Nathan Parker, 2009).

The performance artist Stelarc often uses machinery in an attempt to confirm, with Nietzsche, that we should resist saying death is the opposite of life, and this is true of storytelling in general. We would be forgiven for thinking why be restricted by such boundaries and that a focus on boundaries is far from creative, but we need to know the parameters we are working in. Most books and classes on screenwriting leave format to the very end but this is key, as this is the mode we are writing in, so we need to understand the framework immediately, otherwise we waste time. Some might argue that generating ideas is far more important, but if we fail to understand the mode and framework we are working in then this could be a fruitless practice. Unless we know the format we are writing in then we might end up writing something that will not be a screenplay.

Into the Wild (directed and written by Sean Penn, 2007, from the book by John Krakauer), concerns a rich American young man Christopher McCandless (Emile Hirsch) who leaves university and gives up everything to get back to nature. The film uses excerpts from the book it is based on innovatively, with the words appearing inside the screen frame. As the film comes from the true story that was found when the protagonist was discovered dead, the literary element combined with the visual has a powerful impact. While it is therefore fallacious to say these forms are totally divided, focusing on the visual is of paramount importance. The screenplay overlaps with other forms, such as the stage play, short story and novel, and can be blended with poetry to good effect. The format is our boundary we must work within and this boundary gives us the rules of play. Every game has rules and it is not a game without them. Many people write poetry but have not read a great deal of poetry. We have probably seen thousands of films, but how many short films have we seen or screenplays?

The material known as the black stuff is the heading words in each scene we write explicitly to describe what's happening. This is usually written in the present tense. We might find this difficult at first, as it may not come naturally, given we are often taught at an early age to write stories in the past tense, narrating events after they have occurred rather than in the moment and directly. This leap to the now is what makes screenwriting exciting. Whether screen events are occurring in the past, the present or the future, we experience them as an audience in the moment, and so they need to be written in the moment. If we can always bear this in mind then our screenplays will be fresh and we will be showing events occurring in the here and now rather than telling events.

EXT. PARK. DAY.

A bright, sunny day. Twenty-four people, aged between 18 and 25, are having fun in their local park. Three of the twenty four play football:

John, 25, good looking but vain

Ray, 25, a good natured hard case

Amanda, 18, likeable and witty

Two of the twenty-four are tipsy, and play patter-cake games, pretending they are kids.

Two are kissing intensely, and play fighting at the same time.

Six are playing cricket.

The other twelve indulge in a sumptuous picnic, spread over brightly covered rugs, gesticulating wildly, playing pranks on each other, listening to music, lying in the sun, and having the time of their lives.

Of these twelve, EMMA, 19, blonde and pregnant, is talking to CARLY, 23, dark haired and large. They are sipping white wine, in a civilised fashion, having a heart-to-heart.

This is from the start of my screenplay, *The Four Minute Warning*.[22] There is a lot wrong with it. On occasion I am using what might be termed a cliché, 'having a heart-to heart', but clichés can work as a shorthand. Sometimes you need to cut to the chase. Typically, when I wrote it I thought it was excellent but with distance I now know the faults. The trouble with many writing courses is that there are tight deadlines within short semesters, which means developing work is difficult. In industry a screenplay can take many years to develop, moving through various people's hands. Originality is obviously related to origin but once taken out of one or two people's hands, the origin becomes dispersed, as may the originality. In whatever the circumstances, it is important to have objectivity and this can only come through stepping back. You are not the best judge of your work, as you are too attached to it. If you put your heart into the work you are one with it. There is nothing wrong with this initially, as you are the origin of the work, so any criticism of the work can feel like a criticism of you.

An important question with any writing is: can we ever have objectivity when it comes to our own work and is all writing autobiography? The writer will bring part of who they are into what they do, the work containing their thoughts and their ideas. If you see you and your screenplay as one then a script editor will be chopping off part of you when deleting some of your work, and this will be as painful as castration without an anaesthetic. Formatting prevents this pain, or at least alleviates it somewhat, and can create objectivity, as we can see our work more objectively on the page. For example, we can see simple things, such as whether a piece of dialogue is too long, or if a scene just does not work. This stands out on the page. Without the correct format, the piece might be a great idea, but it is just an idea. We need to be able to stand back from our work, and formatting is one tool that enables this.

Not fixing the time and place of a script is slack and I have neglected this here. A local park, but where, or was that my point all along? I might not be able to argue that here, given that time period and specificity of place is normally all-important, although this is more of a metaphysical screenplay. London, Bradford, Skegness, Barcelona, Melbourne, Tripoli, where exactly? Plus most places have an underbelly, a shadow land, so we need to go further than that. London is a vast sprawling metropolis; is it set in a rough or an exclusive part, or even a road where both are combined? There needs to be a balance. Locations may change at the last minute when shooting and flexibility is necessary. It is so easy to forget the obvious. You can keep it simple and then have two worlds collide. Setting your screenplay in one location does not mean that these so-called separate two worlds cannot collide, for your apparently uncouth villain may have gone up a few notches in the world due to his wealth. But, of course, if it is set in Britain this is often not allowed, so she will be mercifully punished for it. The more we think about format the more we think about our screenplay itself, so it is far from a mechanical exercise of just thinking about what comes where on the page. This is why it should never be left until the last minute but thought about early on.

You may have what you consider to be a really brilliant idea but what use is it if you do not know where to situate it – if you cannot actually visualize it. Even if your screenplay is set in a world that does not really exist, the location is crucial – you need to flesh it out, really visualize your world and make it so believable others will enter this world. Exercises such as imaginative contemplations can help. And you need to achieve this in the minimum amount of words. And this is where some of the boundaries between types of writing break down, because we see screenwriting is akin to poetry – saying the most with the least amount of words. This forms part of the editing process but starting with the correct format saves us time because we can see how long each of our sections are. It stops us overwriting which can be a danger. While we can still have complex and interesting dialogue and suggestive and playful description, anything that gets in the way of our script being read for its visual intention does it a disservice. Fundamentally, it could be our ego getting in the way of our script, so we need to put this aside. Study Paul Schrader's beginning of *Taxi Driver*. This is a very literary opening and sets the picture well. We do not have to be too worried that our skills with language may work against us but just remember that we need to be so dextrous that the language itself becomes invisible. Again, it has to appear as if it was supposed to be. Like the finger pointing to the moon we want to visualize the moon not the finger. As soon as the screenplay gets in the way it is not a screenplay.

We can say a lot about character from just two words but is 'dark haired and large' detailed enough, would 'raven haired and podgy' be better? This is difficult. We want the words to be interesting. Podgy is an interesting word compared to large but we also do not want them to detract from what we are writing. The words are supposed to conjure up visual images and 'podgy' is better than 'large', which is too relative and not as affectionate. This brings us back to Buddhism where we try and live in the present moment through meditation techniques and living more consciously. As mentioned, the black stuff, also known as the business of screenplay, is normally written in the present moment but we are used to telling a story in the past tense: Joanna had sex, or Joanna was having sex then she sparked up, then finished her tab, made a coffee and retched, and scrambled to the toilet. Joanna lights a post-coital cigarette, her lush lips lingering on the butt, is more like it. If there was no lover in the scene we would have to have an image of a condom, or some other prop, to let us know this was a post-coital cigarette. In order for us to conjure up in the reader's mind the image so it is occurring right now we need to use the present tense. We live in the present tense, although our minds may be fixated on the future or the past, and we experience film in the present tense.

An important paradox is that to make our film believable we need to believe and to put it across that it has been 'lived' before. This is how we truly confirm our existence, the feeling that things were meant to be, that the script was right and had been written. By this I mean it has to absolutely ring true, so in this sense past and present are one with the future – the film was inevitable, predestined. Does writing actually cause this inevitability? There is the idea that what we write is stored in a form of 'collective memory bank' and we are just channelling it and we do not own it. This notion of ringing true and of having lived everything before is close to Freud's uncanny, and the notion of being haunted. There is a level of inevitability, where we think in some ways we could have predicted what would happen, even if we are not correct, which leads to a sense of satisfaction. In this uncanny sense the audience believes they actually wrote the screenplay, that it is their story. In the screenplay the beginning is often the end and the end is the beginning, so the future and present are one, and time is collapsed and condensed. This occurs in the majority of good films.

Psychologically, this is interesting, particularly with regards to suspense. Many scenes will end on an open question – such as where next and can you guess – to lead the reader and audience on so that the reader is the detective attempting to work out the secret. But if, simultaneously, they have the feeling they have read or seen this before then it might be assumed that the suspense dissipates. Just as the audience watching a film feels they themselves are projecting images from their mind, so the reader thinks that *they* have shaped the screenplay, for they are seeing in words what they mentally perceive. Paradoxically, therefore, in some sense the originality of the screenplay stems from how unoriginal it is. Writing what was meant to be sounds like a mystical task for how can we write what was meant to be if it is not written yet? But we all know the feeling of seeing a film that is so perfect it comes straight from the collective unconscious. This actually liberates us because the obsession for originality can override our ability to connect, making us only connect with an audience of one – our self. Knowing intimately the boundaries of format will help us overcome this.

The psychology of ideas

What are the commonalities in the following, apparently diverse, films? *Star Wars* (directed and written by George Lucas, 1977); *Lost in Translation* (directed and written by Sofia Coppola, 2003); *The Godfather* (directed by Francis Ford Coppola and co-written with Mario Puzo, 1972, from Puzo's 1969 novel); *Breaking the Waves* (directed by Lars von Trier and co-written with Peter Asmussen, 1996); *Dead Man* (directed and written by Jim Jarmusch, 1995); *Rear Window* (directed by Alfred Hitchcock and written by John Michael Hayes, 1954, based on a Cornell Woolrich short story 'It Had to Be Murder'); *Natural Born Killers* discussed in Chapter 1. All of these films are about dealing with a force, either outside or inside the self, or both.

Most interesting drama, in whatever form, concerns a force, inside or outside the self, that breaks out; so the human psyche confronts this darkness within the safe confines of the cinema. This is straightforward. Everything can come down to physics or metaphysics – there is a battle going on between life and death, good and evil, and what is interesting is when they are not superficially divided, when contradictions rule, and we do not know where we are. The only person without contradiction is a dead man. What if the dark side actually is our origin (Luke Skywalker being Darth Vader's son in *Star Wars*), what if we are an alive man who someone thinks is a dead man but we are really a dead man (yes, you guessed it, *Dead Man*). So when generating ideas we need to think of scenarios of contradiction, high drama and conflict. Some people find this difficult, others have so many ideas they do not know where to start. 'What if?' scenarios are the best place to begin.

So what makes a good idea; anything containing paradox. It is great to have ideas but putting them into practice is important and the first step is getting things down on paper. Get into a habit of writing continually. What if we all lived our lives as if this was the final day we had left on the planet? There's a premise to a film there. Maybe we can see the film panning out in our heads, how the central character realizes that love is important, and he needs to make amends. That's a rhetorical question really, but if we all meditated on this we might waste less time and really focus on what matters. If you want to write something then write something, do not just pretend to write something. Ideas can stem from your own imagination, from your dreams, and you can generate ideas by developing stories you hear in the news. A Latin American woman won a court case against a company because she was traumatized after finding a used condom in a can of food; the company claimed everything was automated, so it was impossible for the condom to get there. This is a real news story with a lot of potential. Along with 'what if' scenarios, your own experiences, your imagination and the news, here is a guide to help you develop your ideas further, so you do not waste any more time, although, as Neil Young has it, 'there's a lot to learn from wasting time, a heart that burns, an open mind'.[23] If we are struggling and stressing to find ideas it can be important to take time out for ideas to find us.

Achievable

For Spanish director Pedro Almodóvar we become our self when we become our dream. Dream the impossible dream – perhaps. Do not hold yourself back. Let your imagination run riot. At the ideas stage why limit things at all, but there is no point dreaming up an idea that cannot be achievable and realized. An idea needs to be understandable and fit within known paradigms, but it also needs to be able to break them. Ask some obvious questions. Writers are often told to write about what they know. In the psychology of screenwriting this could create problems, as you might just be locked into what goes on in your head. Get objectivity. Do you know where it is going to be shot exactly, have you been to the location and scouted about, and taken photographs to help you write the description around scenes? For many it is the location that gives them the idea, and it is this focus that makes it realistic and achievable. Think also about your project from a producer's perspective. It might be good to have an exotic location, but could you do the same with your story somewhere more local?

The quintessential thing to remember is caressing the divine details, as Vladimir Nabokov once put it. This is the way to enter the idea. Really caress the inner truth of what you are doing. Screenwriting is much more than writing poetry, but can be and should be poetic. The poet observes and ought to fully realize the moment, like the Buddhist who meditates on the here and now to enter into eternity. The depth of your screenplay, psychologically, artistically and spiritually, depends on this ability to enter the now, and through this, paradoxically, to transcend the moment. Think of the Psalms; they so clearly relate to a specific time and place and yet they transcend that time and place and speak now as well. Space and time are in many respects constructs and the more you can enter the moment in and through the world of your screenplay the more you can go beyond the superficialities of your screenplay and the world, and connect with others.

Layers

In the psychology of screenwriting, while being realistic, every idea needs to be nuanced. Paradox is the essence of anything interesting. You have a character who is obsessed with identity and with the idea of getting back home (*Moon*, directed and co-written by Duncan Jones and Nathan Parker, 2008), who discovers he is just a copy of a copy of a copy and there is no such thing as self and home as such, no wife and child. Every corner turned can open up into another corner (*Inception*, directed and written by Christopher

Nolan, 2010). Both films play with the concept of identity and the notion that all is a construct, that we never are who we think we are, or are where we think we are. This, of course, does not necessarily lead to the notion that all is a construct, but the opposite. It reinforces the tenacious grip of the notion that identity is fixed, or at least confirms our desire for a grounded sense of being.

Time

Is your story set in a 24-hour period, over a number of years, a few seconds? It is important to consider this when thinking about your idea, for this will enhance your own psychology.

Place

Is your work set in a slum or in a palace, in the most remote regions of Latin America, or the centre of a big city? If you do not get this honed down straight away then you have not got much of an idea that will be transformed into something tangible, concrete and believable. I have mentioned how important location is, and you can learn so much from it. Treat your idea as achievable. Go to the location where you want it set and take photographs. If it is a place from your childhood, notice how much has changed, or has not. Is it for the better, or for the worse? Enter into the sensations and feelings, make it come alive. If you want to set your film in a popular location, such as Camden Lock in London, then have you factored in variables such as tourists during the period it is set? Will your characters have to wade their way through the crowds, or is it a quiet time in the year or the day? This leads us on to another important factor.

Seasons

As indie-rock band Echo and the Bunnymen rhymed sweetly, 'everyone has their own good reason why their favourite season is their favourite season'. Whether we are Gothic-minded tortured souls, loving winter and cemeteries, or cannot wait for the summer, seasons can make a film and actually be the central character in the film. Think of the centrality of the snow in *The Shining*, or the frozen wasteland of *The Sweet Hereafter* (directed and written by Atom Egoyan, 1997, from the Russell Banks novel, 1991).[24] Bond films have an obligatory chase sequence often in the snow, as does *Inception* (directed and written by Christopher Nolan, 2010). Consider the mesmerizing desert in *Under a Sheltering Sky* (directed by Bernardo Bertolucci, 1991, and co-written with Mark Peploe, from the novel by Paul Bowles, 1949), where the desert appears to be a mountainous creature, virtually alive with a presence all of its own. Here landscape and conditions unite, time and space act as one together, so the geology and geography becomes united as a character. This is both physical and metaphysical. Bertolucci has turned the desert into a character. In the mesmerizing film *My Summer of Love* (directed and written by Pawel Pawlikowski, 2004, from the novel by Helen Cross, 2001) two young girls from two very different backgrounds meet one summer, have a sexual relationship, and then return, so we imagine, to their other lives. It is the summer season itself that allows the love, only momentarily, the transgression being contained by the time span of the summer. Time and seasons are deceptive. The summer holidays seem like they are limitless, but are over in a flash, a metaphor for life itself. Christmas movies, dare I mention them, do not have to be mawkish and sentimental, and we can always subvert expectations.

Clarity

If we are not clear on who the central protagonist is, who their nemesis is, and on the plot, how is our reader supposed to make it out? We may only achieve clarity after numerous re-writes, but even at an early stage, when we write out our treatment or premise, or just jot down notes on our plot, try and be clear as to what each character is going to achieve and what they will lend to the story, plot and narrative.

3

The psychology of character

We have seen that there is a complex relationship between cinema and identity. While there is some truth in the statement that Hollywood films are action based and European films are character based these bland divisions are not helpful or particularly accurate. In the psychology of screen-writing it is useful to recognize that relationship is essential. How do we, as writers, relate to ourselves, other writers, our characters, how do our characters relate to themselves and others, and how does our audience relate to them psychologically? E. Annie Proulx, whose short story about two cowboys who have a sexual relationship, *Brokeback Mountain*, was made into an award-winning film directed by Ang Lee and written by Larry McMurtry and Diana Ossana, claimed it was the first fiction she had written where the characters came to life for her and had their own identity and wrote themselves as it were. This is a remarkable statement by an already successful and established writer, but perhaps she is talking about the actual extent to which they came to life. It is worth noting she did 80 re-writes of the story, particularly when we might be struggling with our eleventh draft.

The two central characters had their assumed identities and roles in society but also their secret identities, which they played out with each other. Others did find out about these identities, but the film in part is about how these withheld identities function. As an audience this is what we are interested in. Writing without depth just uses a character as a hook for a plot line and numerous films do that. There are real people who do not have depth, who have very little inner-life, and who are happy operating on the surface, or do not want to look too deeply inside because if they did they would have a shock. And there are successful films which have characters that are cardboard cut-outs, and just perform a plot function. But if we want to create memorable characters and achieve work that is great art, we need to enter their psychology and our own, and that of our expected audience.

So who are you? How we describe who we are will depend on our personality. Someone who rates feelings above all else will say they are what they feel. But are we our behaviour; is it you are what you do? The word 'self', despite being useful, does not refer to anything that persists; it is just that, a word. 'The illusion of continuity occurs because each temporary self comes along with memories that give an impression of continuity.'[1] Where career is often placed above everything else, many people believe they are what they do. One way of attacking materialistic culture is to say people should not identify entirely with what they do. But this is not something new. Think of where surnames came from; often these are from the professions, like Blacksmith. In earlier centuries people were totally identified with their job and position in life. The world is becoming more complex and our tasks are multiplying. While these might define us to others within the pecking order, it is not really who we are deep down.

If we identify ourselves thoroughly with what we do we have a problem but on a more general level, are we what we do? The answer to this is surprisingly yes. We may say we are a Muslim but unless we behave like one are we a real Muslim? This gets complex when we take another religion, like Christianity. Those who follow Christ must attempt to love others as themselves. If they do this they are behaving in a Christian way, but unless they call themselves Christian then they are not a Christian. Part of the faith is to proclaim it. Freud claimed that for the writer words are deeds. Saying something *is* doing something of course, but actions speak louder than words.

Are we who we say we are and who really defines us? The modern and postmodern world has been one of people defining who they are, overcoming being positioned by others into a certain sense of being. So one element of who you are is who you define yourself to be, who you say you are. This will be defined by a number of factors: what you think and feel; your age; the place you live in; the time you live in; what you dress like; what you speak like; how you move and your physicality; your main goals in life; motivation; your education; your genes, and so on. But who you say you are may be nothing to do with who you really are; you might be completely deluded as indeed may others about you and themselves. According to the nineteenth-century psychologist William James, brother of the famous novelist Henry James, whose novels have been made into a number of films, when two people meet there are six people present: how they both see themselves; how they both see each other; and how they both really are. So when building complex characters, while a list covering all the factors mentioned above, and more, is useful, what is paramount is our understanding of how our characters understand themselves.

This is crucial, because often the screenplay we write will be about a path of revelation, about our characters gaining deeper psychological insight, such as an epiphany into who they really are, or who they become. For acclaimed film director Pedro Almodóvar, in life we become ourselves when we become our dream. This is the essence of character development in life and in film. Film can be considered a dream, the projected dream of the audience, and the characters can realize themselves in the course of the film, become who they are meant to be. In this sense, so do the audiences. We are all probably familiar with the idea that everyone in your dream is an aspect of yourself, and writers such as Will Self claim fiction is autobiography. Characters fulfil the dreams of the audience, not merely because the audience is projecting themselves onto these characters, but because part of them is being made whole, or at least a part is being engaged with that is sometimes overlooked.

This is the same for the scriptwriter. Part of the scriptwriter is being made whole through the writing process and this is the essence of the psychology of screenwriting. Writing itself may not lead to deep inner healing, there might not be an ontological teleological linear process, but the process itself is healing, not the product. We want to see dreams played out and we want people to become who they really are, as the film *Limitless* (directed by Neil Burger and written by Leslie Dixon, 2011) shows. Frequently we do not know their potential before we put them into certain scenarios that test them and it is useful to write a number of different endings to scenes. We might know from the start about what is within them and will come forward in our story. Writing can be an unconscious process, but, as with all activity, it is a conscious and unconscious act. We only know what is really there after we have done it.

There are precursors to the unconscious of Freud and post-Freudian concepts of the unconscious. In addition, Jung's idea of the collective unconscious was written about by earlier thinkers. Writing in the 1860s, Eduard von Hartmann maintained the unconscious contained three layers: the absolute unconscious, which was the substance of the universe and the source of the other forms; the physiological unconscious, 'the origin, development, and evolution of living beings, including man; and the relative or psychological unconscious, the source of our conscious life'.[2]

Identity is about commitment and how dedicated we are to certain beliefs and orientations. We label people through their manifestation of a number of categories, such as: gender, class, age, belief, sexual orientation, and so on. While an actor will hopefully get the correct accent, it is up to us as writers to get the correct words. With the ubiquity of American language, we need to be even more specific. If we have an American character can we get the region of America they are originally from by our use of words? As Charles Guignon explained in *On Being Authentic*, in the premodern world people were just what they did, with the idea of an inner self a later modern invention. This might be an artificial binary separation between eras, but the notion of seeking an inner authenticity has become essential to many in the contemporary world, as if this is their only mission in life. Now, however this is changing.

Tim Guest's memoir *My Life in Orange*, about growing up in a religious cult, reveals the lengths people will go to escape their origins, to forge new identities, only to find that by sacrificing everything they have got nowhere. Guignon dismisses the view held by psychoanalyst Alice Miller, and many others, which 'relies on a set of valorized binary oppositions that contrast childhood, understood as what is natural, inner and positive, with what is grown-up, external, artificial and negative'.[3] We cannot assume one moment in life is any more natural than any other. Age, childhood, identity and wisdom, are not necessarily linear processes, and film can be used to spark off memories from childhood. We need to be fully aware of what some literary scholars call the chronotope, that is the time period and place in which we are writing, because this is the world we are creating. These are two key elements, and many new writers forget them, so their writing takes place in an abstract, unreal place. Everything exists in time and space, even if we decide that the world we create is going to be in some way outside traditional time and space. If we make such a metaphysical leap then we have a lot of work to do.

The writer does not do research like the historian or journalist but research is essential. Is it set in 1880s London? What do things smell, feel, or look like; what is the transport like; how do people dress and speak; what do they eat; what are the various positions in society; what are gender relations like; who governs and who makes the decisions; what are the desires of the people at this time; how do they view sex; what are their expectations and are these met; what is the level of communication like; what is known about the rest of the world; how much literacy is there; is the climate and weather different; what is social care like; what are the various belief systems; and how do they influence outlooks and behaviours? This list could go on and on.

Here, getting a level of accuracy involves more than just repeating all the clichés from other films and television shows you have seen; it involves doing proper hands-on research. This research actually might take you down different avenues from the ones you initially set out on, but that is half the fun of exploring a topic in detail. Paradoxically, the harder skill is creating a fantasy world out of nothing. Taking photographs of what you are writing about

THE PSYCHOLOGY OF CHARACTER

might help as will the making of mini-videos on your phone. We do not have the ability to record smells; not yet anyway. We might assume if we invent everything from our imagination this would be easier than trying to stick to accuracy, in terms of a real time and place, but people have to be convinced of the veracity of what you are creating, even if it does not exist yet.

Again, you could play with and subvert some of the usual clichés, like the bar in *Star Wars* full of weird and wonderful aliens from across the galaxy, where Han Solo gets into a fight, and this could work comically. But crucially, you need to be entirely convinced of your world, otherwise your reader and potential audience will not be. This involves using your imagination, in great depth. The Jesuits, and other spiritual groups, have something called imaginative contemplation, and these forms of exercises can be useful. Shut your eyes and imagine your character. What are they doing? Who are they with? And so on. Through this you can develop an entire world and see your characters act. You could be ambitious. You could create a whole new world with even its own language, like *Avatar*, but it has to be convincing.

Names

In the book of Genesis, the first part of *The Old Testament* which is in the Christian and Jewish sacred scriptures, God allows man to name all the animals, and, whether you feel like God or man when you write your screenplay, here is a chance to get creative and take a decision. How to name your characters? Perhaps they named themselves. You are writing about Satan, so his name is obvious, or is it? Beelzebub is a more comical name. In *Reservoir Dogs* (directed by Quentin Tarantino and written by Tarantino and Roger Avary, 1992) naming goes on in the film, with Mr Brown, and Mr Pink, and so on. Everyone knows you are your name, or do they, and how true is that? For every Ben Smart we know, who might be smart, there is a Melanie Pratt who is not one, and maybe Ben Smart is not so smart some of the time, so we can subvert that expectation. Charlie Wax (John Travolta) in Luc Besson's *From Paris with Love* (2010) is a bit of a Charlie, although Chuck might be a more appropriate name. Wax might relate to Travolta's other roles, such as the brilliantly named Sean Archer/Castor Troy in *Face/Off* (John Woo, 1997). Charlie Wax is a squat and brutal name, to the point, and appropriate. Are Kevin, Cuthbert, Quentin, Rupert, and Nigel always squares, and cowards? Even if they are, in general, we might want to subvert expectations, or conclude there is nothing in a name. If we are writing a film with mythical creatures, with certain superpowers, then it is obvious: X-Ray Man, Iron Man. Felicity Shagwell? Or too well?

I invented a character called Johnny Mozzarella, who always 'took care of it'. Granted, he was an Italian stereotype but our knowledge of what we consider to be this type of character is often gained from certain films, so this is bound to be pastiche and this can be subverted. Maybe, as in *Analyse This* (Harold Ramis, 1999) the macho-myth is challenged, where a gangster is seeing a therapist, crying and having panic attacks. It is a big put down to say something is stereotyped or clichéd, but is it not human behaviour to always go in certain patterns? Sometimes stereotypes are correct, and that is the whole point. The problem would be if your central character was just one big stereotype. Then it would all be too predictable, but even that is not completely anathema. Some audiences prefer their experience to have heightened elements of predictability. You need to think about this, but you also need to think about your originality. Are you really creating anything if it already exists elsewhere? Give a girl the name Melissa, and this might conjure up one thing to someone and another to someone else. What is the difference between Melissa and Hannah? For some reason I think of Hannah as a deeper person. And what is the difference between Charlie and Teddy? Not much perhaps, but whatever names we give their characters might subvert the usual associations carried by them.

The essential thing about your character is their motivation. Why do they behave the way they do? If they are the protagonist they need to be the one who feels the most – the one who feels the most agony, who suffers. There is the theory that we are programmed on an unconscious level to behave the way we do, so our choices are out of our hands. Fictional characters need to be offered choices, and whether they go in the right or wrong direction is part of the fun. In the Hollywood formula a character usually learns and develops, and that is the whole point of the film. They make their mistakes, they are taken to the edge, but they finally achieve. Well done we all cheer; what a relief; they made it, and so now we can make it; the whole of humanity can make it. We all feel better. *Avatar* (James Cameron, 2009) is a great example of this. The central idea is walking in someone else's shoes, and learning from the other. Of course, if you walk a mile in someone else's shoes you are a mile away from them, and you have their shoes. And we know they are going to achieve their destiny really, and that is the formula. *Green Zone* (directed by Paul Greengrass and written by Brian Helgeland, 2010 from the book by Rajir Chandra-Sekaran) is another example of the 'alien' (us) entering an 'alien' (them) culture, and realising that there is no 'us' and 'them'. The film concerns a US soldier Captain Miller (Matt Damon) who is tasked with finding WMD, weapons of mass destruction, in Iraq. While storytelling might be about the timing of the delivery of the secret here, as in many other films, we of course already know the story, and the outcome. But we do not know the extent of the corruption, and the betrayal of the Iraqi people, hence the film, while obvious, is gripping.

In standard Hollywood fashion, Matt Damon's character Miller deepens as he wakes up and has his revelation about the depth of corruption in the US government. Both *Avatar* and *Green Zone* are in some respects anti-colonial films for the masses, made without any real subtlety in terms of their scripts but both make us feel the anguish of their central characters. Again, this might lead us to question the role of cinema. Is it to make us feel in a society where the expression of feeling is still often frowned upon, and is it a legitimate release? Cynically, it can be mooted that the audiences goes through the anguish of the hero, feeling they are being political by experiencing a 'political' film, and then they do not get political outside the cinema. As Eric Fromm has made blatantly clear, our heroes are those that move forward and are not afraid to risk everything, but often heroes become idols, and the problem then is 'we transfer to them our own capacity to move'.[4] In this sense they do the work for us. Of course, film may motivate people to get political. There often is a form of rites of passage and a journey that the audience goes on.

With tragedy nothing can be done to reverse the situation. *The Shining* (directed by Stanley Kubrick and co-written with Diane Johnson, 1980, from the Stephen King novel, 1977), despite now being a classic, is not a particularly good example, because we do not feel particularly close to the characters. What are their admirable traits? This does not make it a bad film. Humanity is enhanced through empathy. The narrative is structured so we have empathy in *The Shining* with Danny, and feel sorry for Jack's wife. *The Girl with the Dragon Tattoo* (directed by David Fincher and written by Steven Zaillian, 2012, from the first book of Stieg Larsson's Millennium series, 2005) is another example. While I might feel empathy for Lizbeth (Rooney Mara), as I know her background in a home, even though Mikael (Daniel Craig) has good motives it is difficult to find empathy for him as Mikael. That is why, in the final scene when he returns to his wife, leaving Lizbeth bereft, expectations are more than confirmed which in this instance makes it a comfortable, almost boring, film.

The greatest writers suggest there might be good in evil, or at least they have the same origins, but many films have their characters as irredeemable, so why should anyone care? In crime films often the antagonist is a mentally ill person, who might be terminally ill, while in horror the protagonist becomes mentally ill, tainted by evil, as the story progresses. These characters allow evil to be looked at. In theatre it is more obvious. *Othello* (written by William Shakespeare, 1603, from a short story by Cinthio, 'A Moorish Captain', 1565) is an important example. There are numerous adaptations for film, perhaps most famously the Oliver Parker directed 1995 version, with Laurence Fishburne as Othello and Kenneth Branagh as Iago. Duped by his right-hand man Iago into thinking his new wife Desdemona is having an affair with Cassio who has been promoted over Iago, Othello kills Desdemona and then himself. Othello does learn what a fool he has been, but it is too late to do something about it. There is still a certain awareness, a reflective knowledge. Depending on how vast you believe Iago's skills of manipulation are, and they are vast, Othello's insecurity about his wife's infidelity was already there, so he could be duped. Iago is given all the opportunities he needs to dupe his master. The mad tragedy is Othello needs to kill Desdemona to be aware of her loyalty. And we easily forgive him. Coleridge called Iago's act of revenge 'motiveless malignancy', but A. C. Bradley saw it as more complex than this.[5] If, as Coleridge suggests, there are no clear motives, this would place Iago with characters such as Patrick Bateman in *American Psycho*.

More interestingly, Iago parallels Othello in the traditional way that a screenplay has the protagonist and antagonist often as different aspects of each other. Iago understands Othello so well because he understands jealousy, the green-eyed monster, so well. They are mirrors of one another, with Iago suspicious that Othello has cuckolded him. Iago is no monster because he is concerned for what others think of him.[6] This is actually his main problem. Strengths can be weaknesses, weaknesses strengths. His concern with what others think of him is a strength, leading him to ambitiously perform and compete, but might also lead him to be entirely ruthless. Also, his desire for power fuels his desire for hurting others and there is no real strategy here.[7] What is remarkable about this play is that in Protestant England, that celebrated choice and free will as the bedrocks of true faith, all the main plot points and overall metanarrative come down to luck, chance and fate. This brings us back to the James Bond quotation at the start of this book and to the work of Nietzsche in Book II of *Daybreak* already quoted.

Each hero needs a flaw, a weakness, an Achilles heel. Often their flaw makes them heroic but if their so-called 'over-heroism' is akin to hubris this might be unforgivable. In the case of Chief Miller in *Green Zone* it is his desire to go over and beyond the script laid down to him by the army which is dictated by the government and divorced from truth and reality, his need to take risks, and not follow the party line. Here we have the conundrum of a hero having their own reality, which is then questioned by and not accepted by the outer environment. They are the demon other. Numerous stories engage with this form of characterization, and the narrative arc is about their point of view being accepted by the wider community.

The goodness of evil

We have looked at evil and knowledge. Doing English at college we were given the question: is Shakespeare's Iago a credible character? This is a good question. Is he believable, or is he just too evil? I turned the question into an even better one. Is Iago a creditable character? Despite writing down the question wrong I still got a good grade. How on earth can one of the most so-called evil characters ever invented for dramatic entertainment deserve credit? Maybe he deserves credit for being so evil, so cunning, and so able to duplicitously manipulate everyone around him. Or is this just their stupidity? I have already mentioned that he just seized opportunities from the mistakes of others, so to say there was a clear strategy involved might be giving him more credit than he is due. Iago was overlooked for promotion, so we might have empathy for him, the underdog, and he does get a lot of soliloquies, taking us into his confidence. We need to feel something for all our characters, good, bad, or in-between, and the more in-between the better. There have been a number of film versions of *Othello* and it is a good example as it raises key questions found in numerous screenplays: fundamentally, we want to know what makes someone do so-called evil and what are their motivations; Bradley is right, it cannot just be 'motiveless malignancy'. Is it as simple as greed and the desire for power over others, or is this in itself a weakness? The more questions raised the better.

What are the chinks in the armour? Do the ends justify the means? Characters have an inner and outer life. Sometimes it is difficult to see a character as a rounded person; they are just a person to fit a scenario. *Leaving Las Vegas* (Mike Figgis) does not feel like this, maybe because it is based on a real life experience. It is sometimes difficult to step outside the story and conjure up a real character but that is what is necessary for it to be believable. Bad turned good, good turned bad – these simple reversals form large parts of many narratives. The weak person is the person who believes they are the fight. If the character can go beyond the battle then we are developing strong characters.

For Baudrillard, 'there is a perverse fascination with returning to the source of the violence: a collective hallucinatory vision of the historical truth of Evil'.[8] But he goes on to point out that speaking of evil is impossible and we are stuck with discourse on the rights of man. This stems 'from the Enlightenment belief in a natural attraction of the Good, from an idealized view of human relationships (whereas Evil can manifestly be dealt with only by means of Evil)'.[9] Darth Vadar can only be tackled by his son, and when his son accepts his own 'Evil'.

What is more, even this Good *qua* ideal value is invariably deployed in a self-defensive, austerity-loving, negative and reactive mode. All the talk is of the minimizing of Evil, the prevention of violence: nothing but *security*. This is the condescending and depressive power of good intentions, a power that can dream of nothing except rectitude in the world, that refuses even to consider a bending of *Evil*, or an intelligence of Evil.[10]

Myth and psychology

Myth has been central to a great deal of writing on the screenplay. For Robert Segal the development of a theory of myth in relation to literature is linked to the outgrowth of myth tied to rituals. The same could be said for film, although there are many ritualistic elements about film, in the writing process and in watching.

> For literary myth-rituals, myth becomes literature when myth is severed from ritual. Myth tied to ritual is religious literature; myth cut off from ritual is sexual literature, or plain literature. When tied to ritual, myth can serve any of the active functions ascribed to it by myth-ritualists. Bereft of ritual, myth is reduced to mere commentary.[11]

Importantly, a whole history of literary criticism, such as 'myth criticism' in the Northrop Frye mode, exists, along with the Jungian and post-Jungian work of archetypal psychologists, such as James Hillman.[12] Frye contends that Jung's work and that of J. G. Frazer is just literary criticism, but this is a step too far for Robert Segal: both Frazer and Jung 'intend to be accounting for the origin and function, not merely the meaning of myth'.[13] Segal goes on to explain that the 'grammars' that Frazer and Jung wrote are supposed to be proofs, not just compendia of symbols, and they are for Frazer and Jung based on some form of historical truth. In Frazer's case, 'divine' kings were killed and replaced; in Jung's archetypes do exist in the mind and the world.[14] We could contest Segal's interpretation of Jung's archetypes here, but his point is to show how Frye has turned all forms of investigation, including anthropology and psychology, into literary criticism. This in turn has had an impact on film theory and screenwriting.

Christopher Vogler became an iconic figure in the field of screenwriting reworking these earlier writers and reframing them for screenwriting. Vogler's work is interesting for this study because he delves deeply into psychological archetypes which are not always Jungian and sees them as intrinsic to the fundamental structure of the screenplay. In *The Writer's Journey – Mythic Structure for Storytellers and Screenwriters* (1999) he splits the bulk of his book into two sections. The first consists of quite Jungian archetypes a) 'Mapping the Journey', which includes – a practical guide, archetypes, hero, mentor, threshold guardian, herald, shapeshifter, shadow, and trickster. Those familiar with anthropology might recognize that some of these figures are within many different cultures across the globe, such as Native American cultures. Often it is through a journey and a relationship with these figures that the twists and turns of a story are played out.

In many respects Vogler's work is watered down Jung. He does not reference any of Jung's work directly in his short bibliography. His main source is the work of Joseph Campbell, particularly *The Hero with a Thousand Faces* (1949). Interestingly, Otto Rank's *Myth of the Birth of the Hero* (1914) was not utilized by Vogler as extensively as Campbell's work. Rank deals with the hero myth as ending in young adulthood, whereas Campbell, despite citing Rank, depicts the earlier part of life as mere preparation for the heroic undertakings of the second half of life. 'Antithetically to Jung, he dismisses birth itself as unheroic because it is not done consciously!'[15]

Charles Guignon dismissed the view held by psychoanalyst Alice Miller, and many others, which 'relies on a set of valorized binary oppositions that contrast childhood, understood as what is natural, inner and positive, with what is grown-up, external, artificial and negative'.[16] We cannot assume one moment in life is any more natural than any other. The second section of Campbell's book, b) 'Stages of the Journey', includes the pathway of the journey – ordinary world; call to adventure; refusal of the call; meeting with the mentor; crossing the first threshold; tests, allies and enemies; approach to the innermost cave; ordeal; reward (seizing the sword); the road back; resurrection; return with the elixir. Even if we find a step-by-step formulaic approach repellent, this second section is fundamental to our understanding of most of the stories in existence and is useful to the psychology of screenwriting. The various elements, not necessarily in the same order, seem to underline our most powerful myths that are in turn embedded within our most popular stories. Cinema and television have in many places replaced oral storytelling but the underlying structures and functions of the stories being told may not have changed.

Some writers might not like this structuralist approach but when Vogler breaks down certain films we can see how appropriate his mythic framework is in so many contexts. Clearly it will be more than appropriate for films like *Star Wars* or *The Lion King* (directed by Roger Allers and Rob Minkoff and written by Irene Mecchi and 27 others, 1994) that are based around huge mythological frameworks and are overtly revealing this without attempting to disguise it. But, more interestingly, his other examples in the third section, 'Epilogue: Looking Back on the Journey', include an analysis of low-key British film *The Full Monty* (directed by Peter Cattaneo and written by Simon Beaufoy, 1997) about a group of unemployed men in the poverty-stricken North of England who come together and form a strip act, and the cult classic *Pulp Fiction*. The very fact that what appear to be on the surface quite disparate films do indeed follow a traditional mythic format suggests this format is useful for the screenwriter who needs to be sure of a structure. No matter how creative and imaginative we think we are, or how many or how few ideas we have, or the copious nature of the notes we take, if we cannot engage our reader, and our audience, in some form of deeply symbolic psychological mythic journey, then the structure will not be there.

At times it seems for Vogler there is very little differentiation between real life and the symbolic life of film. It is important to be cautious before we enter fully into the idea that everyone is indeed a projection of everyone else. Whilst stating there are many archetypes, Vogler claims that the most common are: hero, mentor (wise old man or woman), threshold guardian, herald, shapeshifter, shadow and trickster. He makes the interesting point that we may go through relationships, forcing our partner to match up to our projection, our anima or animus and gives the example of Hitchcock's *Vertigo*. Here, John Ferguson (James Stewart) forces Madeleine Elster (Kim Novak) to alter her hair and clothing to become a woman, Carlota, who never existed in the first place.

> The animus and anima may be positive or negative figures who may be helpful to the hero or destructive to him. In some stories it's the task of the hero to figure out which side, positive or negative he is dealing with.[17]

The projection of our concealed contradictory sides, images and ideas about sexuality and relationships construct the archetype of the shapeshifter and, as Vogler has explained, this appears especially in the film noir and thriller genres, *Chinatown* (directed by Roman Polanski and written by Rober Towne, 1974) being a classic example.[18] The femme fatale, such as Wendy Kroy (Linda Fiorentino) in *The Last Seduction* (directed by John Dahl and written by Steve Barancik) is this archetype incarnated. Interestingly, Vogler also discussed the positive and negative implications of the shadow, which we can see incarnated in numerous stories, such as *The Strange Case of Dr Jekyll and Mr Hyde* (originally written by Robert Louis Stevenson, 1886, with numerous film adaptations, such as the 1931 remarkable Rouben Mamoulian version written by Samuel Hoffenstein and Percy Heath) plus in superhero sagas such as Batman. The shadow archetype is good for understanding villains and antagonists in our stories, because they can also contain an unreconciled energy that can lash out in a destructive manner.[19] Humanising these villains is essential and Vogler references novelist Graham Greene as a master of this, but often in film the hero vanquishes the external shadow. Perhaps, using a lesson taken from Derrida, we can go so far as to say that nothing is natural or good in and of itself, and move our characters into hidden depths by exploring this idea further. Numerous novels and films dwell on this, such as Anthony Burgess's novel *A Clockwork Orange* published in 1962, turned into a film by Stanley Kubrick in 1971.

Some might want to blame Vogler for the similarity in blockbuster stories, as if his formula gives guaranteed success, but what is so satisfying about Vogler's take is that it parallels such simple psychology. We know the human psyche is complex, but Vogler's structure makes it look simple although he does engage briefly with philosophising about psychology which is reminiscent of Buddhist approaches we have touched on. As he has put it when explaining the archetype of the Hero under the heading 'Psychological Function', the archetype of the Hero represents in Freudian terms the ego. At first, all Heroes are all ego, but, ultimately, they shift to transcending this ego and this is the journey. They may need to do so by leaving the group, and this represents the search for identity and wholeness.[20] The quotation below summarizes the main message.

> The Hero archetype represents the ego's search for identity and wholeness. In the process of becoming complete, integrated human beings, we are all Heroes facing internal guardians, monsters, and helpers. In the quest to explore our own minds we find teachers, guides, demons, gods, mates, servants, scapegoats, masters, seducers, betrayers, and allies, as aspects of our personalities and characters in our dreams. All the villains, tricksters, lovers, friends, and foes of the Hero can be found inside ourselves. The psychological task we all face is to integrate these separate parts into one complete, balanced entity. The ego, the Hero thinking she is separate from all these parts of herself, must incorporate them to become the Self.[21]

There are some other archetypes Vogler does not mention.

A Pair of Fools (Twins, see the Tarot)

Scouring literature, drama and film, from Shakespeare's *The Tempest* (written in 1611, adapted and interpreted a number of times on film, including *Prospero's* Books, directed and written by Peter Greenaway, 1991) to *Pirates* of the Caribbean and Prometheus (directed by Ridley Scott and written by Jon Spaihts and Damon Lindelof and two other credits for the story, 2012), there are numerous examples of two fools thrown together, in some cases based on reality, as in The Social Network (directed by David Fincher and written by Aaron Sorkin, 2010) where there are twins. Duplication is comic, and revelatory. In Prometheus, which is a didactic science-fiction film about teamwork, the biologist and geologist are the pair of fools. Typically, they are the cowards, and are the first to recognize the danger, because they are more individualistic, as in selfish. Then they get punished, attacking each other, which again is typical for 'Narcissus dies after he has seen himself'.[22] This is an archetypal pairing. The caves they enter in this film are significant and, in general, this form of pairing goes back to Roman and Greek stories.

> In the earlier Narcissus-Dionysos couplet to see one's double may have been less a source of melancholic loss than ecstatic abandon – an erotic reunion with the flowing ambivalence of (m)others before, after or alongside the sacrificial violence of language. This signifies a return to the labyrinth but hardly a solidification of the imperial fortress of one's ego.[23]

Indeed, it has already been shown, with reference to Elaine Showalter, how, post–9/11, a syndrome that relates to doubling became widespread. This clearly is influenced by a threat to the ego, as if one psyche is not enough. Having such a pair can create light or heavy relief. In Adaptation, where Nicolas Cage plays two brothers, these fools rule the film. There is a good case to be made that contemporary capitalist society is merely concerned with the pursuit of ego, where there is a narcissistic pursuit of this object of desire, rather than anything external or foreign. Following Freud, 'Unlike "civilized man" the ambivalent consciousness of archaic peoples "unites determinants from both sides" rather than elevating one to the repression of the other.'[24] Within this paradigm, so-called primitive peoples are involved in a primary narcissism and ambivalence where the conscious and unconscious blur. The relief the so-called civilized receive comes at the cost of repression so there is a split between what is consciously memorable and what is unconsciously perceived. While the writer might write from the latter zone, in the editing process the former is utilized. The more the latter is accessed the deeper and of more psychological benefit the screenplay. In the previously mentioned film Dead Man a certain doubling takes place, given Johnny Depp's character William Blake is not the real William Blake but Nobody the Native American believes he is the real William Blake. Blake and Nobody also mirror each other. They both are each other's spirit guide which, according to Freud, is a way of overcoming a fear of death. The question still remains whether William Blake is physically dead already, even at the start of the film.[25]

The Wounded Healer

When writing a screenplay we will have a protagonist who encounters an antagonist, and the battle commences. We immediately ask the question: will they achieve what they set out to achieve? Underlying this, as a reader and an audience, is a question about our own position, a deep question that essentially asks, can I survive. The opposite of love isn't hate but fear. These different characters might not be human beings, but places, other forms of creatures, or even inanimate objects. Regardless of whether they are animal, vegetable, or mineral, they need to be understood deeply by the writer, and fully rounded, and I do not mean literally here as in the ball Wilson in *Cast Away* (directed by Robert Zemeckis and written by William Boyles Jr., 2000). Before Picasso began painting in a more Cubist individual style he mastered standard portrait painting, and eventually wanted to paint like a child. Similarly, even if you wish to discard straightforward narrative and character development, you still need to know your character inside out. Screenplays that are really not worth reading are those that clearly are informed, or misinformed, by a writer who has never even taken the effort to develop their character/s, so we are left just not believing in them.

It is popular to have characters that have parts of their memory missing, such as *Memento*, and then the audience has to work out what is real, and what is not. In *Inception* there is a multilayered narrative being played out, a dream within a dream as it were, as in *Avatar* where one world feeds into another, a metaphor for the viewing process, and the writing process. You need to be passionate enough about your character so they live. What we find with the best screenplays is that eventually the protagonist, the one who is suffering the most and fighting whatever battles they find themselves in, actually finds out they are not too different from their antagonist, their nemesis. It is the greatest revelation to truly acknowledge that we are one with our enemy. In simplistic Freudian psychological terms this is an aspect of owning up to what we project onto our enemies, and in more behaviourist terms this is acknowledging that what we dislike in others is often what we are denying in ourselves. This splitting, or rejecting what we hate about ourselves and placing it on others, is quite typical behaviour. There cannot be a standard definition of normal or sanity, and so we create one by demonizing the other. For the many strong atheists or even weak agnostics among us, the following may seem strange, or even offensive but, as Terry Eagleton has explained, what Aristotelians call virtue, the spontaneous capacity for acting well, Christians call grace. And this, Eagleton goes on, 'is the reverse of a laborious Kantian conformity to the law'.[26] Happiness might be a warm gun as the Beatles sung, it might be acting on sexual instinct, but here grace is when the will of the individual combines with the will of God.

This is central to the revelation involved inside the character psychologically and perhaps this is also manifested in the external world of the character through a journey or change of place and the audience identifies with this. Writer/directors like Mike Leigh continually stress the lack of mobility in the external world, reflecting the lack of psychological change and desperation of his characters. More traditional film screenplays reflect an element of Jungian psychology here, where the dark part of the personality is integrated into the other part so a more fully human being results and the world can move on. If you manage to find your central character's wants, needs, desires and problem, you will probably already have your plot. You are what you focus on. Luke Skywalker searching for his real father only to find he is the evil Lord Vadar is an archetypal myth, hence everyone relates to it. If you are what you focus on, you will become your father if that is all you focus on. In *The New Testament* Jesus declares I and the Father are one. It is typical for a son, who for many years may have rejected the father, as in the story of the prodigal son, to then return to him, actually take his place and become him. The stories show that difference can be overcome, and what we at first consider to be our enemy is actually who we are. So many films concern children searching for their parent, who they believe will be perfect, and bring them happiness, only to be let down. This then leads to catharsis for their inner wound, their inner delusions, can heal and then they face reality.

In Pedro Almodóvar's *The Skin I Live In* (2011) adapted from the novel *Tarantula* by Thierry Jouquet (1984) by Augustin Almodóvar, the wound of the protagonist Robert Ledgard (Antonio Banderas) is extreme. Skin itself is a metaphor for his pain and the operations he does are akin to him operating on himself, trying to get the underlying truth of his situation. Robert, played by Antonio Banderas in extremely interior acting mode, is a surgeon who has developed a new type of skin through genetically mutating human and animal skin. The benefits are enormous, such as the end of malaria, but the ethical side cannot be overlooked by the scientific community, and he is ordered to stop his experiments. The skin Robert is in is clearly an unfeeling one, partially due to having to cut off his pain as his wife was burnt to death in a car accident. Robert has a daughter by this wife, who commits suicide after being raped. He then kidnaps the rapist, turns him into his former wife through a sex change, and keeps her locked in a room where he occasionally smokes opium with her and watches her through a screen. Eventually he gets to sleep with her but she escapes.

As with many Almodóvar films, the protagonist's relationship with their mother is core and here Robert does not know that his housekeeper is his mother although she treats him like a son and they have a close relationship. History repeats itself, for his first wife ran off with a man who was his half-brother, although Robert does not know they are related. This half-brother, who grew up on the streets of Brazil, is now on the run from a jewellery theft and returns to see his mother, the housekeeper, to hide, then spies Robert's experiment, and rapes her. Robert's wound is being attacked repeatedly, while all the time he is attempting to reverse people's sexuality and has made a skin which means people cannot feel. A producer might read a premise similar to this and see this has great potential to be a fantastic script. All films need an ontological question about the human condition; the film's ontological question is – we may want to feel the depths of the human condition, but how deep do we really want to go? This is a powerful question, and the more powerful our one-sentence summary of our script the better the script is going to be.

The psychology of mirroring

As human beings we mirror each others' behaviour, to a greater or lesser extent. This is how basic robots learn. We communicate by mirroring each other. The greatest screenplays contain numerous amounts of what I call mirroring. The more we can mirror each other the better our communication. This is central to the core thesis of this book concerning predetermination in writing. 'Is there then a world where I rule absolutely on fate? A time I bind with chains of signs? An existence become endless at my bidding?'[27] Not only is it important to have inevitably part of the end, even if this is a total surprise, contained overtly in the beginning, as in *American Beauty* (directed by Sam Mendes and written by Allan Ball, 1999), so when we reach the end we have a deep eureka moment, but throughout a great screenplay each scene is constructed to mirror another scene. In David Fincher's *The Girl with a Dragon Tattoo* (directed by David Fincher and written by Steven Zaillian, 2011) the opening credits contain the horror. Of course there will be a rhythm and flow to each scene and sequence, so after high drama, we may get a poetic peaceful moment to accentuate the difference. This mirroring also adds to the layering of meaning creating a super-structure of echoes and repetitions. There is a poetic sensibility that can infiltrate film here to even lend your screenplay a spiritual quality.

If a writer follows their premise and treatment correctly, then nothing will be superfluous, but what I am getting at here is something deeper than this. For example, in *The Skin I Live In*, Vicente (Jan Cornet/Elena Anaya), the young man who is kidnapped for raping Robert's daughter, works in his mother's dress shop. Our clothes are almost part of our skin and, depending on how much we love fashion, we may even conclude that it is a statement about our identity. We judge people not just on their clothes, but what lies underneath their apparel, their skin. If skin can be so easily manufactured like a dress, as this film maintains, then this questions who we are fundamentally. Robert is playing with nature and this in itself questions what nature may be. It certainly questions what is natural.

Vicente wants to escape his small town, and the fact he has told his workmate and friends this means the police are less keen to look for him when he goes missing. Over the course of him going missing, approximately the four years he is held captive by Robert and turned into a woman, he realizes what he had and how important it is: his low-key job and his mother and friends. What is quite an original and strange story follows the standard format. If we see Vicente as the anti-hero, he learns to cherish what is important in life, moving from a life of mindless hedonism, including drug taking and sex, back to his mother. Along the way he is tortured in a dungeon, has his penis removed and gains a vagina. Do we conclude that the only way Vicente can be reunited with his family, friends and previous life is through him making this journey from one sex to another, or that it does not really matter what sex you are, people will accept or reject you on the basis of something far deeper. A good screenplay really just needs to open up these questions and Almodóvar does not really answer these questions but asks them quite directly. Robert is shot dead by Vicente, as is Robert's mother, so their unhealthy partnership is laid to rest, and in this sense normality is restored. Vicente's skills in dress-making mirror Robert's medical skills in altering skin but Robert in Frankenstein fashion is trying to make the dead live which is one transgression too far, whereas Vicente and his mother are merely enabling the living to live more fully.

In *Tyrannosaur* (directed and written by Paddy Considine, 2012), Hanna (Olivia Colman), a Christian and charity-shop worker, befriends a man who appears to have an alcohol problem and admits he beat his deceased wife. Joseph (Peter Mullan) is mirrored by James (Eddie Marsan), Hannah's husband, and so-called 'Evil' appears to be tackled with evil, when Hannah kills James. Nobody would blame her. He has urinated on her, beaten her, and humiliated her in a number of other ways. The Christian culture she is from means forbearance, turning the other cheek, and the woman submitting to the man. Nobody is going to believe her story about her husband abusing her and, of course, sacrifice and forgiveness is everything. Traditionally, she must sacrifice her own happiness for his. What makes *Tyrannosaur* a perfect script is the mirroring effect. Joseph has kicked his own dog to death, literally. And yet we still feel for him. He himself is the underdog, as is Hannah. Hannah stabs her husband to death and yet we still feel for her. Joseph hammers his neighbour's dog to death. Remarkably, in some way we accept he is putting the dog out of its misery, as the dog is being abused. So, make sure the ending mirrors the beginning and vice versa and have each scene mirror each other. Have characters mirror each other. As explained, the paradox is we want expectations to be subverted, while confirming the predetermined: in the cartoon *Megamind* (directed by Tom McGrath and written by Alan J. Schoolcraft and Brent Simons, 2010), for example, the 'evil' Megamind changes and becomes good, the initial hero turns absolutely neutral, and then later supports Megamind.

The psychology of the self/limit

If the mind, deep down, is nothing, as is the body, then the self does not exist. Buddhism in some respects claims this is the case. Our identity is formed from our behaviour and this stems from our desires. Feelings come before thoughts. Our desires stem from craving what is outside us so would anyone exist without these desires? There is a long history of writers who believe that through imbibing a drug the self, which is always limited, can be bypassed, and we can enter into the unconscious world. Meditation can also offer this. Following C. G. Jung, the collective unconscious 'dictates' our world, and is packed with archetypes. While this is true, I argue this is limitless.

> As God is dead then there is no limit to infinity, there is nothing exterior to being, and consequently we are forced to a constant recognition of the interiority of being, to what Bataille calls sovereignty – the supremacy, the rule, the responsibility, and the monocausality of the self.[28]

We might wonder why there are so many violent films or television shows, but it should be obvious.

The only way a limitless world is provided with any structure or coherence is through the excesses that transgress that world and thus construct it – the completion that follows and accompanies transgression. Transgression has become a modern, post-God initiative, a searching for limits to break, an eroticism that goes beyond the limits of sexuality. God becomes the overcoming of God, limit becomes the transgression of limit.[29]

But contradictions and paradoxes abound. A world without God is a world without the ultimate Law, without the ultimate limit, and without a teleological framework, boundless. And yet, in a world without endless resources, regardless of how limit is being used here metaphysically, limitless seems banal. Being unable to think or exist otherwise, accepting our humanity, might be under-ambitious but realistic. Jenks's comments here on transgression perfectly match both the building of character and the overall screenplay. God, defined as that which is infinite, that which is without limit, sets the boundaries for humanity to exist within. Anything contained within this framework will be limited. If breaking the limits only reconfirms them, there is no escape.

'True poetry is outside laws.'[30] Good writing breaks conventions and is transgressive, and subversive. Whether this then reaffirms the status quo is another question but for a moment it takes us outside convention. Audiences are interested in what is outside law. We want to see characters on the limit that go over the boundary, with the cowboy and the vampire being the two most popular characters of film and television. This is not only to see them pass the test. We want to see what happens to people when they do not fit in, and when they no longer behave in the way they are supposed to behave, when they are not dictated to. The outsider has been the quintessential figure of the twentieth century. Since the 1990s in the UK there has been a reversal of social mobility, but from the Second World War there was a movement between classes. Going back to the nineteenth century there was less movement. People were born into their situation and questioned it less. Audiences and readers want to see characters placed in situations where they question their role in society and have a desire to move beyond it. Whether these limits are placed outside or inside, limits must be overcome.

The world may view disability as a weakness, but this may not be how the so-called disabled person views their disability. It is not my intention to glamorise disability, or to lessen the adversity that people with disabilities overcome, but the point is that frequently our weaknesses are our strengths and vice versa. We might condemn someone for being too emotional, when their strength is they actually are aware of their feelings and those of others. In *Broken Embraces* and *The Diving Bell and the Butterfly* the two central characters lose their sight. This takes us back to the limit, as to many this would be the limit of endurance as would be cutting your own arm off, such as in the film *127 Hours* (Danny Boyle, 2011). Not only are audiences interested in stories where characters are pushed to the limit – how to make a film when blind, how to write a book when severely disabled, how to survive when trapped – audiences are interested in what makes us human. It is in these most severe situations when we discover what makes us human. The limit, the boundary, defines us, and once the limits have been exceeded, this structures our world. Film does create reality, as well as vice versa.

The psychology of machines

Feelings come before thoughts and yet in Western culture thought is deified and rationality rules to a degree. In some cultures to express feeling is transgressive. This suggests that fully encompassing our humanity is transgressive, breaking an unwritten law. This is explored later in terms of the Enneagram where we find that it is important to ask what passions are in possession of you. 'The secret of the interface is that the Other here is virtually the Same: otherness is surreptitiously conjured away by the machine.'[31] Jean Baudrillard here is talking about screens, particularly computer screens where most screenplays are written. The end conclusion is that we are plunged into sameness, homeostasis, by machines, and we could add the cinema industry to that. But this implies there is something wrong with sameness. Deep down, at the very deepest level, are we not all the same, or is this nightmare of sameness why many are more attracted to the nightmare of alienation? Our unconscious drives are in many ways all the same, or at least they exist within the same parameters. Paradoxically, the masks we wear are our so-called identities and these change continually, from one context to the next, so arguing for a fixed identity is absurd. We are shaped continually by circumstance.

In his classic book *To Have or To Be?* Eric Fromm, with reference to Freud, Spinoza, Marx and Ekhart, explained that a concept of being is 'unmasking' and the unconscious is, apart from irrational passions, 'almost the whole of knowledge of reality'.[32] Technology is an 'originary phenotype', in a way meaning technology is in our genes.[33] It is only a small step on to saying machines were God and we should become machines, or we are machines, or we are a slave to machines as Adorno and other theorists believed. This could be the truth already; Baudrillard seemed to think so. This makes nature transgressive. But what is natural or unnatural is a difficult question. We cannot really separate and divide up the natural from the unnatural, just as dividing up the body from the spirit is problematic.

The psychology of the Enneagram

As we have seen, in our postmodern world the idea of a core identity seems anathema, although it is central to the Jungian notion of individuation and to other forms of psychotherapeutic practices such as psychosynthesis. Interestingly, while Jung is well known for his psychological typology, he made the following point that:

One can never give a description of a type, no matter how complete, that would apply to more than one individual, despite the fact that in some ways it aptly characterizes thousands of others. Classification does not explain the individual psyche. Nevertheless, an understanding of psychological types opens the way to a better understanding of human psychology in general.[34]

This illuminates the point already made that deep down we may be all the same yet we are all intrinsically different. There is the belief that our consumption defines us and technology is at the heart of this, given it moves so fast we continually consume more of it to keep up, technology then consuming us. Paradoxically, to be the most fully activated human we must be hooked up to the hottest technology. So the more posthuman we are the more human we are or, at least, the most connected. As we have seen, Keith Ansell-Pearson may have maintained technology was 'an originary phenotype', but he did not maintain it was *the* originary phenotype.

As early as 1999, when most people were just becoming used to the internet, Margaret Wertheim in *The Pearly Gates of Cyberspace: A History of Space from Dante to the Internet*, warned of the dangers of believing the internet could fill the gap humans have in their search for spiritual meaning. Despite governments now tracking every move people make on the internet, today some still celebrate technology zealously as the new messiah, particularly social media, for its apparent part in bringing down governments and breaking down boundaries. Issues concerning control and liberation are central to these debates and with confessional television and blogs we have a world on one level where so much is being said that there is nothing left to say. Cinema did go back to its origins, with the success of the silent film *The Artist* (directed and written by Michael Hazanavicius, 2011) speaking volumes.

In the apparent freedom of our interneted worldwide situation, where all is so intimately interconnected, and you can make a film for virtually nothing and screen it for nothing, there is also the web that traps, where all communication is traceable, every communication monitored, so nothing is free. There is no autonomy and independence with observation. This, on one level, should not be a problem, if we have nothing to hide, but what about the essential right to privacy. Privacy is an element of identity, and without it we can lose our identity. What is remarkable is when individuals lose their identity, through a psychotic episode for example, they are often placed in environments, such as psychiatric wards, where they lose all privacy, which just exacerbates alienation. We may have a public persona, but this hopefully is different to the private persona. With the advent of social media, everyone, regardless if they are a public figure or not, in some ways has a manufactured public image and persona and a private one.

Way before social media, the media and communications guru Marshall McLuhan had it right when he said Americans wish to be public in private and private in public. Regardless of whether someone can really become addicted to social media and technology, the jury is still out on whether social media, through the playing of roles, has watered down the notion of a true core identity. Clearly, people can take on different personas through social media, and are less likely to get found out than in the 'real world'. As we have seen, more screenwriters are picking up on the idea of transient ambivalent characters. The future of screenwriting will move away from the traditional base of fixed characters that predominated in previous work. We can also link this to the dominance of the gaming industry, which in revenue far outweighs the film industry. Psychological personality systems may be resisted because, following Jung's quotation, they may appear to put people in boxes and look too limiting but that is only when these are used from a non-nuanced perspective.

The Enneagram is a workable, accurate, and highly nuanced psychological tool for developing characters and understanding human behaviour in general and has been used for millennia. Its origins have been traced to 2500 BC, Sufi Orders in the fourteenth century, and it has been more recently used by the Jesuits.[35] Like any other psychological tool it can be used simplistically, to label people, as with psychiatric disorders, or in a complex fashion for deepening understanding. It is currently used in an array of fields, from personal growth to business management. In the psychology of screenwriting deep understanding of this system will help us become deeper writers, writing more profoundly. If we know more about the psychology of characters within this framework, we know how to situate characters against each other and it can help us to plan writing in certain genres.

The word comes from the Greek ennea meaning nine and gramma meaning point. As Jerome Wagner put it, we can look at this spiritually, philosophically and psychologically, where 'human nature is expressed in nine natural fundamental ways'.[36] These different ways are our core areas of belief and these not only influence, but 'even determine our perceptions, thoughts, values, feelings, and behaviours', and while the origins of the Enneagram are disputed, it has been validated in widely different cultures, such as Japan, Africa, India, Europe and North and Latin America.[37] What we find with the Enneagram is not merely a way of explaining behaviour but of changing it for the better. If we want to get behind our characters, ourselves, and our audiences, psychologically, then the Enneagram is the perfect tool.

Here are questions that Wagner formulated in his work on the Enneagram and we could answers these from our own point of view, from that of our characters, or both:

1   What is the purpose of life? Wagner asks us to answer this as if we are talking to a six-year-old, or to a Martian.

2   If you or your character only had one year to live, what would you do and why are you or your character not doing this now?

3   Write your own personal mission statement, and/or get your character/s to. What do you believe is the purpose of your life? We have already looked at this with regards to what drives us as humans.

4   What do you want deep down?

5   How has your character survived so long? They may have avoided something important but this, paradoxically, has kept them surviving. What drives us insane keeps us sane, and vice versa; this could be the key to our screenplay.

6   Are there places/things that you/your character has been looking for what you/your character wants in the wrong places? We all know what harms us and yet we have a tendency to move towards this.

7   Me and Not-Me. Set up two columns. The first will contain qualities that you want to identify with, and find acceptable. The other column is that which you find unacceptable and which you might place on others, including strengths and weaknesses.

8   Re-own the not me.

9   Re-frame the not me so you can own it.

10   What are you afraid of?

11   How do your fears keep you trapped in your false personality or ego? 'Are you afraid there will be no one there when you finally come home to yourself?'[38] That is a strange one. The theory is we cannot know ourselves until we fully accept we are alone, but the paradox is we can only know ourselves through others.

12   What are the edges of your paradigm? 'Does your own paradigm create certain perceptions, interpretations, rules, limits, boundaries, or taboos that keep you fearful?'[39] This use of the word paradigm is beneficial. Write down how the fears around this prevent you from doing what you want.

13   What are you afraid will happen if you break this boundary?

14   What do you/your character need to cast out this fear?

15 Your defence mechanisms are?

16 Consider a time when you were in the here and now and connected to self and others.

17 When in a non-resourceful state, what are your distorted perceptions and interpretations, and/or those of your character/s?

18 What are the virtues, strengths or good habits needed for living a balanced life? Do you have all the nine virtues of the Enneagram? Virtue comes from the Latin virtus, meaning strength, and passions and virtues oppose each other.

19 What passions are in possession of you? As Wagner put it, these passions are experiences like addictive energy that drive you to think and feel and do what may not be good for you.

20 What is your main fault? What passion dictates the rest of your behaviour? How does this influence your choices? Write down your observations on this.

21 What is impossible for you to do within your own style? What can't you imagine yourself doing (i.e. if you could or would do it, it would fundamentally change your style)?

22 What happens to you under stressful conditions?

23 What are you like in relaxed, not threatening situations?

24 Which is your preferred centre: head, heart, or gut (body)? In making decisions Wagner has argued it is best to use all three of these but one will be the deciding judge. He has explained the three layers of evolution in the brain: the reptilian brain, located atop the brain stem, which equates with self-preservation and the gut and controls breathing and movement; the old mammalian brain, which is the limbic system, encircling the reptilian brain that regulates the emotions and is focused on the heart; and then the neocortex, which is surrounding the mammalian brain, which is the head centre and involves direction, meaning and purpose.

Each type within the Enneagram comes from each of these centres, with 8, 9, and 1 being from the gut; 2, 3, 4 from the heart; and 5, 6, 7 from the head. We can equate these zones non-specifically and simplistically with three film types, such as action movies, melodramas, and intellectual films. I call these 'types', as these categories are so open they are not really genres. So, in this sense, people are 'pre-programmed' to like certain films, which correlates with the central thesis of this book concerning writing that is 'predetermined' and, to be sure, viewing that is 'predetermined'.

Of course, the best films cross types, zones and genres, but this in some way indicates, biologically, why they are so popular. As a writer we need to tune into these zones, from our own perspective, from that of our characters, and that of our audiences. In developing a screenplay we can use the Enneagram, not just for developing deeper characters, but for developing a range of characters, and for developing our own psychology which impacts on our life and writing. Developing an understanding of our own psychology will enable us to write better.

25   What is the condition of your physical centre at this time?

26   What is the condition of your emotional centre at this time?

27   What is the condition of your head centre at this time?

28   What does your head need and want?

29   What does your heart need and want?

30   What does your gut need and want?

Answer these questions from your own perspective. Put these questions to your characters. Each point, or person, on the Enneagram has a positive way of being and a negative. They may be moving to another point of the Enneagram, but it is not a mission to become another number. One point, one type, is not any more important or better than another. The point is not to move to another type as this is who we are. Wagner calls them styles, and from style One to Nine we have: One the good person; Two the loving person; Three the effective person; Four the original person; Five the wise person; Six the loyal person; Seven the joyful person; Eight the powerful person; and Nine the peaceful person.

One element that is important about the Enneagram is that it teaches us that our strengths are intimately connected to our weaknesses. What is less obvious is that sometimes our strengths can be our weaknesses and our weaknesses our strengths. This is obviously true for character development as well; innocence can be a weakness, or a virtue. For example, Sally Potter when developing the novel *Orlando* (Virginia Woolf, 1928) for screen (1992) wanted to make the central character appealing and she did this through developing Orlando as the embodiment of innocence, which lends itself to comic naivety. But without a certain innocence risks are not taken, so this can lead to heroic behaviour.

In the following section I shall be utilizing Wagner's and Don Richard Riso's clarification of these types, with the examples from Riso.[40] We can use these when developing our characters and differentiating them. To gain a real understanding of how useful the Enneagram is consider people you work with or have worked with, your family and friends and which style they are coming from. Sometimes it will be startlingly obvious, in which case we can learn how to relate to people better; in other cases, it will take some time to establish which 'style' is their style, or, indeed, which style is our own. There are healthy elements to styles and unhealthy elements and it is important to remember that no style is any 'better' than any other.

The Nine Styles of the Enneagram

The One – The Reformer – is principled, orderly, perfectionist, and punitive.

The Two – the Helper – is caring, generous, possessive, and manipulative.

The Three – The Status Seeker – is self-assured, competitive, narcissistic, and hostile.

The Four – The Artist – is creative, intuitive, introverted, and depressive.

The Five – The Thinker – is perceptive, analytic, eccentric, and paranoid.

The Six – The Loyalist – is likable, dutiful, dependent, and masochistic.

The Seven – The Generalist – is accomplished, impulsive, excessive, and manic.

The Eight – The Leader – is self-confident, forceful, combative, and destructive.

The Nine – The Peacemaker – is peaceful, reassuring, passive, and neglectful.

Style One – The Good Person/Reformer[41]

Positives include high standards and conscientious, negatives slave-driver and uptight.

Core values: you want to make things better and help others actualize their potential; you have a highly developed critical faculty and are good at quality control; you have the ability to be exact and to get to the point; you like to be precise.

Distorted values: you over-identify with being good and only by being good do you think you are acceptable; you are afraid to do anything unless it is done perfectly; you have difficulty accepting yourself and other people and reality as it is; you become pre-occupied with what is wrong or missing and may not appreciate what is actually there; you become pedantic about what is right and the details.

Objective paradigm: wholeness.

Distorted paradigm: perfection.

Virtue: serenity.

Passion: anger.

How the distortion of this style developed –

- You were expected to grow up early;
- You may have been the eldest child;
- You came to believe others would not like you unless you were perfect.

You can move to a high side of Four and a low side of Four, a high side of Seven and a low side of Seven.

The One with a Nine-Wing

They reinforce each other and both tend to be removed from the environment, Ones given their ideals, Nines given the ideals they set around people: Margaret Thatcher, Katherine Hepburn, C. S. Lewis, St Ignatius of Loyola, Mr. M. R. Spock. They are not warm or personable, even if really healthy, but they are devoted to principles, if average they are obsessed with elitism and class.

The One with a Two-Wing

There appears to be some conflict here, between the dispassionate One and the warm Two: John Paul II, Jane Fonda. The Two-wing softens the judgemental and harsh nature of One. Average Ones want to control themselves and the average Two wants to control others. They might be prone to resentment and anger.

Style Two – The Loving Person/Helper [42]

Positives include caring and nurturing; negatives non-confronting and infantilizing.

Core Values: you enjoy giving to others.

Distorted Values: you can over-identify with being loving and helpful and you can be out of touch with your own needs.

Positive Core Values: you are a good listener and are non-judgemental.

Distorted Core Characteristics: I am somebody if I am needed.

How the distortion developed –

- You were made to feel guilty if you expressed your own needs and cared for yourself;
- You had to provide emotional support for your parents;
- You got rewarded for empathizing with others and making them feel better;
- Even when they are not good, they must see themselves as good, such as when they are extremely manipulative and coercive.

You can move to a high side of Eight and a low side of Eight, a high side of Four and a low side of Four.

Twos deny they have any feelings of hostility. The source of their motivation is the desire to be loved, but this might make them controlling of others. Their aggressive feelings come out in physical problems that force others to look after them, out of love. Twos fear that others only love them if they are good.

The Two with a One-Wing

There is a conflict here, with the emotionality of the Two and the rationality of the One. Examples Riso gives are: Mother Teresa, Mahatma Gandhi, Florence

Nightingale, Lewis Carroll, and Jean Brodie. There is the tension between professionalism and idealism. The average person of this type is very controlling, and they are egocentric, but this is hidden by their idealism. Twos are usually able to empathize but with a strong One-wing this might make it difficult. Unhealthy people of this type cannot allow themselves to be wrong.

The Two with a Three-Wing

These go together well, as both are people who relate well with people, and include: Luciano Pavarotti, Pat Boone, and Lillian Carter. There is genuine warmth, and in the average subtype is competitiveness.

Style Three – The Effective Person/Status Seeker[43]

Positives: being self-assured and a team-builder and negatives: being self-promoting and ignoring feelings.

Core Values: efficiency, productivity, industriousness and competence, a good team person.

Distorted Values: over-identify with doing rather than being, substitutes projects for persons.

Positive Core Values: friendly and sociable.

Distorted Core Characteristics: you may sell out and lose your personal self for the sake of a public mask.

How the distortion developed –

- You were rewarded for achievements rather than yourself;
- Your worth was dependent on what you did instead of who you were;
- Performance and image were rewarded in place of emotional connections and deep involvement with others.

Shifts to the high side of Nine and the low side of Nine, the high side of Six and the low side of Six .

The Three with a Two-Wing

Extremely sociable people; examples Riso gives are: Burt Reynolds, Brooke Shields, Richard Gere, Arnold Schwarzenegger, and Lady Macbeth. Threes with a Two-wing want to be loved and they are able to project their feelings, so actors, models and singers often come from this subtype. Moving into problem areas, they can be possessive, controlling and obsessed with competiveness and their own self-importance.

The Three with a Four-Wing

Usually the Three is interpersonal but the Four withdraws, examples are: Sting, Mick Jagger, Sylvester Stallone, Henry Winkler, Truman Capote, Andy Warhol, and Iago. They have a better ability at gaining self-knowledge and developing emotional lives than the Three with a Two-wing.

Style Four – The Original Person/Artist[44]

The positives include being sensitive, creative, expressive, questing and cultured, and the negatives include being aloof, dramatic, possessive, overly-sensitive and up and down.

Core Values: I feel therefore I am; you are highly individual and value originality, making the ordinary extraordinary like a poet, you are in touch with your own and the collective unconscious.

Distorted Values: you over-identify with the idealized self-image of being unique, and believe you must be different to be somebody.

Positive Core Values: self boundaries are fluid so you can understand others; you have a sense for the drama and tragedy of life; feel fulfilled and whole in the present.

Distorted Core Characteristics: self boundaries become too permeable so you lose your sense of self, you focus on what is missing in the present and become nostalgic about paradise lost.

How the distortion developed –

- You originally felt close to a strong parent (often the father) then that parent went away (perhaps because your parent died, or your parents divorced, or the parent became busy at work, or a sibling was born, or the parent withdrew or for another emotional reason);

- You felt abandoned and turned yourself into a special person so people would notice you;
- You received attention if you were sick or suffering otherwise you weren't noticed;
- You got attention from living at the extremes;
- Fours felt essentially alone in life, so the mission was self-knowledge.

Shifts to the high side of Two and the low side of Two, the high side of One and the low side of One.

The Four with a Three-Wing

Fours tend to have low self-esteem, Threes high; this can co-exist within the same person. The examples Don Richard Riso gives are: Tennessee Williams, Maria Callas, Rudolf Nureyev, Marcel Proust, Harold Pinter, Lawrence Olivier, Robert DeNiro, Walt Whitman, Albert Camus, E. M. Forster, and Blanche Dubois. Interestingly, the last in this list is a stage character that is in a play written by the first person in the list, with two main film versions. Importantly, these types are competitive and yet fear success. The Three-wing has narcissistic tendencies that partially motivates behaviour.

The Four with a Five-Wing

Examples include: Virginia Woolf, Franz Kafka, Ingmar Bergman, J. D. Salinger, Bob Dylan, Hermann Hesse, William Blake and Hamlet.

As Don Richard Riso put it, Fours direct their hostility towards themselves because they fear there is something wrong with them. With regards to creativity, the Fours can only maintain their inspired creativity by transcending self-consciousness.

Style 5 – The Wise Person/Thinker[45]

The positives include truth-seeking and philosophical, the negatives include uncaring and a fear of feelings.

Core Values: I think therefore I am; the aim is knowledge and understanding, and you are an original thinker.

Distorted Values: you can over-identify with the idealized self-image of being wise and perceptive and live too much from your head, forgetting you have a body and feelings, overly analytical and sceptical, remaining the observer rather than participating in life.

Positive Core Values: appreciation for solitude, independent and resourceful.

Distorted Core Characteristics: addicted to solitude.

How the distortion developed –

- You experienced mother and/or father as withholding so you became withholding;
- You retreated into your mind and books;
- Your inner world became more interesting than the outer.

Shifts to the high side of Seven and the low side of Seven, the high side of Eight and the low side of Eight.

The Five with a Four-Wing

These can be in conflict with each other, given Fives are cerebral which puts things at a distance, but Fours intensify things via their feelings. As Richard Don Riso put it, despite, or because of this, this type combines to make one of the richest subtypes in terms of artistic and intellectual achievement: Albert Einstein, D. H. Lawrence, Friedrich Nietzsche, Hannah Arrendt, Emily Dickinson, Italo Calvino, Jean-Paul Sartre, Elvis Costello, and Stanley Kubrick. There is the combination of knowledge and intuition in the healthy person. In the average Five, they might keep people at a distance.

The Five with a Six-Wing

For Richard Don Riso, these two reinforce each other, and this means out of all the personality types they are the hardest to have intimate contact with or to sustain a relationship with, and he gives some great examples: Sigmund Freud, Simone Weil, James Joyce, Charles Darwin, Karl Marx, Doris Lessing, B. F. Skinner, Isaac Asimov, Ezra Pound, and Stephen Hawking. If healthy, they are extremely hard working and are concerned only with their work and family, rather than their own well-being. If unhealthy, they find their feelings very difficult, and are the classic nerd, as in *The Social Network*.

Style 6 – The Loyal Person[46]

The positives include: cautious, reliable, determined and sensible, devil's advocate, and the negatives include: catastrophizing, timid, status quoer, security conscious.

Core Values: you are attracted to and value loyalty.

Distorted Values: you can over-identify with this, and you can polarize people into friends and foes.

Positive Core Values: you have a sense of propriety, always constant, you can be an adventurous explorer.

Distorted Core Characteristics: you may be overly cautious and spread fear.

How the distortion developed

- You learned that the world was a dangerous place to be guarded against;

- You had to assume the role of being an adult before you were ready;

- You experienced a parent as being incompetent, and so you began to doubt authority.

Shifts to the high side of Three or the low side of Three, the high side of Nine and the low side of Nine.

The Six with a Five-Wing

There is some conflict here as the Six is about dependency on others and Five is about detachment. Again, Riso gives some good American examples: Richard Nixon, Robert F. Kennedy, Robert Redford, Rock Hudson, Paul Newman, Billy Graham, and Joseph McCarthy. If healthy they are interesting people with a strong intellectual and practical streak. If unhealthy, they are constricted in the expression of their emotions, suspicious and fanatical.

The Six with a Seven-Wing

More extraverted: Ted Kennedy, Marilyn Monroe, Diane Keaton, Elton John, and the Cowardly Lion in *The Wizard of Oz* (directed by Victor Fleming, King Vidor and Mervyn LeRoy and written by Noel Langley and Florence Ryerson, 1939).

They are likeable and sociable and probably involved in a vast array of activities, including politics, sports and the arts, and usually playful and funny. The average person of this subtype does not handle anxiety well and if unhealthy over-reacts.

Style 7 – The Joyful Person/Generalist[47]

Positives include being light-hearted, spontaneous, extravert, planner and excitable, and negatives include being superficial, irresponsible and narcissistic.

Core Values: the purpose of life for you is enjoyment.

Distorted Values: you can become over-attached to pleasure.

Positive Core Values: creative imagination.

Distorted Core Characteristics: can confuse map and plan with reality.

How the distortion developed

- You got approval from being light-hearted;
- You did not learn to deal with pain except by avoiding it;
- You got more enjoyment from planning projects than from executing them.

Shifts to the high side of One and the low side of One, and the high side of Eight and the low side of Eight.

The Seven with a Six-Wing

Examples again from Riso are: Mae West, Elizabeth Taylor, Robin Williams, Liberace, Mel Brooks, and Miss Piggy. This might seem strange, viewing a muppet through the Enneagram, but we can see her behaviour on and off stage in the show and as with all characters and actors, it is from what is known about them. They are light-hearted and playful, and even though essentially aggressive want to be liked. If they are unhealthy they are highly insecure.

The Seven with an Eight-Wing

These people are a combination of aggressive tendencies, and Riso gives as examples: Joan Collins, Barbara Streisand, Joan Rivers, Lauren Bacall, and Martha in *Who's Afraid of Virginia Woolf?* (written by Edward Albee, 1962). The healthy version is passionate, and with the Eight-wing has great will-power, with strong egos, and if unhealthy they are totally ruthless.

Style Eight – The Powerful Person/Leader[48]

Positives include being hardworking, confident and competent, negatives include being dictatorial, possessive and bullying.

Core Values: you are attracted to and appreciate power; you know how to get it, keep it and use it.

Distorted Values: you can over-identify with the image and become addicted to power, and rely on it to manipulate others.

Positive Core Values: you can be inspiring and charismatic and fight for the underdog.

Distorted Core Characteristics: you can alienate others and use up people in your path.

How the distortion developed

- You became tough and aggressive to protect yourself;
- You learned when you challenged others or bullied them you got your way;
- You learned never to show weakness if you wanted to survive;
- You enjoyed being in power and felt more secure when you took control.

Shifts to the high side of Five and the low side of Five; shifts to the high side of Two and the low side of Two.

The Eight with a Seven-Wing

The most outwardly aggressive type, and again Riso gives some great examples: Mikhail Gorbachev, Franklin D. Roosevelt, Lyndon Johnson, Indira Gandhi, Mao Tse Tung, Frank Sinatra, Howard Hughes, Idi Amin, Muammar Qaddafi, Don Vito Corleone. Healthy versions are outward, energetic and task focused; those who are average are money driven, and unhealthy are ruthless.

The Eight with a Nine-Wing

More orientated to people and less to possessions than the other sub-type, and Riso gives examples from politics and culture: Martin Luther King, Pablo Picasso, Johnny Cash, Fidel Castro, Darth Vader, Othello, and King Lear. Healthy versions of this type are still aggressive on occasions but less obsessed with asserting themselves, and can form deep bonds with others. Less violent than the other sub-type, but they can move into a dissociated framework and crush others ruthlessly without remorse.

Style Nine – The Peaceful Person[49]

Positives include being reassuring, down to earth and receptive; negatives: tedious and neglectful.

Core Values: peace through the tranquillity of order, you possess diplomacy and see both sides, and give others freedom and space to let them take the lead.

Distorted Values: you can over-identify with this and avoid any conflict, assuming a passive unassertive approach.

Positive Core Values: calming non-judgemental presence, no need to show off and even-tempered.

Distorted Core Characteristics: you refuse to recognize real problems.

How the distortion developed

- You felt neglected growing up but instead of acknowledging this you took the less painful approach saying it does not matter;
- You turned down your energy and lowered your expectations;
- You took both sides instead of choosing sides;
- Your solution was not to decide, to postpone, to wait and see, to allow events to take their course.

Shifts to the high side of Six and the low side of Six, the high side of Three and the low side of Three.

The Nine with an Eight-Wing

If they are strong Nines then they remain peaceful and receptive, with an assertive streak, but because of the contradictory combination they are the hardest sub-type to understand. Riso's examples are: Ingrid Bergman, Bing Crosby, and Marc Chagall. The healthy version can be strong, and the unhealthy can be dangerous.

The Nine with a One-Wing

They repress their emotions to remain peaceful, and Riso's examples are: Ronald Reagan, Queen Elizabeth II, Gary Cooper, Jimmy Stewart, Ralph Waldo Emerson, and Desdemona. The healthy person within this subtype has extreme integrity, while the average may be on a mission to improve the world, and the unhealthy becomes retaliatory.

Concluding the Enneagram

Once an understanding is gained of all the styles, and the various sub-styles, we can begin to see complexities in our characters that at first might just be sketches. This could give us ideas for characters or enable us to write our characters and then establish what it is we need to do to make them more whole. The different components to the different styles briefly outlined offer us a variety of plot developments based on the different styles. Importantly, the Enneagram also gives us a framework for back stories. We may know what our characters are like now and how they behave but do we know what made them this way? In a group situation a number of different styles might be present. Using the Enneagram we can fully develop scenes that have more drama, sequences, plots, our overall structure and the genre of our screenplays.

The complexities of the Enneagram can also be considered through Deleuze and Guattari's work on the 'paraconceptual' figure. Just as Nietzsche wrote through a framework of personae, including Dionysus, Zarathustra, Christ, the Priest, the Higher Men, everybody is a collection of individuals.

> The conceptual persona is not the philosopher's representative but, rather, the reverse: the philosopher is only the envelope of his principal conceptual persona and of all the other personae who are the intercessors, the real subjects of his philosophy. Conceptual personae are the philosopher's 'heteronyms', and the philosopher's name is the simple pseudonym of his personae.[50]

As has been touched upon, not only is the Enneagram useful for developing characters but for understanding and utilizing film genre. As well as using the Enneagram to work on your own psychology and that of your characters, consider writing a screenplay from a particular position on the Enneagram. From using the Enneagram we can creatively engage with the directions characters develop in when they are fulfilling their destiny or working against it. Remember, fictional characters, as with all people, will come from one of these styles and will be making any one of a number of movements within the Enneagram as has been outlined.

In creating screen drama we can use the Enneagram on a micro and macro level. This is where using the Enneagram can get interestingly multifaceted. For example, we have seen that Iago is a Three with a Four wing. However, it is clear that Othello sees him as a Six, the Loyalist, 'oh faithful' Iago. The point Shakespeare is making here is that we see what we want to see. Othello is in need of someone he can trust and sees Iago as this, when in fact he is the antithesis. This is an interesting multilayered example of a character relating to another character. Knowing the Enneagram inside out also enables us to write accurate dialogue. The person speaking will be addressing another person in a manner that indicates how they perceive the other person to be, as in *Othello*. It will also reveal what position they are coming from within the Enneagram. On a macro level, with a variety of characters, plots, and subplots, these can be mapped out, using the intricacies of the Enneagram, so our reader and audience gain a clear perspective of character and therefore plot development.

The psychology of instinct

For Nietzsche the modern is defined as 'physiological self-contradiction'.[51] By this he refers to instincts, for instincts are inevitably curbed. Humans are born with more instincts than other animals, and yet we are trained to dismiss them. This dismissal of instinct can cause psychological problems. In *Broken Embraces* (directed by Pedro Almodóvar and Jirí Chlumsky and written by Pedro Almodóvar and Jan Novák) the central character, Mateo Blanco/ Harry Caine (Lluís Homar), a screenwriter who goes blind after an accident, re-writes a film he was working on when he was sighted over a seven-year period. This initially raises the philosophical question: can someone who has this form of disability, sightlessness, work in a medium that is for the sighted? Inner vision is more important than outer vision, we might tritely say, but *Broken Embraces* is far from trite, and has a number of intricacies that make it worth studying.

Mateo had another name in his former life, Harry Caine, who becomes larger than life, even more than the principal persona in the Deleuze and Guattari sense previously mentioned, although originally before the accident he could be termed a principal persona. Once the accident has occurred, Harry cuts off his former identity completely, so without Mateo there is no real persona of Harry Caine, confirming the idea of the reversal that now the name of the writer is the pseudonym of the persona. Furthermore, with Harry Caine as one of the heteronyms, the screenwriter can achieve anything. A deep sense of comic abundance and hope is central to many of Almodóvar's films, but here it is remarkable, given we have the whole gamut of human misery, with blindness, stomach cancer, and violence leading to broken bones and drink spiking leading to an overdose and hospitalisation, to name a few. Without the illnesses there would be no space and time to tell the number of stories that interweave in the film.

The film is highly contemporary, given it concerns observation in all its forms and it also confirms ideas already addressed concerning predetermination and free will; that our fears come true just by us considering them, be it going blind if we work with images in Mateo's case, or having our lover fall in love with someone else, in the case of Ernesto Martel (José Luis Gómez). Almodóvar tackles our worst nightmares. There is also the notion of repetition, and of people repeating the past, but the real optimism is that storytelling, and re-telling, can set people free by re-writing the very script of life. In this instance, script writing changes real life, rather than vice versa. This empowers the script writer, making them the maker of reality. In this sense, once more paradoxically, nothing is predetermined or inevitable, but this is only achieved through storytelling within the confines of a predetermined paradigm.

When we write we are re-telling life. We can reproduce archetypes from the collective unconscious. This could lead to inevitability, as if actions are prescribed and predestined in our work, plus we can then break this inevitability through our re-telling. Ernesto Junior makes a documentary for his father about the film Mateo is making, starring Ernesto's lover Lena (Penelope Cruz). The beautiful Lena is indebted to the older rich man Ernesto threefold, given, firstly, he has paid for Lena's father's cancer treatment, secondly, he was her boss when she was working for him as a secretary, and, thirdly, he has been going to an agency for sex, where Lena has been working and asking for her.

Ernesto agrees to let her work on Mateo's film if he directly funds the film and is the overall producer, and observes everything that happens. This form of total control might seem shocking on the surface, but is essentially just part of our observational culture, Ernesto Senior typifying our current ideology in the extreme. We might read this as Ernesto Senior representing not just a type of fascist control that may exist in the film industry, or indeed being a hangover from the dark days of Franco's Spain, but also this represents the audience. We confront our demon, ourselves, through him, the film's central demon. The audience, like Ernesto, may attempt to have a closed and defined ending, demanding a less original script.

Surprisingly there is no real tragedy here, if we look at the film overall, and with regards to the screenplay in general this is important to consider. If we have such tragedy it is a greater achievement to have this tragedy overcome than have people dwell in it. Mateo opens the film having sex with a blonde woman he has just bumped into helping him across the street. This is clearly a stroke of luck. Fate and luck again. His masterpiece, a film that is a tribute to the dead Lena, who was killed in a random accident whilst being followed by Ernesto junior, Ray X (Rubén Ochandiano) gets made with Mateo, despite being blind, individually re-working many scenes. He is on a mission to reclaim Lena from the hands of Ernesto Senior. Thus Lena is immortalized correctly and their deep love carries on. Furthermore, the younger generation can get to continue to work on films that interest them, with Mateo as their mentor, and people are now fully realising their dreams. The greatest screenplays clearly show great suffering, as in the case of Mateo and Lena and the dreadful events and circumstances that befall them, but also they reveal how this is overcome. Essentially, Mateo overcomes it through art. Writing itself is the new religion. In a complex fashion, the screenplay and filmmaking become a cure in themselves. This self-reflexivity is at the heart of much contemporary writing, in many forms.

Hot-seating

There is an essential way to get to the core of your characters. Instinctual answers to questions are often more honest and truthful, than those that are more considered, where the interlocutor has time to couch their response into a framework which may suit the questioner. The best way to really get to the heart of your character, and to your story, given character equals plot, is through hot-seating. This is where you sit in a chair where you can be seen by all, this is the hot seat, with a group of people asking you questions while you are in character. You answer these questions as the character, not as someone talking about the character. 'My favourite underwear is ...', not 'her favourite underwear is ...'. Some people find this easier than others, especially if they've done some acting, but it is important to get over the nerves and get into your part.

Remember to stay in character throughout and do not drift into explaining your plot or the story or why things happen the way they do. So again do not say: 'my character would ...' but answer straight as your character: 'I like sausages.' Your questioners can ask anything they like, the wilder the better, so be prepared for that but do not be self-conscious and think too hard: what's your favourite book?; are you close to your dad?; are you a happy person?; are you religious?; how would you describe your childhood?; what animal do you relate to?; how boring are you?; what's your most embarrassing sexual moment?; do you like yourself?; what's your passion in life?; what's your darkest secret?; lowest point in your life?; favourite serial killer?; and so on, and so on and so on. All of this is very entertaining and really is the most comprehensive way to unlock your character's potential.

This makes the character live and is the paramount method to develop a full and rounded character. Your questioners will inevitably ask questions that are really off the wall and playing your character you will have to think of something, and fast. Before this moment your character is probably a loose gathering of an idea that fits your plot. After this your character lives and, importantly, it is your audience that has blown life into the lungs of your character. As a writer it is important to develop your character with those around you. You can get way too fixated on how you see them and miss the obvious. Hot-seating, even if you have a full-fledged life-line for your character and believe you know them inside out, enables you to iron out any anomalies, plus really flesh out who they are. Once you start thinking as your character, you will know how they act, and you will then see how the scenes can be built.

There are obvious power questions you can ask: What does s/he want? What does s/he need? What does s/he dream of? What does s/he fear?

What is his/her main strength? What is his/her main weakness? What are his/her main problems?[52] Naturally name, then: all that is observable e.g. ethnic background; age, gender; sexuality; height; how they dress; where they live; where they work; where they shop; where they holiday; hobbies; family; relationships; children; friends. Then significant life experiences: background; illnesses; accidents; beliefs, hopes and ambitions; triumphs and disasters; likes and dislikes. Everything under the sun is unnecessary, but covering a lot of ground is, so check the development of your characters and make them realistic. You may need to change your ideas and have a rethink. Do not get stuck on your original ideas. New writers think that their character needs a dark history, a certain shadow, but this is not always necessary. They can have dramatic potential without any such special history. You might want to bring in details of significant others, but do not overwhelm the context with detail.

Other strategies

Consider all of the following about your characters. Introvert or extravert; high energy or low; mentally active or physically active; expressive or inhibited; optimistic or pessimistic; openhearted and optimistic; or mean spirited and pessimistic; do they need to be in control; do they need to win; do they find it hard to say no; are they imaginative; are they literal; are they practical and organized or happily chaotic; are they fearful; are they gregarious; are they easily overwhelmed; do they finish what they start; do they get dogmatic; do they stick to their guns in an argument; can they stand their ground in a conflict or are they a pushover.

Physicality

Do they have a disability, how does it affect them; long, thin, short, fat, inflated round the chest or collapsed; piercing gaze or warm look to their eyes; strong jaw, or weak-chinned; start observing people's physical types and see how this relates to their energy and typical patterns of behaviour. As Oscar Wilde once put it, only a fool does not judge someone on their appearance. How do they move: tentative, impulsive, insistent, demanding, composed, or aggressive? They need to live and breathe.

Throw the grenade

What is the metaphor that runs throughout your screenplay and how does this relate to your characters? What are the main aspects of your character?

Write these down: quirks; something distinctive; not just how they look. Write your character's life-line from beginning to end. Now how can you upset your character, impel the story, where is the best spot and moment to throw your grenade to cause havoc and put your character to the test? A good exercise with a group is to get people to pick a card telling them where they are in the pecking order and have individuals act out that role, without telling others where they are in the pecking order. Through acting their roles members get an indication of which position each person is at and then the group must line up in the order of power. Only after this point are the true positions revealed.

Scene and structure

Because the scene is intimately entwined with structure, which equals character, you can see the relevance of having this section in a chapter on character and Robert McKee gives the following definition:

> A scene is a story in miniature – an action through conflict in a unity or continuity of time and space that turns the value-charged condition of a character's life ... A scene may be infinitesimal. In the right context a scene consisting of a single shot in which a hand turns over a playing card could express great change.[53]

Knowing when to change scenes can be confusing. We need separate scenes if there is a change in time and/or place. These are the two key elements in a scene. For example, a man is walking to his house, so this is one scene; he enters his house and is in the hallway, and this is another scene; he is then in bed with his lover, another scene of course; and then waking up in the morning is another scene; and so on. Sometimes it is not clear-cut so it is important to learn when there is a new scene beginning, paying close attention to time and place. Even if there is just a minuscule difference in time and place, such as a short car journey, this needs different scenes being written as time and location will change.

For McKee there are only two emotions – pleasure and pain.[54] He goes on to explain we experience this through a transition of values; we empathize with the character, through knowing what the character wants and wanting the character to have it. A change in values moves our emotions. So ask these questions of each scene: What happens in the scene? What is the purpose? Why is it there? How does it move the story forward? What aspect of the character will be revealed? Where does your scene take place? Write the scene at first without dialogue. You do not need to number scenes or have any headings other than ones similar to the ones shown here.

Transition scenes

Writing transition scenes is an art form. There is no better example than in Hitchcock's 1959 film *North by Northwest* (written by Ernest Lehman). Roger O. Thornhill (Cary Grant) is holding Eva Marie Saint's (Eve Kendall) hand, as she dangles off a cliff near Mount Rushmore, then holding her hand pulling her up into a bunk bed on a train, which is then followed unsubtly, yet comically, by the train going through a tunnel. Other techniques can be identical dialogue in each scene, or the same word repeated, or similar action, such as the holding of the hand just mentioned, or one character picks up a glass full and another puts it down empty. Charlie Moritz covers this area well.[55] In the masterpiece *Crash* there are numerous examples. In one scene a woman slams a door. In the next a man geographically nowhere near the previous person wakes up with a jolt. Similar or identical imagery can be used, or similar subject matter and, as Moritz has indicated, the same mood can be resonated, including the pace, tone and feel. Attention can also be paid to interesting use of carried-over dialogue or sound effects. We may hear the aeroplane taking off at the end of one scene, and then see it in the next.

Structure

Briefly, it is useful to consider Linda Aronson's nine-point model, taken from Paul Thompson and Sam Smiley's work: Act One: Normality, Disturbance, Protagonist, Plan, Surprise … this turns into the Obstacle – end of Act One. Act Two and Three: Complications, sub-stories, more surprises and obstacles and climax (end of Act Three), followed by Resolution, i.e. how the world goes on.[56] In this nine-point plan mirroring develops. 7. – Complications can be viewed as a later development of point 2. – Disturbance and so on. Just as characters and scenes can mirror, so can structure.

Aronson has shown how this works for the fairy tale Cinderella. For this division into three acts the obstacles can be adapted. We may not need that many obstacles, but the obstacles we do have may look at first insurmountable. Take Cinderella's step-sisters for example and her step-mother. How far will they go to prevent her from seeing the prince? The fact the prince wants her, a scullery maid, over the sisters, suggests that all manner of obstacles can be overcome. This is a wish fulfilment and we do not need to go into a detailed Freudian reading of the shoe fitting her foot. As it stands, the Cinderella story is a good example of a three-act structure with all the significant points.

The function of STRUCTURE is to provide progressively building pressures that force characters into more and more difficult dilemmas where they must make more and more difficult risk-taking choices and actions, gradually revealing their true natures, even down to the unconscious self.[57]

I have emphasized throughout the primacy of the unconscious. What is significant is that the unconscious essentially has a will of its own and is beyond the will of the individual. Whatever choices are made, this unconscious true nature comes to the surface and not only reveals the true inner nature of your protagonists but the structure of your screenplay.

4

The psychology of dialogue

Psychologically, in real life, why do we say anything? Why say anything if we are just a word? This textualization of everything became very fashionable during the 1980s but we do need to move beyond such a reduction. It might be to fill the gaps and from anxiety. Generally, it is to make a connection, to get closer to someone. Whether it is to get something off our chest to an intimate friend or to tell a stranger directions it is about expressing ourselves and communicating. Importantly, in a film we can invariably do all of this without dialogue, and we should do this without dialogue if possible. People go to see a film to be visually stimulated. Great characters and witty dialogue might be part of it, but the best form of dialogue is no dialogue. It is as simple as that. Or is it?

The Social Network, which I have mentioned twice before, opens in a bar with geek Mark Zuckerberg (Jessie Eisenberg) swigging a beer, on a roll, trying to impress his girlfriend with his witty tales, including how his friend made three hundred thousand dollars one summer. There is a mantra in most screenwriting books 'avoid talking heads', literally a section in Linda Aronson's 2006 book.[1] She points out that you can have exposition, just do it with some action, such as the walk and talk scenes in *The West Wing* (1999–2006). This is not a great example, given these have become heavily satirized in a number of comedy shows, such as *Armstrong and Miller* (2007–10). Personally, I have nothing against the talking-heads type of scene, if it is done in an intelligent, or even an avant-garde fashion, as in the work of artist Bruce Nauman who has used television screens to address the notion of being talked to and at.

Back to *The Social Network*, where in the opening Mark Zuckerberg seems like a nervous nerd, but it is electrifying banter, as if the character is high on amphetamines and unstoppable. The irony is that within a few years 500 million people will be using computers to 'social network' due to

Mark Zuckerberg and this form of banter will be far less important in some respects. Perhaps this is the screenwriter's point, because Mark never gets his girl, no matter what he tries, which reveals, moralistically, that no matter how much money you make or whatever cool things you invent, it does not automatically buy you love. Mark blows it in this opening scene by mentioning they only have access to the bar because of Erica Albright (Rooney Mara).

Erica has a lot of the best lines in the film: 'you're probably going to be a very successful computer person. But you're going to go through life thinking that girls don't like you because you're a nerd. And I want you to know, from the bottom of my heart, that that won't be true. It'll be because you're an asshole.' Or: 'As if every thought that tumbles through your head was so clever it would be a crime for it not to be shared.' And: 'Dating you is like dating a Stairmaster.' Not only are they the killer lines that hit Zuckerberg in the heart, they are comments on the FaceBook and Twitter generation, and mirror society.

Given the above, it is obvious that rules can be broken, such as having a talking-heads scene, if it works. *The Social Network*, about a type of genius, is a work of genius in some sense, but it is far from visually compelling, contradicting in part the dictum – be visual. If the dialogue is that good then this is not as paramount and, in any event, cinematography is not your job. The opening fast-fire banter in *The Social Network* might alienate some of us and, quite innovatively, it was recorded with the extras at 'normal volume' so it is difficult to hear without concentrating, which hooks the audience in. Plus there are references a non-American audience just might not get and some of it might be difficult to follow even if you are American. But it clearly establishes the quest, the objective of the central protagonist, that is about to commence.

Mark is discussing with Erica his desire to get into the elite clubs of Harvard by doing something people will look up at. From a loose comment he loses her and the film is essentially about him trying to win her back. In the brief opening scene we get the social position of the key characters, the atmosphere of the time-period, and the inner workings of a young apparent genius who will influence a generation in such a phenomenal manner social communication will never be the same again. What makes it so interesting is its slippery genre: it is a legal drama, a bio-pic, partially a comedy, plus a romance/bromance story.

Essentially, it is important to be able to communicate visually, in an interesting fashion and to try and do so at all times. Dialogue could interrupt the flow and wooden dialogue stands out a mile. As a rule, any dialogue we use needs to be moving the story forward, or showing us something about the character. Perhaps people do speak the same, use the same language, and express themselves in a similar clichéd fashion, but in a screenplay the dialogue needs to be distinctive, even if the characters are similar. Paradoxically, realism in film means the realism inside the film, and authentic dialogue does not necessarily mean authentic to real life but authentic to the characters and the piece. We do not want films to thoroughly reflect reality, as that would be boring. A film critic in Jonathan Coe's masterful novel *The House of Sleep* (1997) pitches his film idea to a top producer. The idea is simple: following someone throughout their whole life, without edits. If they live to 70 years old, the film is 70 years old. It makes Andy Warhol's *Empire* (1964), a film with the camera just set up filming the Empire State building, look like an action movie. For comic impact we might have characters being identical, and then the love interest tries to find out who is who. Each character needs an individual speech style so the character becomes more rounded. In *The Social Network* we have twins, and this is played for comedy by the same actor, with one being more aggressive than the other to differentiate them. Realistically, this is quite accurate, given even twins have an age difference, and one is normally the dominant one. Here, both have the husky, resonant, accent of money and are preposterous in their vanity and arrogance. They are both comical due to their body language.

When the popular British stage and television actor David Jason reads scripts he is not looking for anything in particular, as you never know what will get the best laugh from the dialogue. Having worked on hit television shows, such as playing Granville in *Open All Hours* (1976–85) and Del Boy in *Only Fools and Horses* (1981–2003), he knows how to work with good dialogue. And yet, having done an 18-month stage play, *No Sex Please We're British* (written by Anthony Marriott and Alistair Foot, 1973), he also knows that communication and comedy is about the body. Verbal and oral comedy is not always the funniest. Great British comedians, such as Eric Morecambe and Tommy Cooper, and more recently Vic Reeves who is similar to Eric Morecambe, had the audience laughing even before they said anything. So why was this? It was because they took on a comic aura that people related to, the same as Del Boy for David Jason. While new writers fear dialogue and most know writing good dialogue is difficult, let us confirm the old adage – if in doubt leave it out. Let your action do the talking. You are not writing a stage play. Mike Leigh's *Naked* is one of a number of exceptions, where David Thewlis gives a mesmerizing monologue on metaphysics. If you build your characters well enough, through hot-seating and other good methods, you will get to the very heart of them and their speech patterns and dialogue.

As Charlie Moritz has pointed out in *Scriptwriting for the Screen*, the best dialogue is that which is *repressed*, rather than expressed. What intrigues us and keeps our interest is what is not said, rather than what is said. This leaves it up to us to do the work and read between the lines. What we do not want is talking heads banging on expressing what is an unexpurgated version of the writer's ideas. Leave that for the stage. You can do so much more with the visual medium of film. Another main point Moritz has made is that dialogue is not just about words but the spaces between them. Famously, the writer Tom Stoppard has a reputation for this kind of spacing, or pauses, and we can tie in Stoppard with Harold Pinter and Samuel Beckett as playwrights and screenwriters who delve deeply into the human psyche through this particular method. By using silence these writers, and others, actually get us to question the ability, or inability, of language to express what and who we really are. Language, as well as being a device to free us can trap us. We are so immersed in language that these techniques, like the phrase that comes from literary theory known as defamiliarization, get us to stand back and think about whether the language we use is really achieving what we think it is.

Most of these writers make us feel very awkward. In social situations people often gabble on, sometimes inanely, because they do not want any awkward or difficult silences, as if any gaps would be too much, or a gap would reveal that there really was no connection. It seems that if they allowed the gap, the meaninglessness of existence would swallow them or, or conversely something out of their control would enter the situation, and this must be avoided by any means. So it is worth asking philosophically why this is, given today with regards to verbal and written communication, there is often the cacophony of noises of ipods, phones, televisions, DAB radios, computers, ipads, and many other new and yet to be invented technologies, demanding and competing for our attention. Why is there such a desperate need for noise?

A study found that bird song had significantly shifted due to the sounds of mobile phone ringtones. If we were extreme about this we might conclude that this excessive noise, which is only increasing, is actually preventing us from confronting our fundamental aloneness in an existential sense. There are many religious orders that have as part of their novitiate a time spent alone, just so people can get clarity as to their true calling, and many religious houses offer silent retreats. From attending these retreats people get clarity about themselves and the world, and see the world afresh. Both Jesus and Buddha spent time away from the world.

Psychologically, this relates to the point about repression. Often, there is far more meaning in what is not said than in what is said. The following personal example, if you will allow such self-indulgence, sums it up for me. I once gave the reading at a friend's wedding in the main church in Tavistock, Devon. He was an evangelical atheist, on a par with Richard Dawkins, a real Nietzschean, but wanted me to read from an ancient King James Bible that had been in the family for generations. The text was tiny, but I thought nothing of it. I got half-way through the popular wedding reading, 1 Corinthians 13, and then to my horror lost my place. I could not believe it, but kept my cool and just looked at the text as if I was discovering a new meaning in it for the first time. There was a Pinteresque pause. I could feel the people in the church with me, hanging there.

Then I just carried on again, as if nothing had happened. Afterwards people congratulated me wholeheartedly on the 'pregnant pause'. They said they were drifting off, but this brought them back into the reading, and it was a very moving experience, and helped them understand things anew as all great works of art should. The gap gave their brains time to wake up and be drawn back to the moment, like a Buddhist meditation. I do not even know to this day whether I carried on again from the correct place in the passage or not, but it did not matter. The process and the feeling created by the performance had the desired impact. Unconsciously or consciously here I let the congregation do the work, and gave them space to enter the piece in the silence. They had to fill in the gaps with part of themselves, despite not even realising there were any, this being the power of the pause, the gap.

We often write to work things out for ourselves but we need to remember that the audience have seen a lot of films. Unless we hold back, or offer layers of meaning, then what we write will be just like wallpaper, background filler. Once something is definitively articulated then the number of ramifications, levels of nuance, and the metaphorical layers are finite. Creative writing needs to be open, rather than locked down. We all should be aiming for a number of levels of meaning in our writing, a number of avenues. If something is uttered that is more ambiguous and multilayered then this is open to interpretation and may leave your audience having more of an opportunity to enter the world of your film. They have to step in and do the work. New writers tend to be quite didactic. Let the reader and audience ask: does she mean this; is he really saying that; what are they reflecting upon then?

All of this builds up meaning and creates a richer work of art. Have your character circumnavigate what they really mean, or have a number of double or triple or multiple meanings. Most comedy is based on this; something meaning two things concurrently. One of the greatest moments of screened miscommunication, guided miscommunication, is *The Two Ronnies* (1971–87) 'Mastermind' sketch. Ronnie Barker asks the questions playing Magnus Magnusson the quizmaster, and Ronnie Corbett is the contestant answering them. His answers are in the wrong order, as he is answering the question that was given before. Amazingly, eventually his answers do start to relate to the question being asked, often explicitly. What kind of person lives in Bedlam? A parachute. What is a jockstrap? A nut case.

This comedy sketch indicates how far we, as an audience, will create meaning, and how much we want traditional meaning to be broken and dislocated, plus it confirms the thesis concerning the need for predetermined meaning. As with the Bakhtinian notion of the carnivalesque, the brief transgression of meaning within the safe confines of a film, stage play, or television show, may only serve to reinforce normality in the end, and re-establish the status quo, but at least it goes across boundaries. We need to try and steer clear of being didactic. There is a way of using dialogue that creates tension or using repetition and key phrases that threads the meaning and wider theme of the screenplay throughout your work, again adding richness. This in itself can function as a form of Chekhov's Gun, as with the *Old Testament* quotation Ezekiel 25.17 that Jules, Hitman 1 (Samuel L. Jackson) uses in *Pulp Fiction*, or 'feel the force' in *Star Wars*.

We can develop the work of Moritz who has identified the following pitfalls in writing dialogue, into a number of clear points:

Some points about dialogue

- Avoid relentless chatter, meaning, characters just going on and on ad infinitum. In real life people might do this, of course, and there is some leeway. Establishing a character that is garrulous might be a major part of the plot, and this could be part of using the Enneagram, as they might be a friendly Three, and this might contrast with someone who is laconic and withdrawn, such as a depressive Four. But a screenplay is not real life. This obvious point is worth making again. True art does not merely reflect life, it engages with life in a paradoxical, ironic, and skewered fashion, offering us further truths through fiction.

- Paradox really is the key to anything interesting, including dialogue.

- Focus on telling the story in the shortest way possible. Some incredible dialogue might not seem to follow this instruction, such as that in *Naked* previously mentioned, but it is essential to always focus on the visual. Director David Fincher attempts to have the scene on the screen for the shortest possible time, but he said this before making *The Social Network*, which has a long opening scene. Although for this film there was three weeks of rehearsal time where Fincher went behind every word with the writer Sorkin, to really establish what was meant. The opening scene is unusual, ten pages of dialogue with just two people sitting at a table, and took 99 takes, and is worth studying to understand how to write long blocks of biting dialogue.

- Think about the reality and practicality of this. Get into the scene much further on, as late as possible, and leave at the earliest opportunity. There is the useful term 'in medias res', where we begin in the thick of it, in the middle of the action, or the dialogue. This will influence the way you write dialogue and should definitely influence the way you edit dialogue.

- Be careful about the balance between what you believe to be witty banter and talk for talk's sake. We are not interested in a random conversation down the pub or in a house. What we want to know is something interesting that reveals something about character. At first what seems like a random discussion about burgers and beer in Europe in *Pulp Fiction* is surreal, hyper-real, and comic, as the killers are on their way to slaughter a bunch of students. Of course balance is also crucial. Here there is a superb rhythm to the dialogue between scenes, with the apparently banal dialogue followed by a scene of vociferous biblical language and violence. How random is random? A conversation might seem random at the time, but every word really does need to have significance. Again, Johnny's long rant in *Naked* is beautifully constructed. It might break the 'rules' of dialogue, but it does so in an entertaining fashion and contains within it the existential heart of the film.

- Know when to shut your characters up. Let the dialogue reveal something about your character and the story; that is it.

- Avoid: using unnecessary formalities, e.g. Hello! hello you, how are you? very well, and you, pleased to meet you, and so on, cut all that; over-explaining; unnecessary repetitions; losing the tone; losing the rhythm.

- Do not say it if we can see it – this is important but, like with anything, there are exceptions.

- Normally there is no need to name names in dialogue; we never use each other's names, unless it is for a particular emphasis, such as a parent perhaps telling off a child and using their full name 'Edward', instead of Ed for example, or where it is necessary to indicate to everyone, the audience and other people involved, who it is, e.g. if someone is on the phone.

- Write the dialogue in the way the character would speak it, so do not let yourself get in the way of the character.

Here is an example of a script; a short film about six minutes long, called *Stormy Weather* (directed and written by Ben Richards, 2011).

```
FADE IN:

Instrumental music from 'Stormy Weather' over
titles.
```

EXT. FLORIST - NIGHT

A calm fills the air as the colours of various
flowers and bouquets illuminate the inside of
the store, seen through a large window.

A few drops of rain fall from the sky and
bounce off the canvas awning. A sudden, and
torrential, rainstorm starts. Water hurls
itself from the clouds to the ground.

HANNAH - late twenties, plain and bookish -
comes running in out of the rain for cover, her
smart clothes completely wet through. She holds
a sodden magazine above her head.

She catches her breath and wipes the black
smudge of mascara off her face, using the
window as a mirror.

JOHNNY - late twenties, slightly geeky and
lean - runs to take shelter under the awning,
his suit drenched. He is pointlessly holding a
newspaper above his head. As he tries to stop,
his shoes slip and he crashes into Hannah.

They manage to steady themselves with the aid of
the window, despite their limbs being entangled.

                    JOHNNY
          I'm sorry. It's these new
          shoes. I'm really sorry.

He reaches out and brushes water off of her
shoulder. She takes a quick step away, taken
back by his breach of her personal-space.

He lets out a deep sigh and turns away, running
his hand through his hair, causing it to stick
up at a strange angle.

She casts a few glances his way, looking at his
hair. He notices her looking and casts a few
glances back, oblivious to his hair. She steps

in close to him and smoothes his hair down. He
smiles, embarrassed.

He holds his hand out to her.

                    JOHNNY (CONT'D)
          My name's Johnny.

She shakes his hand.

                    HANNAH
          Hannah.

Just as she says her name, lightning CRACKS
across the sky. Hannah jumps and grabs Johnny's
arm, frightened. She continues to hold his arm
in nervous anticipation of the thunder. As it
RUMBLES, she buries her head into his shoulder.

She quickly becomes embarrassed and steps away.

                    HANNAH (CONT'D)
          I'm sorry. I'm not good with
          lightning.

                    JOHNNY
          It's okay. I wasn't, you know,
          using… it.

He gives a nervous laugh and she looks
confused, but laughs politely.

They both look out at the street as the rain
continues to pour, no sign of letting up.

                    HANNAH
          How long do you think it'll last?

                    JOHNNY
          What the rain? Hopefully not
          too long. I need to get home.

                    HANNAH
          Someone waiting for you?

                    JOHNNY
          Just my dog. He'll be starving.

                    HANNAH
          Ah, what kind?

                    JOHNNY
          A puppy lab.

                    HANNAH
          What's his name?

                    JOHNNY
          Kino.

                    HANNAH
          Oh, that's… unusual.

                    JOHNNY
          Yeah? Well, I just wanted
          something that would stand
          out so, you know, fifty dogs
          don't come running if I shout
          'Buddy'. Or something.

                    HANNAH
              (understanding)
          Of course.

                    JOHNNY
              (excitedly)
          One of my favourite things is
          to try and run faster than
          Kino. He can just about keep up
          now, but soon he'll…

     He notices the sad expression on Hannah's face.

                    JOHNNY (CONT'D)
          What's wrong?

                    HANNAH
          I don't have a dog waiting for
          me.

She says this trying to hide her loneliness and slight desperation.

                    JOHNNY
          Oh.

He smiles at her reassuringly. Another CRACK of lightning fills the sky and, once again, Hannah grabs Johnny. He puts his hand on her shoulder and she draws comfort from this gesture. They slowly disengage.

He looks at her and gently wipes some more mascara off her cheek and lifts some wet hair away from her face. She straightens his suit jacket and fixes his collar.

ALICE – just twenty and obviously pretty – comes running in from the rain, breaking the mood. She has no idea what she has done. She straightens her short skirt and tidies her blonde hair.

                    ALICE
          Phew. Oh, it's really coming
          down out there huh?

She looks at Hannah and Johnny for a response, but nothing comes. She looks slightly confused.

                    JOHNNY
               (brightly)
          Oh, yeah. Really coming down.

Alice and Johnny exchange a polite smile, causing Hannah to dart an angry look at her. Alice notices the tension and begins to feel uncomfortable.

                    ALICE
          Err… Well, bye.

She braces herself before running back out into the storm. Johnny watches her leave.

                    HANNAH
                 (upset)
             Who was she?

                    JOHNNY
             Who? There's only us.

Another CRACK of lightning fills the sky but
Hannah doesn't jump. She squeezes Johnny's hand
tight, trying to control her fear.

A MOTHER runs by pushing a buggy that has more
protection against the rain then she does. Both
Johnny and Hannah laugh at this sight.

                    HANNAH
                 (conversational)
             Do you think you'd want
             children?

                    JOHNNY
             Yeah.

                    HANNAH
             How many?

Johnny goes to speak but Hannah interrupts.

                    HANNAH (CONT'D)
                 (seriously)
             You can't give them funny names
             though. You shouldn't give people
             any reason to pick on them.

                    JOHNNY
             Okay.

He puts his arm around her protectively. She
snuggles into his embrace as the rain slows,
then suddenly stops.

They both look out into the street and Johnny
tentatively holds a hand out to see if it's
stopped for good.

```
                    HANNAH
          Do you think it'll last?


He looks up at the sky and then to Hannah. He
reassures her with a smile then takes her hand.

                    JOHNNY
          I do.


Together they step out from under the awning
and into the street. As they do, Johnny's shoes
slip on the wet pavement and he falls, smacking
the back of his head on the curb.

                         CUT TO BLACK.


The song 'Stormy Weather', and rain falling,
plays over the end credits.
```

This is a wonderful example of what I call 'fully loaded' meaning. Everything has a powerful subtext and double meaning. Each phrase means more than its surface meaning, and this is a perfect example of intriguing dialogue. Two people meet 'accidentally' outside a flower shop, in the rain. The location is romantic with the flowers and rain creating an almost mystical and mythic setting. Perhaps this is love at first sight. These things do happen, not only in the movies. They initially collide in the rain, as Johnny (Napoleon Ryan) dashes out of the rain into the shade of the shop awning and skids in on the wet pavement into Hannah (Jessica Sherman). We should pick up on the fact there is something wrong with his shoes, as this is the Chekhov's gun, a subject addressed in pages 151–2. This in some senses confirms this book's overall thesis concerning 'predetermined' screenwriting being the best form of writing. We may only pick this up unconsciously, or dismiss it, but we have witnessed it and so whatever happens is inevitable, even though it may come as an incredible shock.

Johnny apologizes for bumping into Hannah, and then the double meanings start, with Johnny responding to Hannah's comment 'do you think it will last' with 'what, the rain?' and, immediately, we have two strangers discussing their relationship. This may seem surreal and absurd, we may think, as they do not have a relationship as such. Plus, it highlights the ephemeral nature of a lot of relationships and the power of cinema to transcend time for everything that can happen in life can happen in film in less than seven minutes. Johnny and Hannah come across as middle-class, well-dressed and apparently normal people but they are intrinsically lonely. There is something deeply existentialist about this.

The film takes us through their encounter, the falling in love, the jealousy of the threat from a younger 'obviously pretty' outsider whom Johnny did not even notice, discussion about babies and the naming of babies, and the phrase 'I do'. This moves from just an encounter in the rain, to indicate a permanent commitment. The beauty of this is that it seems so normal and rational within the world of the film. Anything can happen in a film if the world of the film is built to be believable and works in its own world, regardless of whether it contradicts the 'laws of reality'. We want our reader and potential audience to inhabit the world we have created and we can only do this if we inhabit this world.[2]

And all of this is achieved in just a few minutes, during a brief rainstorm. In real life of course all of this takes place over a number of decades. The film ends with Johnny's accident, bringing us back to his slippery footwear, so there is a supposed death as well. We should realize that the article that brought them together is the same as that which rips them apart. And all the while the flowers watch on, like a screen themselves, as they are needed for each of the ceremonies: marriage, birth, and death. To me this is a perfect short film screenplay, where the awkward stilted dialogue encapsulates the caricatures while concurrently offering a significant subtext.

Finally, there needs to be more of a poetic approach to dialogue. We can be poetic in our work, and, discussing theatre, Antonin Artaud called for a return to magic and incantation.

> The theatre should aim at expressing what language is incapable of putting into words. My principle is that words do not mean everything and that by their nature and defining character, fixed once and for all, they arrest and paralyze thought instead of permitting it and fostering its development. I am trying to restore to the language of speech its old magic, its essential spell-binding character.[3]

Language, discourse, and dialogue have become corrupted, words being empty and deceptive, according to Amos Vogel. Given the visual characteristics of film, it is important for us to stress what cannot be verbally expressed. Filmmakers such as Jean Luc Godard, Alain Resnais, Michelangelo Antonioni, Werner Schroeter, R. W. Fassbinder have chosen to use language semi-abstractly, for example preceding or following action, rather than the traditional way of accompanying it, or to use it in a way similar to music, 'as poetic, associative innuendo'.[4]

5

Individuation

The timing of the secret

We all love hearing and even telling a good secret. To know something someone else does not know makes the knowledge more precious and exclusive. Secrets are about power and can involve power over others. What is a good story? Is it just like a joke, and more about the way it is told, the timing, than about the content? All good stories involve some form of revelation, even if the epiphany is some form of anti-epiphany, such as a secret being unfolded and a story's energy concerns the evolving nature of this revelation of the secret. All good stories concern a secret and the real secret of screenwriting, as with any story, is how the secret or secrets is revealed. Because, in many respects, with the access of the internet, all secrets are available, the screenwriter needs to think harder. We have seen that for T. S. Eliot, in our beginning is our end, and the end is where we start from. *American Beauty* encapsulates this. It seems that in life the biggest secret of all, that we die, is always pushed to one side, but in this film one big 'secret' is revealed immediately. The voiceover tells us this is the last day of the central character's life, but the real secret is the answer to who did it?

In many films it is about people facing up to uncomfortable truths, after possibly years of repression, and *American Beauty* involves a whole host of characters who are led to face up to these uncomfortable truths. We cannot escape the fact that it is our deep-seated psychological need to engage with the deep psychological needs of others that keeps us going. As James Hughes has shown, our own identity as creative artists is intimately tied up with our creative products. Hughes, quoting Jung, asks: is it Goethe creating Faust, or Faust creating Goethe. This leads to a more interesting question about the psychology of screenwriting. Characters may not only be writing themselves, or indeed may write us, but they are part of us, and crucial to our own psychological development. Hence the attachment we have to our creative forms, and why editing, rewriting and receiving criticism is so difficult. The deeper we understand them, the deeper we understand ourselves and vice versa. Creative forms, like scripts, involve battles between the many sides of us, which is, hopefully, a never-ending process, unless we are dead that is. We need to witness the struggle.

In the acclaimed French film *I've Loved You So Long* (directed and written by Philippe Claudel, 2009) one central secret is the question over why the protagonist Juliette Fontaine (Kristin Scott Thomas) was sent to prison for 15 years. Yes we can guess, as others do, and it is not too difficult. To receive such a long sentence you would have had to have had committed something drastic, such as murder. And this is the case but, of course, there is more to it. Murder is so taboo in most societies, that it fascinates us completely. This is the ultimate transgression: thou shalt not kill, so it dominates real stories on the news, plus fiction films and novels. What would drive someone to step over this boundary? We like to believe, even in irrational circumstances, that there are reasons for our behaviour. We are dominated by this cause-and-effect thinking from science. For Thomas Szasz, in the past when religion was strong and science was not developed, magic was seen as medicine, but now with science strong and religion weak, medicine is seen as magic. But it is not as simple as that. Religion is not weak and there has been a theologization of politics, but both science and religion offer explanations. This act seems so off the radar, so forbidden, something must have caused it. It is even more drastic here, as she has killed her own son. Could anything be more unforgivable? Understanding is forgiveness, according to Voltaire, and we do essentially want to understand. We want to know the depth of the human condition. That is central to why we listen, watch, or tell stories. It is about entertainment? Maybe it is about 'humilitainment', as in a lot of horror films. If we do not learn anything about the human condition from your script then what is the point?

In *I Have Loved You So Long*, Annette is asked where she has been for such a long time by a drunken writer who is hosting a dinner party. She tells everyone the truth, but they roar with laughter, unable to believe her shocking revelation. A good story is about the timing of revealing the secret. This is the secret nobody wants to accept. If she had been a large, aggressive-looking man then maybe they would accept she was a killer. Only her friend, who has worked with prisoners and has an empathic sensibility, believes her. When it is finally revealed she killed her own son, because he was dying anyway, the main thrust of the drama comes from the sister: why did you not tell us; why did you not allow us to help you? The real depth of the film comes in the sister acknowledging she could have done absolutely nothing to help her killer sister anyway. And she is the younger sister, which adds a further psychological dimension. Not only did the older sister kill her son, but she was not there for her younger sister but banged up in prison, virtually killed off by her own parents, and not discussed. There might be a core, existential message here, such as life goes on, which is a repeated phrase throughout *21 Grams*. While this is a hopeful message, to a degree, it also can provoke further questions concerning meaning and purpose. If life goes on, then what about the depth of meaning of what life there was before, is that all meaningless now?

Despite popular notions to the opposite, people basically want to help each other, love thy neighbour as thyself, but this is probably for selfish reasons, as Matt Ridley explains in *The Origins of Virtue*. As with all animals, we do favours to others in the hope they will do them back. In *I Have Loved You So Long*, the two sisters can be reconciled after such a long time, and they are finally there for each other. In an American film about two close sisters, *Rachel Getting Married* (directed by Jonathan Demme and written by Jenny Lumet, 2008), Kim (Anne Hathaway), a television star, returns from rehab on the eve of her sister's wedding, and we soon have the first revelation: aged 16, when on drugs, Kim could not free their baby brother Ethan from his car seat, and he drowned. Is that not enough for now?

Again we have the deep psychological theme of sisters and death, but in this case it is a dead brother, not son. If that was not enough, Kim then bumps into someone from rehab in the hairdressers', whilst with her sister and the bridesmaid. They did an exercise in rehab which was supposed to be anonymous but he remembers Kim's story about her sister, child abuse by her uncle, Rachel getting an eating disorder, and so on. He goes on about it, saying how much of a hero she is. Not only is a secret revealed, perhaps the worst secret of all today, child sexual abuse, but it is said in public, so Kim's sister can hear everything. And it is pure invention to impress everyone at rehab. The film cranks up the tension exponentially.

The major revelation in the hairdresser's might be considered a 'plot point' in Syd Field's terminology: 'an incident, or event, that "hooks" into the action and spins it around into another direction'.[1] According to Field a screenplay will contain as many as 15 plot points, and those at the ends of Acts I and II are stressed. But this incident does not really spin things about, as we have heard about Rachel's anorexia. For Field, you need to know what these points are before you start writing, but I would argue this really depends on how you write. The basic point, that you need a trajectory and something to aim at, is a sound one, but being so prescriptive might be counterproductive. We do not always know where we are going until we go there. It is in the process of writing that you work out what you want to achieve. Field is correct to warn some writers about getting 'lost in the maze' of their own creation but some people need a fixed plan, others do not.

The secrets can be anything you like, but they have to be entertaining enough to sustain our interest. Often people like delving into their own past, their own family history, or that of those close to them. There is nothing wrong with that, for the writer everything is material, as long as you can keep a certain distance, and that can be difficult. There is no real truth in this context, just perception of the truth, and with perception comes interpretation, so truth alters in the process. You might want to get mystical about it and find the heart of your story, the key, but these can be scrapped. You may think you know the truth and this is probably the moment you do not.

This resonates with Syd Field's plot points and with screenwriter William Goldman's great example in *Which Lie Did I Tell* when he discusses working on *Misery* (directed by Rob Reiner), for which Kath Bates won an Oscar in 1990.[2] In the 1987 novel by Stephen King, a famous author has a crash and is rescued by a mad fan that, amongst other pursuits, uses a propane torch and an axe to cut off his feet when he tries to escape. Goldman believed this was crucial to the film version he was writing and goes round the bend about this but then eventually realizes he is wrong. Everyone would have hated Annie after that, so a little ankle breaking was done instead; much more acceptable.

There are a number of lessons we can learn from this. Firstly, in adapting work, even if you think it must be literal, it does not have to be. Secondly, a different way of doing things can have a similar or better impact. Thirdly, you may need your audience to love your monsters, so try and be more complex. Fourthly, as Goldman pointed out, as with life, you need all the help you can get. Fifthly, despite the need to push boundaries and show every secret imagined, or yet to be imagined, and the belief that everyone is craving for more and more horror, blood and gore, there are more subtle ways of achieving your desired impact or a greater impact. They just might take more thought.

Break a few rules and home

We have already seen how some of the best screenplays break all the 'rules', and if we want a rule this should be it – break the rules. But once again paradox rules, for is it ever possible, or desirable, so even this 'rule' must be broken. Some of the best screenplays seemingly break all the rules but if we look under the surface they are simultaneously keeping many of them, so paradox is part of the rule. Take the film *Buried* (directed by Roderigo Cortés and written by Chris Sparling, 2010), which has the 'what if' scenario: what if an American truck driver in Iraq is buried in the ground for a ransom. We may think a film that has the protagonist stuck in a coffin and basically has no other action is going to be tedious in the extreme but it is not as simple as this. The fact the protagonist Ryan (Paul Conroy-Reynolds) is isolated is perfect, for there is nowhere else for the audience's attention to roam.

Ryan speaks with the police, the FBI, the state department, his company, the group for hostages in Iraq, and his kidnapper, his wife's friend, his mother, and eventually his wife. Speaking to the video recorder he also broadcasts to the world; moments after he sends out a video and the request of his kidnappers it has received 48,000 hits on YouTube and has been broadcast on Al Jazeera. The box he is in becomes his testament, diary, notebook and manuscript, as well as cage and tomb, as he has a pencil which he uses to scribble down numbers and a name, Mark White. Interestingly, it in effect becomes a form of screenplay in itself, or at least notes on a screenplay, within the film. For Won Kar-wai, fully formed scripts are restrictive, given the complexity of what is required, the script being unable to portray the extent of images, sounds, music and tempo intended for a film, other than in a boring fashion, so he uses a form of notation instead which might be unreadable to others.[3] Here, in the inner sanctum of the coffin, another form of notation takes place.

The British-accented head of the hostages group that is supposed to be finding him informs him early on in the film that Mark White was rescued three weeks ago, and is back home in the US at medical school. There are two major plot points in the film. One comes seconds before the end, when we hear the rescue mission, as they claim to be coming closer. The hostage begins to hallucinate he is being rescued with a bright light above his head and the audience might at this moment believe this is real. We then hear the voice of the head of the hostage group say, 'Oh my God, it's Mark White.' So they have been lying all along. An Iraqi has taken them to a spot where he knows an American has been buried, but it is the man the group claimed was rescued before.

Not only this, but his company claims he has no insurance because he has no contract – they have invented a story that he has been romantically involved with a colleague, thus nullifying his contract. His worst fears about his government are confirmed, and also there is no future for his family. He laughs, giving his last will and testament into the phone; leaving 700 dollars to his wife, and his clothes to his son, who will grow into them, but jokes over the bloodied clothes he is currently wearing. Bombs are going off around him, but the killing of Iraqis above his head may also kill him, with sand entering his wooden prison. All he wanted to do was do right by his family, he says.

On one level Ryan is a totally innocent victim wanting to return home and yet he represents the invader, despite being part of the mission to rebuild the country, turning the world into an American home. As his kidnapper points out, they have destroyed Iraq and now they are rebuilding it, so it gives the US a lot of business. Behind all these tension-raising plot points is the subtext that Ryan must have been desperate to leave his family, that he probably could not make a living back in the US. Unlike *The Hurt Locker* previously mentioned, which reveals psychologically how some macho soldiers cannot truly live anywhere other than a warzone, *Buried* has the central nexus of economics.

The use of phones, mobile or stationary, has been done expertly elsewhere, most explicitly in *Phone Booth* (directed by Joel Schumacher and written by Larry Cohen, 2002). In *Buried* the British head of the hostage group and the head of personnel are the antagonists. Despite the former maintaining a lie about whom they have previously rescued, he is trying to keep the hope going, hence the lie. The question here is when does an evil deed become a good deed and do the ends justify the means. Should he lie to someone to keep their hope alive; should we invade a country to topple a dictator? This was, of course, an aspect of Tony Blair's reason for going to war. *Buried* breaks a number of 'rules', on one level, because it is not especially visual, but the plot development is entwined with character development and dialogue.

The best paradoxes make the best stories and screenplays and are often intimately connected to the concept of home. In *The Godfather* Michael Corleone (Al Pacino) has just returned to the bosom of his close Italian family after fighting in World War II. But to protect the life of his family, especially his father, he must murder a New York police chief and the head of a rival mafia clan, which immediately means he is personally exiled once more and must return to Europe. In *Moon*, Sam (Sam Rockwell) is working for an energy company on the dark side of the moon. With only three weeks left before he returns to earth and to what he believes is his wonderful wife and daughter, he discovers he is a clone, after being rescued by 'himself', another clone. The second clone we encounter manages to escape back to earth. Why would a company have a clone with feelings and a manufactured past? Despite being a clone, the human in him, and us, always feels the need to go home. Film fundamentally offers escapism, but has to draw on this notion. *The Man Who Fell To Earth* (directed by Nicholas Roeg and written by Paul Mayersberg, 1976, from the novella by Walter Tevis, 1963), starring the father of the director of *Moon* (Duncan Jones), David Bowie as an alien, powerfully plays with this theme. It is hard to think of a film that does not delve into the theme of home, whether it is leaving home, getting back home, or facing the impact of home. We are all from somewhere and the tensions of leaving and returning are essential to the psychology of screenwriting and this also confirms Freud's fort/da theory previously discussed.

Fundamentals

Some new writers forget to put in the basic details, such as the ages of the characters, or where it is set, and the time. Quite often people put 'a typical teenager', but typical does not really make a character live. On occasion, if it is just a background character then maybe we can get away with this, but they still could have a distinctive feature. We want our characters to be real, and to go against the grain. To be complex, like real people, we do need to get specific. In terms of formatting, place and time are the essential ingredients: interior or exterior, in a brothel or church, day or night? For Freud, the first thing we think about someone is whether they are male or female – biology rules. This might not be that obvious. Think of Aerosmith's fantastic song 'Dude Looks Like A Lady', concerning judging a book by its cover, and there will always be androgyny, with Virginia Woolf's *Orlando* and Sally Potter's film adaptation of the novel making this magical. When we are young small gaps in age seem crucial. 'He's three and four months', 'I'm nearly sixteen'. We never really lose this, but we think less about our age and more about how old we believe we are inside. We reflect on how old we feel as we have more years to compare it to. This is useful for developing older characters.

Producers and directors might like a script to be less specific, so the film can be theoretically shot in any similar location, but we need to hook our writing in a time and place. Location, Location, Location, is crucial. Sometimes people just put 'In a pub'. Well, what type of pub is it? An old man's boozer, full of real ale, big beards that people stroke like pets, real pets, and beer bellies, or a yuppy bar, where everyone goes 'ya, ya, ya', and laughs like they have been trained at the same elite college to do so, or which sounds a bit like a mating call, or maybe a bland chain where nothing is noteworthy except desperation. Do the research. If you want to create some form of class conflict then the work of George Orwell is perfect. Some of this is down to an assumption on the part of the writer. My eight-year-old son often asks me why I am asking him things. Maybe he assumes I already know what he is thinking about. He has not worked out that the world and his mind are not the same and some philosophers may argue that they are the same, that the world is mind. Similarly, some writers think their readers have insight into their heads or what they are doing. There is a difficult balance to be had between spelling things out and simplicity, and making things multi-layered and letting the reader and audience do the work.

Key questions are: where, when, who, what, why, and how. For detectives, the how leads to the what, which leads to the who. All throughout your work you need to consider these questions, consciously bear them in mind in your writing, and answer them. They may seem obvious, but if we just take one, 'when', what does this actually mean? Yesterday or tomorrow? Yesterday could be tomorrow, if the film is set in the future. A million years ago or a time before time? A second ago now, or a combination, or a zone outside time? Can we ever be in real time? Some films have attempted it and succeeded, such as *Phone Booth* and *Timecode* (directed and written by Mike Figgis, 2000) and, in terms of television, the show *24* (2001–10). But these are not fully in real time. The film may range over time, and the amount of time might be complex, so the 'when' might be complex. Sometimes it is easier to set the film just slightly in the past, to have more distance and objectivity. Those new to writing often just write everything in the present, without even considering the options. The film is its own world, and whether a fiction film or more factual, it abides by its own systems that need to be consistent.

Intertextuality and the reader

Terms such as inter-textuality, trans-textuality, and post-textuality are contentious and talking about film as if it is a 'text' is also dubious, although a screenplay might be considered something 'other', a super-text if you will. Granted, if such terms distract us from our writing then we should avoid them. They can, however, make us think more deeply about the psychology of screenwriting, what we are doing and how we might do it better. 'The reader takes neither the position of the author nor an author's position.'[194] Every reading of a text is therefore an invention on the part of the reader. Here we are speaking of the reader of the film script that a company may employ. But it is interesting to note how the ideology of the Enlightenment, where books were claimed to be reforming and transforming society, still exists in all the ways in which we are continually told that culture should have this aim. 'Today, it is the socio-politico mechanisms of the schools, the press, or television that isolate the text controlled by the teacher or the producer from its readers.'[195]

Kick Ass (directed by Matthew Vaughan and co-written with Jane Goldman, 2010, based on the 2008 comic, written by Mark Millar with drawings by John

Romita, Jr.), is a superlative example of a genre-bending intertextual film. At first, we may think this is a typical or even stereotypical teens' movie that we have seen so many times before. As the plot unfolds it entwines the teen movie genre, the hero movie genre, the action movie genre, and the comic book genre, producing something fresh and new. The film goes beyond our expectations and always has an ironic take. Not many films can do this, as in general our expectations are so high, having seen so many films, good and bad, and the ubiquitous nature of film.

Dave (Aaron Johnson) is on the cusp of being a loser, the underdog with whom we immediately empathize. He has two close friends, everyone is obsessed with comics, and we imagine he does well at school being a bit of a geek, but he initially does not have a girlfriend. All superheroes are set apart from society, they have some kind of specific problem, usually medical, but all have the general problem of difficulties in finding love. One major issue the film confronts is class. This might seem radical for a mainstream American movie but, since the economic crash that became more overt in 2007, this is mainstream.

When Dave talks about the need for a superhero today that really does clean up the streets we know his friends think he is all talk. This call for social and community engagement with some of the real issues that are important chimes with a call in 2010 across the UK, and beyond, for people to become involved with each other, to take responsibility, to not rely on government intervention or the 'system' to help. Two worlds are presented: one involving people who work hard for the common good and the other where selfishness rules.

Dave initially talks about befriending a boy, Chris D'Amico (Christopher Mintz-Plasse), who is isolated because his father Frank (Mark Strong) is enormously wealthy and when he suggests it in a diner his friends tell him to do it. The script takes us initially from one crisis to another: the rebuttal in the diner, when the rich boy's bodyguard tells Dave to 'fuck off'; to the boys getting mugged, and having their money and phones taken, while a man watches on from his bedroom and does nothing; to Dave getting beaten up, while dressed in a camp green suit as Kick Ass, confronting the same two men who mugged him, who are now trying to steal a car. Kick Ass gives them a lecture on how the person who owned the car worked hard to get it, which may or may not be true, but it is the American-way. We know Dave comes from a single-parent home, his father a hard grafter trying to do the best he can.

Some may laugh mockingly at the triteness of all this American-way nonsense, but it ties into superhero stories from the 1950s in an interesting intertextual fashion and it is a comedy of sorts. In story terms we see the pattern here of the hero falling to the lowest point imaginable. Dave not only does not have any super power, apart from being an ordinary nice guy, but also he has no real strength. There is also the comedy when his father visits him in hospital and asks if his attackers did anything sexual, given he has told the paramedics to say he was naked, rather than reveal he was wearing a camp costume when they found him. This is a nice attack on the paranoia around sexual abuse and victimhood. Plus, back at school, recovering from his injuries and now full of metal, his buddies try and test out the theory he does not feel any pain, sticking forks into him, which is funny, but indicates he has been through an initiation process. He is the returning warrior who has faced the demons and survived.

Superman, Spiderman, and Batman, all have their sense of justice and their stupid side, where they will put themselves into danger for others and it is this element of risk that makes them heroic, and an example to all, for if we all did this then there would be no problems. Kick Ass also buys into this, for he is prepared to be sacrificed and to make a stand for what he believes in. There is a powerful Christian theme, with Kick Ass saying to those attacking a man that he is prepared to die for him. Because Kick Ass states this they back off but not before dozens of people have recorded Kick Ass defending a man. This soon becomes the most watched clip on the internet. The film is incredibly violent but the comedy here lies in the fact that instead of using their phones to dial for help, as Dave begs them to, those watching just want to record it, because it is so 'awesome'.

Technology has become so addictive, it can deny humanity, yet it archives and broadcasts the extraordinary, bringing the magical and supernatural into mundane lives. Mobile phones are ubiquitous, and often make for lazy writing, particularly in television drama and radio, but using new technology in this way here makes the film more powerful. Importantly, the paradox and the film's main message is that addiction leads to pain, despite addictions being an attempt to avoid pain. The main thug in the fight scene, where Kick Ass initially distinguishes himself, has 'addicted' tattooed below his neck, and the drug trade dominates the city.

The social message here, as with the class issues, are only surreptitiously fed into the plot. This is important, as some viewers might walk out if they thought they were being preached to. Katie (Lyndsy Fonseca) falls for Dave because she thinks he is gay and will not try it on with her, which addresses another contemporary issue comically. He goes to find the man who has been stalking Katie, who is a drug dealer, and while Kick Ass might now get his own ass kicked, he is saved by other superheroes, Big Daddy (Damon, played by Nicolas Cage) and Hit-Girl (Mindy, Damon's daughter, played by Chloe Moretz), the message being that you do need others. Those who help him are driven by a desire for revenge over the loss of their wife/mother, which relates to the drug trade. The police are corrupt, so they have to take things into their own hands, Big Daddy once being a cop. With the chief mobster fearing that it is Kick Ass who is killing his men, he orders the man to be executed and he mistakenly kills a man who is just wearing the Kick Ass suit.

The film manages to reveal the absurdity in cult and celebrity worship but also the deep need for people to take on the issues of the day. Addressing numerous contemporary issues in a script like this is difficult but lends it weight, and *Kick Ass* reveals how it can also be comical and enjoyable. In this respect a wider audience is catered for. I think it is important to never go for the lowest common denominator as too many films do, but go for the story that needs to be told. Kick Ass betrays Big Daddy by leading Red Mist (Chris D'Amico, the mobster's son) to him, but this is for a benign reason as he believes Red Mist is genuine. When Kick Ass and Big Daddy are captured and tortured live on the internet by the D'Amico gang, the perverse nature of the internet is made clear. Television stations switch off their broadcasts because it is so horrific. Hit-Girl arrives, and saves Kick Ass, but her father Big Daddy dies, so this is no happy ending.

What is remarkable is that, even with such a ludicrous array of characters, drawing on all the clichés where we are never led to believe this is real, this is highly original and deeply moving. Through its fantasy *Kick Ass* reveals that any backdrop will do. It is not really where your film is set that is important. It could be in a fantasy future New York, like this, or in Roman times, or on another planet. Simply put, something is lost, and the journey is the quest to find it. Dave is the hero because he believes it is worth doing something about the sense of decay in society and puts this into practice. He has reached breaking point and has had enough. Most people believe it is someone else's responsibility to sort things out and are happy to keep their head in the sand.

Intertextuality might go too far and it is worth considering how far you push the readers of your scripts and your potential audience who might not even get a quarter of what you believe are witty references. Breaking genre boundaries and 'shock cinema' is in some sense innovative; James Quandt coined the term 'the new French extremity' in 2004. He used it to describe the 'growing vogue for shock tactics' since the 1990s amongst French directors. Quandt saw this basically as a desperate way to attract the attention of audiences by transgressing every taboo. From playing to what the audience might expect, or sticking with common techniques, films such as this might take cinema a step further. Rape, necrophilia and self-mutilation are issues covered in these films and it has been asked whether they are just offering these acts up for some form of voyeuristic pleasure. There is always danger in trying to go beyond previous films, using any means necessary to depict the greatest of horrors.[6]

> Writing accumulates, stocks up, resists time by the establishment of a place and multiplies the erosion of time (one forgets oneself and also forgets) ... each of the places through which it passes is a repetition of the lost paradise. Indeed, reading has no place: Barthes reads Proust in Stendhal's text; the television viewer reads the passing away of his childhood in the news reports.[7]

The reader can skip from text to text and move inside each text, escaping the law of the text and from the social milieu. As a writer this can be both freeing and unsettling, for are we unsure the reader understands what we mean, given they need to understand what they mean in relation to everything else that might have meaning for them. There is an unmooring from the scriptural place and an acceleration in the reading processes that comes with speed reading, so space is redefined. For Michel de Certeau, the emancipation from places means the reading body is freer than ever, running through the text in 'the way one runs traffic lights'.[8] This is even more the case now we are reading so much on hand-held devices. He references Barthes, who identified three types of reading: the one that stops at the pleasure afforded by words; the one that rushes on to the end and 'faints with expectation'; the one that cultivates the desire to write. There is pleasure to be had in reading scripts, if they are well written, not just seeing them as a potential film. As readers of scripts and as writers of scripts that are read often by speed readers we can relate to all three of these and we will have our own further types.

Theme

This is a difficult area given all screenplays need a theme but ultimately this is inexpressible. The theme is the unconscious or subconscious message, often unwritten and unspoken. If we think of the screenplay in a matrix, we have the mechanical side containing the genre, plot and character on one side. We have the more artistic elements, including the style, form and theme, on the other. These are all intimately interwoven, hence the word matrix, and if we leave out theme, then this matrix topples over. The theme is the universal thread that is invisible that runs through the story and holds it all together, it is the unspoken story. We need to ask the purpose of our writing, in all its elements. As E. M. Forster once put it, only connect. Without a theme there is no story or shape.

Of course some films may not have a clear theme, and are considered more avant-garde, like *Chien Andalou* (directed by Luis Bûnuel and co-written with Salvador Dali, 1929), but there are themeless themes where people are reacting against theme. Themes never pose answers, but just ask questions. There is clearly no real answer to why people fight, why wars happen, why there is a tendency to evil, or to love. Themes may contain your personal point of view or experience, and it might be a learning experience for the audience but it is not about a lecture. In discussion here of films I have mentioned Christian themes, themes of sisters and death, and the theme of wholeness. For Phil Parker, the audience is looking for meaning, something they can relate to. If we can draw on deeper themes, these will relate to the universal shared experience, the collective understanding, and instinctive understanding. We need to go beyond reason.

Themes point to the big questions and dilemmas of the human condition, such as why are we here. If we knew the answer to this the stories would dry up. So, theme is not the same as moral, but often about immorality. Themes are often about power. One of the greatest films ever made, *The Godfather* (Francis Ford Coppola), encapsulates this. There is the question around do we personally have power, and we all seek power, even when we avoid responsibility, say for example when intoxicated.

Adaptation

The word adaptation has been employed already and has a number of meanings. Adaptation studies of one form or another exists in most university film courses. For some it is rich for academic purposes, for it lends itself to discussions of layers of meaning, intertextuality, and infinite re-workings. We have seen that Peter Greenaway believes adaptation of, say, a Jane Austen novel is a waste of time, but surely it is how this is done. He himself adapted *The Tempest*. Adaptation commonly means from book to film but in practice most so-called original screenplays have been adapted from somewhere along the line, whether it is a story someone was told or something they read in the newspaper spliced together with something else. This is not to say in postmodern fashion there are no original ideas any more as some claim, just that the originality comes through re-working old ideas.

Psychologically, we need to get behind what adaptation is. Stories have always been adapted but today a lot of conflict occurs because of our obsession with ownership within capitalist culture which emphasizes the individual above all else. Psychologically, this is unhealthy. Within cultures of the troubadour and the shaman, stories could be shared and passed on, with ownership not such a big issue. Paradoxically, in such cultures stories held more worth because they were treated with more respect and possessed a higher spiritual value. The stories may have been sacred and sacrosanct but simultaneously embellishment and adaptation was part of the process. They came from the gods and were channelled by earthlings. They worked their magic through language, there may have been a fee, but people could not seriously sue people over stealing a story. There is copyright law now, of course, and nobody likes their ideas being stolen. Ideology is when ideas have you, theory when you have ideas. If all reality is created within ideology ideas that are not our own; they form us. Ultimately questioning whether we are individuals at all within this is essential; this is not nihilistic or merely relativistic in a postmodernism sense.

Both flashbacks (analepses) and flashforwards (prolepses) can be utilized. The former can be external to the primary narrative providing useful background information, or internal, offering insight into the primary narrative. If we also add voiceover as a device, this might be trying too hard and complicates the chronology, developing a treatment that does damage to the original idea. This needs to be watched out for. The majority of films in every era have been told chronologically, but with the novel this is the exact opposite.[9] In the first 20 years of film history it is exceedingly rare to see changes in chronology, with one exception being *Birth of a Nation* when the little Colonel tells of the bitter events that have occurred under Reconstruction. Furthermore, while analepses can be found often in genres such as film noir, prolepses are unusual. Nicolas Roeg and Alain Resnais are two filmmakers who have made use of prolepses in innovative ways but they are exceptions.

Of course, cinema has no built-in tense system therefore any deviation must be adequately and often over-adequately indicated, through a plethora of signals, to make sure the audience gets it: voiceover, musical effects, changes in costume or locale, blurring or stippling of the image, turning calendars, whirling leaves, rapidly moving clouds, you name it, all of which guide the viewer. These can seem corny. There is still the commonly held belief that the novel is about the interior world of the character, film about the exterior, and stage drama about the language of talking heads working like some kind of multiple tennis match. This is way too simplistic a view, given the way modernism in literature has absorbed film, stage drama absorbed film, and how film can be highly literary, and stage can utilize multimedia elements.

In *Orlando* (Sally Potter, 1994) we have the central character address the camera with a look, and this sense of humour invites us into their world. According to convention, what the camera 'sees' is called objective, and what the character sees is subjective and the story is the development of both the objective and subjective image, 'Ego=Ego; identity of the character seen and who sees, but equally well identity of the camera/film-maker who sees the character and is what the character sees.'[10] There is a strong tendency in the majority of screenwriting discourse to denounce the camera not as an enemy but as something anathema, to be self-consciously ignored, for to not do so would be to tread on a director's precious feet. For novelist Ian McEwan, when he writes a screenplay he writes for the camera, not the actor or director.[11] The objective subjective is true for the traditional cinema of Hitchcock, for example, but directors such as Pasolini went beyond the traditional story, creating a fusion where the singular vision of the characters are expressed, a form of 'free indirect discourse', poetry if you will rather than story.[12]

In her diaries Virginia Woolf explained that the aim of her novel on which the film was based was to 'exteriorise consciousness'.[13]

In other words, she set out to find images rather than abstract literary monologues to describe the secret machinery of the mind in such a way that the outer world – with its weather, costume and surfaces of all kinds – became an expression of inner complexity.[14]

One main problem if you are adapting a book that has been published, or just working from 'real life', is the belief you should stick religiously to the so-called 'original' material. History is more than a contrived corridor, to paraphrase T. S. Eliot. The source material should not hold you back and stop you making a screenplay that exists in and of itself, as a separate entity. Just as no human is truly a separate entity, neither is a screenplay, an interdependence will remain but there is a time when a work of art becomes truly unique. Potter reveals in the introduction to her screenplay that in the four years it took her to adapt the novel it was during the last year, on advice of her story editor Walter Donohue, that she saw the script in its own right as if the source material had vanished.

This metamorphosis is the beauty of adaptation; despite postmodern theory that might claim it is impossible, something new is created. After such a move, she could confirm that 'the screenplay would have no pretensions of literary merit – indeed, one of my first ruthless tasks was to divest it of redundant literary concerns'.[15] She goes on to point out that cinema is more pragmatic, the obvious notion being that everything needs to drive the story, and that she had to loosen the biographical facts with the book being a spoof biography of Vita Sackville-West. While she does not put it like this, she goes beyond Woolf, as this enabled her to offer 'a more biting and satirical view of the English class system'.[16] Another adaptation where class is at the fore is *The Shining*. For Frederic Jameson, Kubrick's film achieves something greater than the novel because it is a specific historical commentary, rather than King's 'vague and global domination by all the random voices of American history'.[17]

For David Cronenberg creativity involves a lot of waste, just as the spider will lay a thousand eggs and only two of them will end up being a mature spider.[18] Patrick McGrath, screenwriter and novelist, does not necessarily see it as a waste but an opportunity to try out ideas and this occurs in novel writing as well. This is an interesting point given people are continually trying to separate the two writing forms, the only major difference for him being that in a novel you can drift in the story. The same challenges are there in any writing, such as:

> mounting narrative progress, that business of having to build on the scene, or every scene having to work on two or three levels at the same time, giving two or three bits of information about the story and the character, not repeating yourself, sustaining the momentum.[19]

The layered element here is worth noting for this leads to scripts that are rich with depth. He reveals that once Cronenberg saw his script he was good at cutting, e.g. one minute Spider is at Waterloo, then there is a tube scene that is unnecessary. The script was cut down to 78 pages. McGrath thought this too short. 'I will film slow!' said Cronenberg.[20]

The journal Spider is writing is the novel in some ways but in the film it becomes indecipherable which is a metaphor for the word of the artist, the film director even, 'trying to somehow render reality in some kind of design'.[21] The more things become horrific the more he tries to get control of it by writing it down. McGrath did research on the dialogue by reading novels of the period about working-class life, such as George Orwell, looking at movies, and immersing himself in the working-class culture of the 1930s East End. The time period shifted to the 1950s and 1980s, and the voiceover was cut.

If we are involved in an adaptation we can sum up whole chunks of prose in a few words of description, a small piece of dialogue, or one simple movement of a character. This is achieved in the adaptation of Richard Yates' masterly *Revolutionary Road* (directed by Sam Mendes). The film and novel both open on Frank in the audience watching his wife, but Yates explains in detail how embarrassed and awkward everyone is. The screenplay, however, just contains a look on Frank's face and one line of dialogue from a woman behind Frank. There is a form of shorthand in the screenplay here but it is actually just as powerful as the prose of the novel.

Writer and director Darren Aronofsky follows the same advice Francis Ford Coppola gave to George Lucas, 'Just get through it.'[22] Meaning, just go through the entire scene in one sitting, and do not get worked up by the poetry of the piece, and in some cases this will come. When writing an original screenplay he claims the closest he can describe himself is as a tapestry maker, because a lot of different threads are coming together from a lot of different places, and he weaves them together. For example, in *Pi* (directed by Darren Aronofsky and co-written with Sean Gulette and Eric Watson, 1998) we have the Kabbalah, the conspiracy, the paranoia, the sci-fi, elements of the *Twilight Zone* (1959–64) and spiritual elements, which he claims comes from his high-school teacher who taught a spiritual maths class. He also singles out the influence of Philip K. Dick.

With his disturbing film *Requiem for a Dream* (directed by Darren Aronofsky and co-written with Hubert Selby Jr., 2000, based on Selby's 1978 novel), he was taking a 480-page novel and reducing it to a 110-page screenplay. The process was finding out the structure first and then identifying which scenes belonged to this structure, and 'how beat after beat after beat follows'. He goes on to claim 'Syd Field books were evil', and others of their ilk, and 'I was always anti-establishment enough to resist those'.[23] Narrative is the mantra for Aronofsky, so search for it. Break it down beat by beat, then move on to index cards, order with colour and look for pattern, finding out how the whole works. Put them on a whole wall to make a meaning. One card per scene, and then when they are in a good place write each scene. For this film he wrote about 20 drafts and fused this with the author's original screenplay from 1978. Interestingly in terms of adaptation, Harry Goldfarb in the novel (played by Jared Leto in the film) wanted to open a coffee shop. Outdated now with Starbucks, Marion (Jennifer Connelly) wants to open a fashion shop. Now the question, do we update the dialogue? They decided it would be good to make it timeless, like addiction, so they have seventies clothes, despite more recent technology.

In the novel there are four characters given subjective points of view, plus the third-person narrator. In the film no clear narrator, but it is the monster of addiction that is the real protagonist. The screenwriter used a graph to plot the ups and downs of the character and every time something good was supposed to happen something bad happened. And when something bad happened to the character something good happened to addiction.[24] There are three acts – summer, autumn and winter. Selby began writing a movie, and two weeks later had a novel. He did character arcs for the screenplay – each character's progression, a graph, with the time on and different events and where they were; a visual representation. Only write in 'smash-cut' or camera angles if really important; it turns directors off.[25]

Alex Garland, author of the 1996 novel *The Beach*, which was adapted for film (directed by Danny Boyle and written by John Hodge, 2000) and the screenwriter of *28 Days Later...* (directed by Danny Boyle, 2002), writes in long hand exactly what happens, all the major action, and in 24 hours will have a quarter of the screenplay.[26] This is remarkable. He believes he writes so fast because, unlike prose, you do not have to care initially about the sense of sentence construction or how it reads on the page. Then he will have the rest of the screenplay complete in four days. Interestingly, Garland may have his A4 page pinned close to his computer monitor, but if the ending veers away from his initial idea then it does not matter. He believes if you are writing in a genre, the genre dictates, which adheres to the idea already mentioned that the work writes itself, and remarks that people like Charlie Kaufman, who work outside genre, have to be inventive, but for him he is building on the work of all the people who developed the genre beforehand, so it is far easier.[27] He claims to be obsessed with structure, and into the three-act structure, but is not into the Robert McKee style of screenwriting course. The point with genre, Garland maintains, is that it is so easy to subvert. For example, we always have the protagonist getting it together with the girl; well, try and avoid that cliché. He often writes to music to get the correct tone. Working with directors like Danny Boyle who have their own strong idea of the set soundtrack and tone of the film, sets the writing process. Interestingly it was not at the shooting stage when he knew things were wrong, but at the moment when he watched the loosely cut rushes, and he could see that there was in some scenes too much exposition. At this point he knew later scenes would need to be cut or rewritten as well.[28] He was lucky with *28 Days Later...* because he could work with the team on the film and the film was shot in sequence so if anything did not work he could rewrite immediately and rewrite later scenes.

Interestingly, Garland does not care about back story or elements of the story that might not, when considered in detail, be believable. The very nature of film-going entails using your imagination, so the audience can fill in the gaps. Indeed, looking on the Internet Movie Database indicates audiences invent all sorts of elaborate scenarios for why things happen in movies, and they may believe the filmmakers intended this when it is not always the case.[29] Not filling in every gap is important. What comes across from Garland's interview is that his writing process seems individual and manic, and yet as he writes 50 or so drafts with others, and is still unhappy about certain scenes, there is a definite perfectionist streak, both to his process of development and the way he views the final product. Most writers will agree, without a heightened sense of what is wrong with their writing and a real internal critic, most of the writing that is produced will be vanity.

Writing voiceovers

As with all forms of writing, dialogue that is about exposition – telling us stuff – is boring and fake. So cut it out. Voiceovers are particularly annoying if they are just explaining in this expositional way but they can work if, again, they are not just about telling us stuff, as this is lazy, but are about creating a deeper relationship with the audience. *American Beauty*, previously discussed, is an excellent example. The film begins with the voiceover of Lester Burnham (Kevin Spacey) telling us he is already dead. We have an immediate sense of empathy with the protagonist from the voiceover. There are many cases where voiceovers are non-creative lazy ways to impart information, so care needs to be taken to stay away from a mere expositional information style. It works best when the voiceover, as with *American Beauty* and *How To Train A Dragon* (directed by Dean DeBlois and Chris Sanders and co-written by them with William Davis, from the book by Cressida Cowell, 2010), is by one of the characters, bringing us deeper into the world of the protagonist and their story.

Once the basics have been acquired, voiceovers can be employed in interesting ways. In *The Opposite of Sex* (Don Roos, 1996), for example, hearing Dede Truitt's (Christina Ritchi) bitchy thoughts has a highly comic impact that could not be achieved otherwise. In the psychology of screenwriting we need to work out what will deepen understanding of our character and this type of voiceover can work. And let us not forget that classic *Pussy Talk* (directed by Claude Mulot and co-written with Didier Philippe-Gérard, 1975, from the Denis Diderot novel), where a vagina does a lot of the talking, not a voiceover as such but an interesting angle, more a 'voice-under'. In *The Quiet American*, (directed by Philip Noyce and written by Christopher Hampton and Robert Schenkkan, 2002, from the novel by Graham Greene, 1955), the opening voiceover establishes the atmosphere and voice of the central protagonist played by Michael Caine, and lends the film a literary quality. This is quite standard and not particularly interesting.

In writing a screenplay it is interesting to think about diverse ways in which voiceovers might be employed to enhance the overall dynamic. Voiceovers are sometimes seen as lazy, especially for the new writer who is just using them for expositional reasons. They can, however, be much more interesting. The words contained in a voiceover might actually subvert and alter the meaning of the pictures, and say what people are really thinking, for example for comic impact. There are plenty of examples from real life where we say one thing when we actually mean another. Some factors might give what we are thinking away, like body language, but a voiceover that mocks a character's disingenuous hypocrisy, by being close to their 'real' self, can also more overtly express this. *Blade Runner* is the classic example of playing with voiceovers with regards to marketing and artistic integrity. One version is the director's cut, without the voiceover, which is supposed to be less didactic, while the other has the voiceover, and explicitly tells the audience what is going on. Clearly the latter might reach out to the audience and hook them in, so they feel personally addressed and talked to. It depends on how well it is written, of course: so what is a well-written voiceover?

We speak of finding the voice of the character, and ask 'does this ring true' to them? There is the voice of the character that comes through on the page, then we may have another voice that is the voiceover which is supposed to be even more authentic, but we have already seen how authenticity is a questionable term. If you become yourself when you become your dream, as Pedro Almodóvar put it, then it could be argued that this is achieving authenticity. The question is why the voiceover should actually be the inner or so-called authentic voice of the character. We are assuming that there is a singular narrative that speaks for each person. A good voiceover will therefore mix and mash-up the voice, so we have contradiction, drama and conflict. In this sense we get the inner contradictions of the human, who is wavering between self and other, the constant moral dilemma between taking and giving. The latter may, of course, be linked to the former with the benevolence played out for selfish reasons. This does not matter for the benevolence is still there. Ultimately this concerns creation or destruction, and how the inner world and feelings of the character become projected onto the outer world. Woody Allen achieves this in a number of films, and for Allen the script is the film, and he is not interested in the film after the point when the script is complete. John Hurt's voiceover in the film *Dogville* (directed and written by Lars von Trier, 2003) is didactic in the extreme. The film is strange as it is played out in what appears to be the inside of a warehouse, with the rooms of the town drawn in white lines on the floor. What the voiceover does is lend a certain fairytale mystery to the story.

There are two exemplary classic voiceovers in the history of cinema and both are forms of adaptations from well-known novels, *Apocalypse Now*, which is an adaptation of Joseph Conrad's *Heart of Darkness* transposed to Vietnam, and *A Clockwork Orange*, a visionary stricter adaptation of the Anthony Burgess novel, produced and directed and written by Stanley Kubrick. In the former the fact that we hear the thoughts of the protagonist Captain Benjamin L. Willard (Martin Sheen) laconically expressed not only brings us closer to the Captain who is on a mission to get Colonel Kurtz (Marlon Brando), but it enables our own fascination with Kurtz. We travel with Willard both down the river and inside his head, entering his distanced tormented psyche, becoming more obsessed with Kurtz. In this instance, there is not a great amount of exposition, for Vietnam and everything else, whilst being real, is a type of mystery, and verges into a surrealist postmodern nightmare that the poetic voiceover encapsulates.

The best voiceovers raise just as many questions as they answer. Why does Willard take a mission that can really only lead to some form of annihilation, as if he himself is trying to deny all of his past? There are no explanations, and the gaps that are left leave us unnerved and yet hooked. Even with the slightest knowledge of the war, we know this is some kind of hell on earth. But people still choose to enter hell, as if Kurtz is Willard's Shapeshifter, Shadow, and Mentor (Wise Old Man) all thrown into one. Willard cannot resist the mission to go further into the darkness and finally not just encounter his Shadow, but fully become him. Willard is the introverted soldier, highly strung yet highly efficient, who does not do small talk. He cannot believe what is going on around him, such as surfing as helicopters bomb the hell out of 'Charlie'. Fundamentally, Willard is a loner, the existentialist anti-hero, and the only way the audience might get to travel with him is through a mysterious voiceover that functions in its tone and content like a mantra.

A Clockwork Orange, which was completely misread by the censors at the time, is a prophetic analysis of society and still works today, particularly in its analysis of young people, violence, and the state. The narrator is Alex (Malcolm McDowell), a hooligan who to gain release from prison after committing various violent acts submits himself to government treatment as a guinea pig which will make him resist violence and sex completely. He has a desire to be good, even if he has no choice about the matter, a priest who helps him claiming this is not really goodness, for goodness can only come through free will. Doctors and government ministers see this as mere semantics, or high ethics and theology at best, not relevant to real crime prevention. The experiment looks to be a success. Even his pleasure in music, particularly Beethoven's ninth symphony, is accidentally removed via the treatment.

Starting from when Alex's gang of 'droogs' carry out their acts of violence, the whole film is brilliantly narrated by voiceover from the position of the recovering Alex, who has attempted to commit suicide, given the disastrous impact of his treatment. None of this information is revealed until late into the film. Due to the voiceover, we obviously get to really come to know Alex psychologically and, despite committing rape and even murder, we feel empathy for him, particularly when he comes home from prison only to find a lodger has now taken his place in his parents' affections. Late in the film Alex must undertake a form of hero's journey into the underworld facing the obstacles that he created, this section of the film mirroring the first.

He stumbles lost into the situations where he perpetuated violence before. First, he encounters the tramp that the droogs had previously attacked. The tramp reaps revenge, attacking him. This is broken up by the police, who are his former droogs. They then nearly kill Alex by drowning him. Remarkably, he manages to go towards a sign saying 'home', which is the house where he had attacked a writer and raped his wife with his droogs, the writer now wheelchair bound. Everyone wants to seek their revenge, particularly the so-called liberal writer, who is partly based on Anthony Burgess. Each scene of the film is perfect in construction, both in the plotting and the mise-en-scene. There is a bombastic theatricality to the film and again the voiceover at times is comedic. Other films, like *Alfie* (directed by Lewis Gilbert and written by Bill Naughton, 1966), use a voiceover to similar effect.

Most of the examples previously given are quite traditional and it is always interesting to think of more unusual ways of using voiceover. There are really interesting uses of voiceover in *Eternal Sunshine of the Spotless Mind* (directed by Michel Gondry and written by Charlie Kaufman, 2004). The film begins by using what might at first be considered to be a traditional form of voiceover, Joel (Jim Carry) literally telling us these are his random thoughts when they are actually a clear story concerning his disillusionment with his job and relationships and, ultimately, himself. This introduces the film in a traditional way but it is made 'clear' that this is not exactly what 'really' happened, so we understand later not to necessarily trust this voiceover. In this sense the film asks us to question not only conventions of cinema but psychology, in particular memory and identity, making the film remarkable. What is even more interesting is when Joel is having his memories of Clementine (Kate Winslet) wiped by a machine and the voiceover is that of the scientists observing him, following the action of his memories as he relives the experiences giving a commentary. Not only this, but at one point these are on the screen on his own television, which then functions as a visual voiceover. In this way, the more we can move voiceover on from mere exposition the more successful it will be as a tool in screenwriting.

Whose voice?

In Chapter 2 we saw how it is necessary to find the voice of the work and the characters. For Carl Jung we do not create voices, the voices create us. Stepping outside the text we step in, creating objectivity through a knowing fluidity. I am not asking writers to divorce themselves from their writing, and take out emotion. What I am saying is the opposite. I believe it is the constraints of marketing and branding and the notion of 'finding a voice' and obsessions with 'authenticity' which detract writers from writing what is truly alive. What I want is writing that is an entity in itself rather than a construct. I believe we want characters to live, not the author. We can, and should, get away from solipsism and our addiction to the self, which is part of our addiction to therapy culture.[30]

Discussing theories of affect and creativity, Sandra Russ has referred to performers such as comedian Robin Williams who claimed that characters came through him, and he just piped them, which has a clear shamanic ring to it.[31] Many performers, such as Mick Jagger, have a professed shamanic quality to their art, where they appear to move or be moved into and by another being, and become possessed, to truly take possession of their art. Interestingly, Harold Pinter begins his play *The Homecoming* with the sentence 'What have you done with the scissors?' Initially Pinter did not know who was saying this and even whom they were talking to, which brings a level of openness to the concept of voice that transcends convention. Again, this is refreshingly antithetical to the dictum and mantra, 'find your voice', or even the more open 'find the voice of your story'. Borges is another example and he is worth quoting in full.

> Suddenly I feel something is about to happen. Then I sit back and get passive, and something is given to me. I receive a beginning and an end. When I have a subject, the subject tells me the style that he needs. When I write, I forget my own prejudices, my own opinions. The whole world comes to me.[32]

Again, this has a mystical and shamanic ring to it, the creator having to by-pass the conscious mind. Re-working Freudian theory, writing in the 1950s Kris claimed that in creativity there is repression in a controlled fashion that leads to accessing primary thought processes. For adaptive reasons creative writers then evaluate these so-called primitive associations.

A great deal of research relates children's pretend play with creative writing and primary processes.[33] Importantly, 'aesthetic cognition may involve representational manipulation of emotional experiences' and what distinguishes humans from other primates is this feature.[34] While more work needs to be done on this area, it has been clinically proven that children who use play well can maintain more emotional memories to begin with and therefore have better access to these memories than those who cannot use play to deal with emotions. Expressing negative affect was important.[35] Taking this childhood paradigm into adulthood, the shaman, or successful creative writer, has a greater ability to play, to access these memories in play and through ritualistic and/or artistic means to translate them to the wider community. As Ingmar Bergman put it with regards to his screenplays:

> I have maintained open channels with my childhood. I think it may be that way with many artists. Sometimes in the night, when I am on the limit between sleeping and being awake, I can just go through a door into my childhood and everything is as it was – with lights, smells, sounds and people. ... I remember the silent street where my grandmother lived, the sudden aggresivity of the grown-up world, the terror of the unknown and the fear from the tension between my father and mother.[36]

6

Conclusions

The psychology of story

What exactly is a story and how can we understand story with regards to individual and group psychology? This is a simple yet profound question. A 'real' story is one that evokes questions. A nineteenth-century film, if we can use the word film, of a baby in a high chair being fed is not exactly a story as we have come to understand story. It can, however, be interpreted by the viewer as part of a greater story, and it offers the potential for a story, and indeed it does ask us to ask questions, so it can theoretically also be viewed as a story. As we have already seen, very early films do have an implied narrative, if not script. As cinema developed throughout the twentieth century, particular stories told in a certain way became popular. But in this basic example the audience can invent their own narrative around this simple series of images of a baby being fed. Paradoxically, it is useful to think about this early form of film as we want to steer clear of storytelling that is actually just telling.

Exposition for the sake of exposition is the mistake in all writing and needs to be avoided. Moving on from Karl Marx's idea that religion is the opium of the people, and Theodor Adorno's condemnation of the culture industry for dictating to people, what I am claiming is that we must resist this temptation. People want to be left with some work to do. In this sense, they own the film and they are writing it as they watch or read it. The psychology of screenwriting needs to be akin to the psychology of the human – endless, open to twists and turns, full of contradictions and paradoxes, and the shielding of secrets. In many ways, what makes us who we are is not what we reveal about who we are but what we hold back, the gaps, our secrets that drive us, as with a narrative. One danger of confessional culture is that it could lead to the human inner world being made banal, as all is open for analysis, so there is nothing left.[1] A deep story not only evokes questions at the start, including how is this going to go, but questions at the end.

A great example of this is the closing of the film *Lost in Translation* (directed and written by Sofia Coppola, 2003), when Charlotte (Scarlett Johansson) and Bob Harris (Bill Murray) share in a whisper. As an audience, we are desperate to know what this is, but realize this is private, so it would be to transgress a boundary if we did know. We are often told that a good screenplay is about taking a character to a point of epiphany and revelation, and we get that to a degree in *Lost in Translation*, but the main element of their relationship remains hidden. Murray, the disillusioned actor in Japan making an adver-tizement for whiskey, meets Johansson, the disillusioned younger woman straight out of university with a philosophy degree unsure of what to do next, and they make a deep bond. The power of the story here is not what is told, but what remains untold; that which is outside the limits.

All interesting stories concern the limits of psychology, what is at the edge of our map, be it the edge of the world, universe, or our inner geography. A simple ink drawing of an octopus at the edge of the map with the words 'here monsters lie' evokes the idea that there is something beyond, something to be feared. We are fascinated with what might happen – how the secrets will unfold and how far things can be pushed. It is the boundaries of behaviour that absorb us and what it means to transgress them. The most reworked genre is the horror genre, as it constantly deals with this theme: what does it mean to be human? Good stories can offer catharsis and film is a safe way to test the boundaries and limits. *Limitless*, previously discussed, is a film about a drug called NZT that gives the taker 'limitless' powers, the pill offering access to the 'other' 80 per cent of the brain not used. Every positive must have a negative, to create the psychological tension. It has a down side; it can make you sick and kill you. But it is fun while it lasts. There is also another wee down side which some viewers of the film might overlook – you may kill other people after sex with them.

I have emphasized how the unconscious mind is believed to operate one step ahead of the conscious mind and this film explores and verifies this myth. Once a pill is taken the protagonist can remember a book he glanced at ten years ago, and help his landlord's wife write a law paper, enabling him to have sex with her. Eventually Eddie Morra (Bradley Cooper) does not need a drug to function at such a high level. We are unsure whether he did kill someone, which makes the film slightly deeper than it is trying to be, and the subversion which is obvious a mile off is that Eddie is standing for senator without any false stimulant, the message being a Nike advert – just do it! Americans celebrate success while Europeans, particularly the British, celebrate failure – the one that got away; both attitudes if taken to extremes are problematic. But we are interested in extremes, the drama.

Chekhov's gun

'Chekhov's gun' is a term used when writing for the stage, where a prop returns to remind the audience of what has happened previously in the plot, working as a form of foreshadowing, setting up an idea. The phrase 'in my beginning is my end … in my end is my beginning' is vaguely familiar to all of us, and comes from T. S. Eliot's *East Coker*, but he, of course, plagiarized it from elsewhere. It is this familiarity that is central to Chekhov's gun. Numerous films place the ending of the film at the start, and then work up to this point, *My Summer of Love*, and *Lilya 4-Ever* (written and directed by Lukas Moodysson, 2002) to name but two. In *My Summer of Love* the opening is on the central protagonist, whose actual name is Lisa (Natalie Press), but who has been rechristened by her brother as Mona. She is drawing a picture of herself on the wall of her bedroom, but this might also be a picture of the Mona Lisa.

This picture signifies the idea that we can continually change our identity. Interestingly, Mona's brother Phil, played by Paddy Consandine, is just out of prison and he has changed his identity into a born-again Christian. One striking image throughout the film is the telegraph poles that dominate the Yorkshire landscape, appearing like crosses, minus the corpse of Christ. Mona is resting corpse-like in the middle of a grass patch when she is approached by Tamsin (Emily Blunt) who asks if she is OK. She is only resting, after buying a moped without an engine from some gypsies. Tamsin, the upper-class girl, sitting on a horse, looks down on the working-class girl. So, is the Chekhov's gun here the painting, the repeated trope of the telegraph wires, or the moped that is fixed the following week? It is possible to have more than one.

Lilya 4-Ever opens with a death-metal soundtrack accompanying a young distraught girl running away, and then getting up onto the railings of a bridge to jump. We do not know if she jumps, and we can see the plot of the whole film then building up to this point to answer the questions – what put her in this state and does she jump? 'Three months earlier' appears on the screen. Lilya (Oksana Akinshina) is left in Russia when her mother decides to leave with her new man to go to America. We know Lilya is being left alone, as the mother says to the boyfriend when they are alone in bed, 'it's just the two of us now'. Lilya is placed in the care of her aunty, who then proceeds to take her flat off her, removing Lilya to a disgusting flat of a recently deceased man. When she asks for help, her aunty tells her to go and be a prostitute like her mother. Lilya does not want to sleep with men for money, despite being desperate, but her female friend does sleep with a man even though she does not need the money and just fancies some new clothes. When her friend's father finds the money she tells him the money is Lilya's and says Lilya gained it from being a prostitute. The whole estate where she lives then calls her a whore, and she is gang raped.

After having sex to buy food, she develops what on the surface seems a benign relationship with a man who apparently does not just want to sleep with her, but wants them to have a life together. He promises her a job in Sweden, picking vegetables, but says he cannot go with her immediately because his grandmother is ill. She is actually being sold into sex-slavery, and is locked in a flat, and prostituted numerous times, until she finally escapes, plunging to her death on the bridge that was introduced at the start of the film. As with the majority of films, the end is the beginning, the beginning the end, and however much this might be played with, this is the norm and substantiates the overriding nexus of this book concerning predetermination.

While she is dreaming, we see what could have been: how she could have listened to her close younger male friend and told her so-called boyfriend to get lost and not gone to Sweden; how she helped the old woman in her block pick up potatoes that dropped from a bag. Repeating the events that have taken place in an ideal way as a form of portraying regret and wish fulfilment works startlingly well, and relates to Chekhov's gun, even the rolling potatoes in this instance being part of it. In the original sequence Lilya abuses the old woman, calling her an old hag, as she runs out of the block to her 'boyfriend's' car. Escape is at the heart of the film; her mother's escape to America; Lilya's to Sweden; Lilya's from the flat; and finally from her life.

For Aronson, such devices are merely to add pace. I disagree with this view and with the view that it is remarkable that some films do away with the three-act structure. It is not remarkable at all, but clearly indicates that in film writing we need to be careful of imposing a one-size fits all framework. Films like *21 Grams* previously mentioned, *The Hours*, or *Crash*, which start with part of the ending, are not merely 'fractured narratives', as she puts it.[2] They are examples of multiple-layered narratives that, along with many others such as *Short Cuts* (directed by Robert Alman and co-written with Frank Barhydt, 1993, from short stories by Raymond Carver), break new ground and whose screenplays should be studied closely.

The psychology of freedom

Death hangs over us. It is a trap yet it frees us from the trap of life itself, just like an orgasm, la petite mort. A screenplay that exists on the page must exist as a formula that brings about a world that exists in and of itself; this is what culture does. For Adorno, the meaning of culture is 'suspension of objectification', but the critic doubles this objectification of culture making it his object.[3] The 'very rejection of the guilt of a life which blindly and callously reproduces itself' is the essence of authentic art, and this means 'the promise of happiness, the promise of a state where freedom could be realised'.[4] Basically, we have culture because we are not free. There is the cliché that all narrative is about escape, but, as Colin Wilson explained in *The Craft of the Novel*, we essentially are interested in freedom, and the greatest films and novels, and stories in all forms, tackle this on a profound level. We know we are in some senses trapped; this sentence itself has a limit which is a trap to a degree but also freeing by its limitation. Madness can be defined as a place beyond the limit, beyond meaning and thus in many senses is meaningless itself. We are trapped within our own body, our own mind, our own set of external circumstances, and these traps are also the way out of the cage. With regards to the psychology of screenwriting, and our own life, it is battling against this trap that sets us free, even if the freedom never comes, meaning it is the process rather than the outcome.

It is this sense of freedom, and the potential of freedom, more than freedom itself that is the motive. Primarily, freedom comes through the power of the imagination. Without our imagination we are stuck within merely rational paradigms, without the potential to move beyond the materially obvious. Terry Waite during his time held captive for five years in Beirut began going through all the Bible stories he knew in his mind. Even though he was held captive, chained to a radiator, he was still free. Our imagination has the power to set us free, and writing out of this imagination sets us free, and can liberate others. I have already mentioned Zola and disorders connected to obsessive writing. St Ignatius of Loyola, according to one source, was addicted to writing, and it is easy to relate the notion of addiction to the processes of writing. Addiction paradoxically can be freeing, like sex it is also called a mini-death (see work on addiction), and when we write we are free of anything else encroaching on us. Many books on writing encourage us to find a set place, to work at a set time, but all of this goes against freedom. A routine can bring a more fluid sense of writing, and bring about a more productive process but if we latch on to a certain time or place we are limiting ourselves.

Through identification with characters on the screen we gain freedom from ourselves, by stepping into their shoes for the period of the film, or by actually learning from them, taking on their role, characteristics, or way of being. Some characters stay with us, and represent part of us we wish did not exist, but does. A writer is an observer of life, more than a partaker, finding the ability to stand back from the fray. Jack Kerouac clearly partook deeply in life, but then would step back, living in his childhood home, and reflect through writing on his activities. If poetry, for Wordsworth, is emotion recalled in tranquillity, then what exactly is screenwriting? Meditation can be a freeing process for it fosters the ability to stand back and observe.

The psychology of the non-self

There is liberation in creation, so 'art is allowing the anarchy of experience to free itself from forms and methods'.[5] In terms of doing 'real' philosophy, the only method is not to have a method, and it could be suggested this is the same for groundbreaking art. This takes us further than the methods employed in literary and cultural theory for, as Clair Colebrook has explained in relation to Deleuze, these areas rely on deciphering cinematic signs, and are usually about working out whether images are representative, or not. For Deleuze, if we followed this route we would only be concerned with cinema becoming more realistic, but cinema is far more than this – it is about creating new 'intuitive' worlds. This key idea should have resonance for the screenwriter, who might be stuck in trying to convey a certain conventional reality that, paradoxically, actually might be nothing of the sort. Deleuze refers to the time-image that 'gives us time itself, no longer spatialized or derived from movement'.[6] And even more optimistically Deleuze showed how cinema offers the ability to move beyond the detached external observer, perceiving movement from the point of view of the moving thing itself. There is an ethical dimension here. We should see art and philosophy for what they can do, rather than what they are, so it is the potential that counts and, following Nietzsche, artists and philosophers are the doctors of society.

Fundamentally, is it necessary to berate ourselves as writers and ask whether we are truly ambitious enough in our writing, meaning: can we match Deleuze's ambition to find in cinema a mode of seeing 'not attached to the human eye'?[7] Removing the 'eye' and 'I' is truly anathema to many. Such a task can be 'seen' as blatantly absurd, and impossible for is not everything attached to the human eye; such a project is not what we desire in human terms at all. This attempt at the so-called impossible counteracts our deeply engrained belief in there being nowhere beyond the human eye and 'I'. While Deleuze used the term philosophy, we can replace this with psychology, and agree with Deleuze that cinema offers a new way of becoming and vital dynamism in life. Idealistically, so does screenwriting.

Deleuze was fascinated with Spinoza's work which was imbued with Buddhist thinking. Buddhism attempts to get behind what is known as false appearances, false passions, and the numerous deaths we may experience. In the West we worship the individual and have a paradoxical relationship with death. For Deleuze, the ego changes in time so it is impossible to rely on Descartes' explanation. Essentially, what is the 'I' that is doing the thinking? To speak of a subject I must synthesize time. But the ego changes in time and, following Leibniz, there is no subject, just points of view known as monads, which are not particles but waves. This idea of 'point of view' is important when considering the processes of narration. In Buddhism no first cause is accepted. If we place the following in reverse we can cease the process:

1   Through ignorance are conditioned volitional actions or karma-foundations.

2   Through volitional actions is conditioned consciousness.

3   Through consciousness are conditioned mental and physical phenomena.

4   Through mental and physical phenomena are conditioned the six faculties (the five sense-organs, and the mind).

5   Through the six faculties is conditioned (sensorial and mental) contact.

6   Through (sensorial and mental contact) is conditioned sensation.

7   Through sensation is conditioned desire, 'thirst'.

8   Through 'thirst' is conditioned clinging.

9   Through clinging is conditioned the process of becoming.

10   Through the process of becoming is conditioned birth.

11   Through birth are conditioned decay, death, lamentation, pain and so on.

Behind this is the question over the 'I' and the 'me'. For Deleuze consciousness is machinic, and it is always the third party who says 'me'.[8] He moves away from the theatre of the mind. Significantly, language for Deleuze is always metaphorical, and all language is indirect. 'No primary, pre-metaphorical meaning can be attributed to language.'[9] This is because 'all meaning derives from an unstable system of figures which does not have linguistic constraints'.[10] Once we accept this unstable system we are not obsessed with searching for a fixed underlying truth and meaning and we are able to see the multiplicity of meaning. In the main, however, our writing and philosophy in Western culture pretends otherwise. As Foucault showed, with the development of the individual the further societies developed total control of the individual; we pay a high price for our individuality. Freedom in this context is a bogus term, for under observation we are never truly free, the gaze controlling behaviour. Numerous films cover this subject of the individual and observation, such as *Broken Embraces* (Pedro Almódovar), as it seems as if this is the essence of cinema itself, modernity and postmodernity, but we need to be clear that this subject is not necessarily dealt with in a negative or one-sided manner.

We have become so used to art being concerned with tackling issues of truth that Deleuze's concept of truth might make us balk, for it is not at all about 'affinity' but, 'shock, contingency, constraint, chance'.[11] As anyone who works creatively knows, within this chance truth may appear of its own original type and of its own volition. For Deleuze, what is made known here is a world beyond the subject. In Buddhism there is no soul, self or ego; unlike Lacan who separates the ego and the self. There is, of course, the idea of the self, but this is the essentially false belief that causes all our problems, and overall is actually the cause of all evil.[12] Adults and even nations, with immense destructive force, behave like children, when they declare something is 'mine' in a possessive fashion. What is most interesting here is how drama overtly and covertly plays out these different egos and selves on screen or on stage. Through dramatic art the audience can become attached to, or even 'become', a different ego to experience their world and the worlds of others. To slip into this world suggests ego itself might be transient. Simultaneously, without a belief in the ego's permanency the depth of experience might be limited, for only through a limit are we aware of anything beyond a limit. But before we start condemning the non-self as one sided, Buddhist teaching of course has a great get-out clause. For it is pointed out that 'I have no self' is just as much a bind as 'I have self'.[13] Both arise out of the false idea 'I AM'. We need to ditch both sides. So the correct position to take is that 'I' and 'being' are 'physical and mental aggregates, which are working together interdependently in a flux of momentary change within the law of cause and effect, and there is nothing permanent'.[14] We can all buy into this to a degree, but it could be just as easily argued that this non-permanency is not something to be permanently meditated on, because it is the non-permanency itself that causes the pain.

For Andrey Tarkovsky, cinema has a spiritual dimension, and the spectator is reacting against the modern world, seeking to find 'lost time'.[15] Traditional semiotics has been used creatively to analyse cinema, while modernism absorbed cinema, and both the character and the camera have a viewpoint and, crucially, cinema can go 'beyond images which are purely objective or subjective'.[16] There is a continuous place in cinema from the objective perception to the subjective perception. Early cinema, in the form of expressionism, had the character filmed or followed from behind, then with liberated cinema and with tracking shots the camera moved amongst the characters, in doing so creating the 'eye of the camera'. What we have is camera-consciousness, not subjective or objective images. In Deleuzian terms we eventually enter the zone where it is impossible to distinguish between what is imaginary or real, physical or mental. How this may have affinities with the Buddhist notion that all is of the mind is a viable question, although Deleuze is less definitive. For Deleuze, early cinema had been concerned with faith and revolution, and then with directors like Stanley Kubrick modern cinema was concerned with the brain, and with Eisenstein the brain was the problem.

This helps us in screenwriting, because if we cease to see writing as writing about something, as a form representing reality, part by part, like developing a jigsaw, but equate it more with cinema itself, more concerned with an intervention in reality, we can establish our writing and film as a moving image of thought, undermining conventional notions of the subject and object. Freud explained that for the writer words are deeds, and this artistic endeavour therefore truly has the potential to be an original behaviour. We will produce writing that evokes thinking, and extends reality. This level of integration is far-reaching; 'a principle of indeterminability, of indiscernability: we no longer know what is imaginary or real, physical or mental'.[17] This is how far we must aim, without letting limited generic-copying and our own desire to conform stand in the way of this ambition.

Genre

Just as our brains are arguably pre-wired to recognize certain archetypes and tropes, we soon come to recognize certain stories. The convention in which a story is told is known as genre. It can be argued that if we set out writing deliberately for a particular genre our writing might be fake and inauthentic, in that we attempt to meet the demands of the genre rather than being true to our story and character. But we need parameters within which to write and it would be naive to think we can step outside of our culture and cultural history, what has come before, to create something that is an entirely new genre in and of itself – usually the most innovative films combine genres and subvert them. This takes us back to the 'what if' scenarios, which often splice two genres together. Genre is essentially about expectations and as we are, psychologically, constantly trying to subvert expectations, knowledge of genre is essential if we are to transform our reader and audience, and to make them experience the world anew.

We must tap into what our audience is already aware of, and writing within certain genres means a lot of the work is done for us already. For example, *Lock, Stock and Two Smoking Barrels* and *Snatch* (both directed and written by Guy Ritchie, 1998, 2000) are films about criminals and fit a certain genre while adding to them just slightly. A good genre film can do this. Genre helps us understand milieu. Because we know where they are coming from Ritchie can develop plot and character faster, rather than wasting time on background and context. Just as books are classified into certain sections to enable sales, films are classified into genres, so it is worth thinking about market and who will want to see the film of our screenplay. Of course, things are not as straightforward as they may seem. There are the meta-genres of drama, where the protagonist inevitably wins through; tragedy, where there is suffering and usually death, and where people, creatures or things face the consequences of their behaviour and fail to win through; melodrama, where there is nearly always failure; and comedy.

Interestingly, with comedy, characters do face a choice, but characters never really change, so the best comedy is the best tragedy, and vice versa. In the UK the long-running success of TV series like *Only Fools and Horses* (1981–2003) and *Dad's Army* (1968–77) and in the US *Sex and the City* (1998–2004) are good examples. These characters really stay the same. They might marry, or do something slightly different, but essentially they are the same. We are the ones that grow older and usually change, and psychologically there is something reassuring in comedy where people do not change, and innately remain the same. Behind this is partly the comedy of failure, and schadenfreude, which translates as literally damage-joy from the German, laughing at the woes of others.

I am not suggesting creating anything great is easy, but if nothing fits outside genre in some way then our job is in some sense easier. For Robert McKee there are 25 genres, and within them subgenres, involving different subjects, settings, roles, events and values. These are: 1. Love Story, and the subgenre Buddy Salvation; 2. Horror Film (many have written on the different subgenres of the horror such as the slasher movie, but McKee interestingly breaks this down into three main subgenres: the uncanny, where there is a 'rational' explanation, such as aliens or a maniac causing the horror; the supernatural, where the source of horror is irrational, and of the spirit realm; and the super-uncanny, where the audience has to guess between the other two, such as *The Shining*); 3. Modern Epic; 4. Western; 5. War; 6. Maturation Plot; 7. Redemption Plot; 8. Punitive Plot; 9. Testing Plot; 10. Education Plot; 11. Disillusionment Plot; 12. Comedy; 13. Crime; 14. Social Drama; 15. Action/Adventure; 16. Historical Drama; 17. Biography; 18. Docudrama; 19. Mockumentary; 20. Musical; 21. Science Fiction; 22. Sports Genre; 23. Fantasy; 24. Animation; 25. Art Film – for McKee the art film fits two subgenres, minimalism and anti-structure, and embraces other basic genres, such as love story and political genre. Plus, of course, there is the metagenre, or cross over, like the sci-fi western. Think of genre like a backbone to your story, it is there enabling the story to exist, but it does not have to be restrictive.

Editing and the rewrite

Just as there is no fixed way of writing, there is no fixed way of editing. Clearly, we edit as we write, just as when we speak, as we leave out what we believe is superfluous but, initially at least, this may not be beneficial. If we have a scene with a variety of outcomes then it is good to write the different outcomes and be open. Some writers can visualize everything in their heads and know that it has to be that way, but sometimes practicalities get in the way so it might be more beneficial to have an open mind. The screenplay to *Tinker, Taylor, Soldier, Spy* (directed by Thomas Alfredson and written by Bridget O'Connor and Peter Straughan, 2011, from the novel by John le Carré, 1974) is so honed that the tension is phenomenal, every word uttered is significant, and when there is an explosion of words it is remarkable. Just as with the new actor over-acting, there is a danger that the new writer will over-write, and stick in as many witticisms and asides as possible. A flabby script draws attention to itself and the writing, rather than the visual story being told, although if the words are interesting enough then you can get away with anything, such as a really long monologue as in *Naked* previously mentioned.

This leads us back to the idea of removing the ego. If in doubt, leave it out. Deep down we are all supposed to be the same, with the same fears and wants. The deepest writer is the deepest person, but films are not about worlds in words but worlds in images. As scriptwriters our words are doing the acting for us. We still need to construct this world. Just as the actor, in the main, attempts to not draw attention to who they really are but the character they are playing, if our words draw attention to themselves then we are not doing our job. So the paradox of writing in all forms, but particularly scriptwriting, is that it should be invisible. We should endeavour at all times to write our scripts without dialogue, with images and symbols that craft meaning in and of themselves. The American novelist Henry James claimed we should 'dramatise, dramatise, dramatise', which is true of all writing, and no audience wants to be lectured at by characters. Here are some useful areas to think about for your re-write and remember all good writing is re-writing.

1 Stick to the spine.

   Always keep in mind – a) your premise b) overriding theme c) stay faithful to your genre.

2 Cut to the chase.

   Do not leave your characters dangling at the end of scenes. Enter scenes at the last possible moment and exit at the earliest. Avoid superfluous scene description, but make sure you give enough visual information so that a reader can picture the action. Always describe characters: age, dress, and demeanour.

3 Cut the talk, walk the walk.

   Pare down your dialogue to only what is absolutely necessary for comprehension. Trust your audience; they might be cleverer than you think. Say the maximum with the minimum. Show what the characters are thinking through behaviour rather than having them tell the audience.

4 Do not kill the cat.

   Bear in mind audience sensibilities – you want them to care about the protagonist, whether hero or anti-hero. Unnecessary actions, especially if they are gratuitously violent do not impress – they can just turn people off.

5 Make it visual.

   It should be clear by now that scriptwriting involves showing stories through pictures. If you cannot visualize what you intend happening on screen then neither will the audience. Work on your screen descriptions. Create not just a visual identity of the sets, but also ambience and style, and you can have your own voice here. Remember Point of View (POV). Ask yourself – whose scene is it, and tell it through their eyes and their idiosyncratic language.

6   Get your first draft out of your system as soon as possible and avoid editing as you go along.

7   Write the best scene first to set the standard then look back at the previous scene to get in the flow when continuing writing.

8   Read it out loud after finishing the first draft.

9   Get someone else unfamiliar with the work to read it out in a plain way, not doing the accents of characters, and not naming the characters. Have you got the different speech patterns correctly tuned, so we know these are different people?

10   Redefine the premise if the story has changed substantially, and use the premise as your frame, religiously not moving outside the frame. This will save you time in the long run.

A five-point check list

1   Character

Give your character a reality check.

Pump up their backstory.

Identify their traits, are they clearly defined?

What are they missing?

What do they want?

What is stopping them?

What is the internal conflict and what is the external conflict?

Are they a worthy protagonist and is the challenge worth it?

Often the secondary characters come to the foreground in the re-writing process, or even when the project is filmed. At this stage, can you think of how you might enhance them?

2   Plot

Does the plot reveal character?

Are there active questions being asked with dramatic tension?

You need the plot points – the inciting incident, the crises, the climax and the resolution.

Think about pace.

Do the sub-plots enhance or detract from the main story?

Have you really considered the form and genre of your piece?

Is it correct for your story and are expectations fulfilled?

You can try too hard – are you?

Have you thought seriously about locations?

3 Structure

There needs to be a beginning, a middle and an end, but not necessarily in that order. Examine screenplays that play with this successfully, such as *Memento* and *Pulp Fiction* previously mentioned.

4 Dialogue

Keep it short.

Make it believable and in character.

Keep it pared to the bone.

Is it often unfinished and interrupted?

Have it loaded with emotion.

There is always a sub-text (what they are really saying).

5 Exposition

A key rule, other than there being no rules: do not preach.

If you need to impart information, make it invisible.

Hide it in conflict situations.

Remember, show rather than tell – lectures might be interesting but we do not read a film script or watch a film hoping for a lecture. While it may be educational and informative, it needs to entertain.

Finally, the Unholy or Holy Trinity, depending on your story
Re-read your script and ask yourself these following questions:

Is the character's motive clear?

Are they a 'character', meaning – how eccentric are they?

Is a larger question being asked; what is the central moral choice?

If you have a lot of NO answers, then you need to do a lot of re-writing.

The how and the why

Psychologically, we always have the final frame of death as our own point of reference, and cinema plays with this, but infinity is in many respects problematic compared to finality. If we progress Foucault's reading of Nietzsche's declaration of the death of God, we acknowledge this has forced us to place this realm of infinity and finality within the self. When encountering cinema, however, we encounter the self but there are moments when the other breaks through. This other may also be beyond self and other and therefore beyond conclusion. Literature appears to have too many fixated and fixed signifiers, while art has seemingly too few. With its combination of both, film is in many respects the perfect art form, the finite and the infinite.

As Allister Mactaggart has explained, artists like David Lynch are creating moving paintings.[18] And yet, through Mactaggart's explanation of Lynch's non-linear approach in reference to Greg Olson's work, we see these paintings come from the writing, from putting ideas down for scenes on seventy separate cards, three inches by five. This approach is not novel, and indeed is commonly used by novelists, who like magicians then shuffle the pack. From such shuffling a different framework may be had, but its permutations are not limitless, far from it. Even with one definitive ending, a myriad of others might be implied, or could have been written, and even shot, and originally included in the film. A version might have been shown to an audience, their reactions dictating the way the film is then packaged, including a change in the conclusion if necessary.

Take *The Hurt Locker*, previously mentioned. When the hero of the film returns home to his family in America, after dismantling a number of bombs in Iraq, he cannot deal with the domestic milieu and decides to head back for the adrenaline rush of his job. He has befriended a boy in Iraq, who is a surrogate son in some ways. For me, this conclusion takes away the power of the film, for why does he have to return? We know he is reckless and a hero and he cannot escape. But do we have to have our noses rubbed in it and along with the rock music we see it is a glorification of the military and of a certain brand of masculinity. Perhaps this is a feminist statement on men in general – the domestic war of the home front is too much for them and, however difficult, it is easier to be a hero at home if you are never there. We can conjecture about other endings, and in this sense the conclusion of *The Hurt Locker* allows us this space.

Despite the typical Hollywood production, where everything is stereotypically tied up neatly for our own safety, our attraction to open-ended stories I believe has increased. Metanarratives are not over, and trying to establish clearly why modernism is any different to postmodernism might have been fun once, but often any such categorisations are false conclusions. Many works of art can be called premodern, modern and postmodern if we want to incessantly classify and categorize like a nineteenth-century biologist. But our drive to realize that one position may not be the only position has been enhanced, particularly since the 1950s, due to battles for race, class, gender, sexuality and disability equality, to name a few.

The idea that much of reality is subjective and that 'official' ideas of history are being challenged by new discourse is still loathed in some quarters.[19] Clearly, it must not be concluded that these battles are over, but a way forward is to deal with these issues in our work, making them more psychologically powerful for now. *The Elephant Man* (directed by David Lynch and co-written with Christopher De Vore and Eric Bergren, 1980, following the Bernard Pomerance play, 1979), is set in the nineteenth century, but the cry 'I am not an animal but a human being' is being made in the 1980s, when many, particularly people who are disabled, were seeking equality. All of this is still relevant today in a global political climate of economic crisis and cutbacks to the welfare state.

Whatever the truth in clichés, it is often said humans only use ten per cent of the brain, but in the 1970s English literature professor and media guru Marshall McLuhan argued everyone would soon be using different parts of their brains, with future developments in technology. New technology allows us to work with many forms of input, simultaneously, but I would argue our attention span is dwindling. There have been experiments where audiences can choose different endings to films, but these have not been especially successful. When being entertained, how much effort do we really want to make? Dr Johnson's view on the novel being a form of entertainment has already been pointed out, and traditional fiction films, ones condemned by Peter Greenaway, are intimately connected to this form. There is obviously a difference between the creative insights of a Lynch screen painting, formulated from 70 different ideas, and a screenplay that is catering for an audience that does not have an attention span. *Pirates of the Caribbean 4: On Stranger Tides* (directed by Rob Marshall and written by Ted Elliott and Terry Rossio, 2011). is one example from many of a film that, if you will excuse the pun, does not push the boat out in this respect. But it does not need to, as it is a franchize with an established loyal audience. You buy one can of Caribbean, you buy the next. Certain formulas work. As with James Bond films expectations are fulfilled and audiences are satisfied.

To create a full-length screenplay takes an enormous amount of time and effort. As Robert McKee pointed out in *Story*, there is the popular myth of the screenplay being cracked out by the pool, one lazy hot afternoon. Section 1.4 was entitled Inferiority Complex. Clearly McKee feels he must justify the form, making it sound of equal merit to the novel, due to the work that goes into it. But we judge the work on its merit as we usually have no knowledge of the time that went into it. Time actually may not be a factor. Virginia Woolf knocked out the novel *Orlando* quickly, the work just suddenly coming to her, whereas Sally Potter took five years on the screenplay adaptation. As Woolf informed Vita Sackville-West on 9 October 1927, she wrote down the title 'as if automatically' and then her 'body was flooded with rapture' and her 'brain with ideas'.[20] This writing seems to have come directly from the unconscious working as a seemingly magical process. While the process may have been fast, however, the gestation period may have been years.

Realistically, getting the initial screenplay down may be a fast process but it is the editing that takes time and this involves having distance and moving beyond the idea of ownership and subjectivity. Objectivity is essential. While taking a personal interest in our subject matter clearly adds to the passion and may sustain us through the process, we do need to distance ourselves and time allows this. In a world where time is speeded up and everything happens currently, it is easily argued that depth disappears, although this does not stop films like *Dead Man* being made. Our ambition should not be thwarted by time. Writing, while being an art form that comes from creativity which fundamentally is a break in reason, has its framework and boundary, including genre, format, and the Enneagram. But hopefully you have seen even in the brevity of this book that these frameworks and boundaries are so nuanced and complex that they are paradigms to enhance any creative output. Originality comes when we cross the border, it is without conclusion, and it is essential we avoid the full stop, period, by any means necessary …

If we move from soundtrack to title songs, as with *Blue Velvet* (directed and written by David Lynch, 1986), we see there is a more complex approach to both film analysis and film writing, one that is based not merely on imaginative inspiration but the very processes of construction itself. Using Derrida to develop film theory, Brunette and Wills have maintained that in this instance it might be questioned as to whether the film is thoroughly derived from the title song, although such an argument can be purported. They point to a multilayered signification process, through the performances of the song throughout the film, plus 'the extradiegetical snippets of the original recording, and Dorothy Vallens' renditions, all of which remain fragmented'.[21] *Blue Velvet* includes many other songs, of course, such as 'The Bride Wore Black', which represents an open form, a type of 'anti-generic love-story'.[22] Paradoxically, this has an impact on aesthetic practice. The connection with death is overt and while the film is full of death and generic tropes, Wills and Brunette, through maintaining the writer constructs from an already written script, confirm in a sense the core argument of this book concerning predetermined writing.

Screenwriting obviously contains many mini-speeches. Throughout history, speech versus writing has been set up in an oppositional mode, and writing has triumphed, logocentrism. As has been point out by Brunette and Wills in their discussion of Derrida, for a whole range of thinkers from Plato to Rousseau and Saussure, not forgetting philosophers such as Wittgenstein and Rorty, 'natural language' is incorporated in what is known as 'writing'. 'Writing becomes the model for all linguistic operations, including speech, to the extent that they always involve dependence on the difference, spacing, and rupture that the speech model occludes. Writing thus comes to stand for otherness in general.'[23] If, following Derrida, language is an institution, then screenwriting can itself be seen to fit within an institution. An awareness of this allows for subversion, to a degree. The mission, if there is one, of Derrida's deconstruction, is to contest the centre, and to prevent the sameness and the repression of the other which has dominated Western thinking.

In screenwriting it is clear how this relates to genre but, unwittingly, screenwriters like Garland are actually employing a Derridean idea when they step out of their writing, and employ what could be termed an anti-signature stance. Discussing prose writing, Garland, in his interview with Kevin Conroy Scott referred to in 5.6, confessed he has never managed to get past page three of a Salman Rushdie novel because for him the authorial voice was so strong. Being banged over the head by the writer's authorial voice might not be what we enjoy, although some clearly do. Again, there could clearly be a paradoxical side to this, where the writer is leading the reader on in one direction, only for this to be subverted, as with the work of Italo Calvino or Vladimir Nabokov.

Writers, in the main, wish they were more disciplined, not purely with their tongue in debates but with their keyboards. Carlos Cuarón, who wrote *Y Tu Mamá También* for example, follows F. Scott Fitzgerald, who got to the office and wrote dialogue for an hour and then would throw all of this out and start again more seriously. He starts writing in prose, using writing he has done over the years, using random ideas, and creative diaries. He does not mention this, but like Hemingway did, he leaves one good piece of writing in the middle so the following day he has something to come back to. According to Cuarón the hard thing about writing is not the writing itself, 'but the thinking you do before the writing'.[24] Planning and thinking and researching can be the hardest part of the process. Successful writers, in any form, are the harshest critics of their own work, and only want feedback from those who are going to be tough with their work. Some creative writing courses fail because students are not taught enough how to give proper feedback and it becomes just a 'thumbs up thumbs down' scenario or students just cannot cope with criticism.[25]

As long as you accept that your script will be edited and can deal with the triple MC: that is, the three Ms, the masticated, manipulated, mutilated and the three Cs, chopped and changed and culled, then you will do well. You might have to fight for what you think is right but accepting someone else's opinion is no sign of failure but often a sign of maturity. If you have not shown your script to many people who are independent in the first place, to those who will not just say it is good because they know you wrote it, then you are making a significant mistake. We can only understand ourselves through others and we only know our script through others, the more independent the better. When you start writing it is important to remember each word you write is precious, every phrase can be a gem. But when you have passed this on to others that is that, everything is up for grabs. In many respects every word you write is a victory, an achievement, but it is important to learn to deal with rejection and be able to let things go.

Finally, there is an important question to ask: 'why do I write?' There could be thousands of reasons, and these will change over time. Try asking this from time to time.[26] It will have an impact on the way you write, your own psychology of screenwriting, and what you write. And also behave differently and do something different if you want your writing to be different. Changing our own psychology will obviously have an impact on our writing.[27] So how is the end point reached? The chances are if you get as far as writing a feature film screenplay that is of any interest you are in some ways a perfectionist. When do you stop re-writing? For Joel and Ethan Coen it is only the amateur 'who lacks the imagination' who works 'beyond the point when their script bores them'.[28] Ultimately, we write and read and watch films to understand the human situation. We know when our script is ready because it contains the feeling that it had to be written, that it was predetermined to be written in this way. The question 'why?' is the question that breaks the machine. In the psychology of screenwriting and the psychology of life this is the question we need to constantly ask of ourself, our characters, and our screenplay. We will hopefully not be answering this question in full in our screenplays but playing paradoxically with this question. This will ultimately lead us, and others, to a fuller understanding of the human situation.

Mediated fate

In the modern world believing we are free to make choices in our lives, that we have free will and are not dictated to by fate, is frequently seen as being intrinsic to identity and to liberty. And yet there is a form of popular philosophy that propounds that, ultimately, fate is in control, fate being a force beyond our immediate influence. Plenty of people believe their lives are scripted, even predestined. For two decades I have been analysing how this relates to fictional narratives. The central theme of this text has been the relationship of predetermination to psychology and screenwriting.

Frequently defined as the power that determines events, there is an aspect of fate relating to Greek and Roman mythology, with The Fates being three goddesses, Clotho, Lachesis, and Atropos, who dictated the destiny of humans. Drama, whether in the form of ancient stories about gods, acting on the stage, or on the screen, always involves an element of fate, this being central to narrative. Characters have obstacles placed in their way and we as an audience ask, will they succumb to fate or break free?

This format is not new, with dramatists using similar devices throughout history, such as playwright William Shakespeare, including a play within a play in *Hamlet* which comments on the main action. But things have shifted considerably following the explosion in screen media in the 1970s. The majority of the world has become a mediated arena, with the screen replacing reality, everything swallowed up by the media and the plethora of narratives it produces. In such a position, these narratives, which are fed by a form of fatalism, start to dominate. All the best stories concern paradox. We see an inherent contradiction here, or paradox, because if the modern world concerns the core issue of identity and choice, how does this fit within a belief in what I call mediated fate?

According to British behavioural psychologist B. F. Skinner, each individual, from Alexander the Great to the girl next door, is solely the product of their heredity and environment, so freedom and dignity are futile objectives.[29] If this is the case for everyone, including fictional characters, a series of pertinent philosophical questions arise: Does any character act freely? Furthermore, are we personally free to conclude whether any character acts freely or not, or to judge them at all? And, personally, do we want to be free, that is free to do anything, to be anything? And, what about being free to think, or say anything, or to be free of the pressing questions concerning free will itself, to even be free to be subsumed by fate?

Free will has been a central subject of philosophy for thousands of years and is essential to screened drama today, which engrosses us through offering us characters we are concerned about. We are aware that there is a certain destiny for characters, which could be fated, and part of a greater scheme of events, but we are desperate for them to make the right choices. Depending on the intensity of our viewing, and our level of empathy, we will virtually feel we control characters, as if we are determining their destiny. The depth of feeling people have for their favourite television soap stars exemplifies this. In these circumstances there is the strange phenomenon where the spectator believes they control the show. But, there is always the paradox that we love our expectations to be subverted. For Socrates, we act on our own choices. But these choices are geared towards the good. So, if the great Socrates is correct, how free are we to behave badly and, if we did, would this be our fault?

Fast-forward over two and a half millennia, more recently a belief in fate has been fashionable. Since the 1960s, with the popular acceptance of a blend of Eastern belief and the development of New Age philosophies, when things went wrong the belief was it was fated to be that way. Embracing this was believed to be part of the path to enlightenment, particularly in so-called cults, such as that headed by Bhagwan Shree Rajneesh. Ironically, when things went wrong or right, the implication was that this was out of our hands anyway, with the concepts wrong and right meaningless. This is a form of Zen Buddhist acceptance, and Eastern and Western philosophy and beliefs merged.

'Good, bad, what's the difference,' asked the Indian Jesuit priest Anthony de Mello, rhetorically. Anthony de Mello's point was that to judge any event as ultimately good or bad is missing the point, for we never really know the final outcome, or true cause, of events. There are plenty of examples from drama, such as the television series 30 Rock (2006–): something supposedly bad happens but the show must go on and eventually a better 'product' is created by overcoming the odds. The expectations of both 'good' and 'bad' are subverted, this being the essence of creativity and of narrative development.

The term 'simulacrum' was popularized by Baudrillard, who believed everything was 'the look', everyone desiring that which is more than real. All is multiplying and this is with a mad over-determination. In terms of determinism, for Baudrillard things are always in advance of their unfolding causes, reality has stopped and history has ended. There is no way out in this philosophy, with all things being determined. But, once more paradoxically, this is no cause for despair. The paradox is that the world is saved by the spectacle, so celebrate mediated fate. There is no chance of escaping a predetermined destiny for Baudrillard but as with the beliefs of Nietzsche, appearance saves us from chance. This is crucial to our understanding of both free will and fate and narrative.

Importantly, chance is always the spanner in the works, both for those who believe in fate and believers in free will. Fate cannot dominate if chance always breaks through. You cannot really be free in your choices, and in life generally, if random chance constantly gets in the way. But, paradoxically, just as philosophies concerning belief in fate have grown since the 1960s, through an acceptance of ideas drawn from theoretical physics, particularly quantum theory, belief in chaos, chance, and randomness has become popularized.

Quantum theory has been called the language of nature. When these beliefs combine, fate and chance go hand in hand. We can have our cake and eat it. Paradoxically there might be a force in control but it is chance.

In this mediated simulacrum, narratives concerning co-incidence and fate are intrinsic to all existence, with rampant conspiracy theories now part of the mainstream. Do all forms of established media offer a fatalistic view of life, or is this itself too much of a fatalistic statement? Events occur, and then are documented, and stories are invented, and then performed in some way. This form of entertainment can give a sense of mediated fate, as if the events were meant to be, all stories having the same elements, and that they should have happened in the way they did. This 'I told you so' attitude is a way of staying in control, but there is something more insidious here, as it re-affirms the status quo.

While they may appear contradictory, free will can exist alongside determinism, and this position is known to philosophers as compatibilism. For libertarians, those that solely believe in free will, the problem is not determinism, but how free will can be reconciled with chance. Roman-born Bishop of Hippo, Saint Augustine, observed that created things should not presume to create. This was not as a rebuke to artists but to reject claims of self-origination; for Eagleton, self-authorship is the bourgeois fantasy par excellence.[30]

A branch of philosophy concerned with being is known as ontology and a number of ontological questions arise from this. Who, or what, am I really part of? Do I need to sacrifice part of me for true fulfilment? How can I fully experience reality? There is the profound notion that true understanding can only be gained through the other. This confirms the work of recent philosophers concerned with ontology, such as Emmanuel Levinas. Included within this is the notion that a relationship with unreason, that is 'madness', must be found.

Paradoxically once more, man becomes inhuman to be human; a robot is the only really 'human' person, as many science fiction writers reveal. For Joseph Brodksy, 'should the truth about the world exist, it's bound to be nonhuman'.[31] What and who actually rules? As we have touched on: 'To identify freedom with reason is in fact to deny the very nature of freedom.'[32] To be free means there are alternatives but, paradoxically, for the rationalist believer, God acts in the most perfect way, so God is not free to act otherwise.[33] We can extrapolate from this an understanding of characterization. When we say a show contains 'perfect' casting we mean characters function in such a predetermined fashion that they fulfil our expectations. And, of course, this may be achieved through subverting our expectations.

Free will concerns responsibility within a moral framework and may have religious and political components. Fate and predetermination are encapsulated in time. A well-programmed machine is predictable, and for Theodore Roszak it is the attempt to make society run like one that removes joy. For Lewis Mumford, 'the clock ... is the paragon of automatons. ... The automation of time, in the clock, is the pattern of all larger systems of automation.'[34] As we have seen, technology 'is to be regarded as constitutive of the extended phenotype of the human animal, a dangerous supplement enjoying an originary status'.[35] In this context, the more machine-like we become, the more natural we are.

If technology has been within nature since the beginning of time as it were, or even before, fate makes all seem natural, fate here being akin to the evolutionary narrative. And we are now at a point where, 'it is no longer possible to determine whether technology is an expression of our genes or a sign of nature's cultural conspiracy'.[36] There is an element of fear in both of the philosopher Keith Ansell-Pearson's comments, but the biological language, whether interpreted literally or metaphorically, implies that this is fated and predetermined. There is nothing we can do about it. We are at the mercy not of the ghost in the machine but the animal-machine, at the core of both our internal nature and the external culture.

We think of fate, determination and predetermination, as part of discovering a pattern and an overall meaning, which in itself is predetermined. In this sense, while not a modern phenomenon, it has a contemporary resonance, because it is linked to conspiracy theories that we have seen have become endemic in contemporary culture. These have become more rampant, the more information and misinformation have become widespread. These more complex conspiracies, involving governments, world authorities, or even extraterrestrial beings, have overtaken grand narratives, often linked to religious stories. As with fate, whether good or bad, these conspiracy theories banish the lack of insignificance, with collective delusions bolstering a fragile sense of agency.[37] Once we believe there is a pattern, we set about 'discovering' it everywhere, like a psychotic delusion.

There are elements of these theories which involve looking back and fitting the jigsaw together, through a certain lens, to prove a certain theory, but what about fate looking forward and prediction? As mathematician and children's author Lewis Carroll put it, 'It's a poor sort of memory which only works backwards.' Here we see the relationship between predetermination, determination, fate and prediction. All good drama engages with the essence of the human condition and asks the audience to move away from individualism and narcissistic solipsism into a freer, less determined, life. This can only come by working with and within the whole. Given this is the essence of existence the final paradox is if we want to survive and thrive we do not have a choice in this after all.

Endnotes

Chapter 1

1 Francis Wheen, *How Mumbo-Jumbo Conquered the World* (London: HarperCollins, 2004).

2 Rita Felski, 'Context Stinks!', *New Literary History*, 2011, 42, p. 583.

3 Terry Eagleton, *The Meaning of Life* (Oxford: Oxford University Press, 2008), p. 80.

4 Erich Fromm, *To Have or To Be?*, p. 122.

5 *The Cloud of Unknowing*, (ed.) Halcyon Backhouse (London: Hodder and Stoughton, 1985), p. 30.

6 Erich Fromm, *To Have or To Be?* (London: Abacus, 1988), p. 124.

7 In *On the Nature of Things* 3.157–160, quoted by Adriana Caverero, *Horrorism: Naming Contemporary Violence* (New York: Columbia University Press, 2011), p. 4.

8 Douglas Kellner, *Critical Theory, Marxism and Modernity* (Baltimore: Johns Hopkins University Press, 1992), p. 199.

9 Theodor Adorno, *The Culture Industry* (London: Routledge, 1991) p. 163.

10 Ibid., p. 3.

11 Edward W. Said, *Culture and Imperialism* (London: Vintage, 1993).

12 Marilyn Beker, *The Screenwriter Activist. Writing Social Issue Movies* (New York: Routledge, 2013), p. 57.

13 Jack Stevenson, *Dogme Uncut. Lars von Trier, Thomas Vinterberg, and the Gang That Took on Hollywood* (Santa Monica, CA: Santa Monica Press, 2003), p. 153.

14 Ibid., p. 289.

15 Ibid., 153.

16 This is the view of Jean Luc Godard phrased by Deleuze, who comments that this shows not much of an understanding of what theory is, given theory can be made no less than its object. Gilles Deleuze, *Cinema 2. The Time-Image*, trans. Hugh Tomlinson and Robert Galeta (London: Continuum, 2011), p. 268.

17 Kellner, op. cit., p. 232.

18 Elle Leane and Ian Buchanan, 'What's Left of Theory?', *Continuum. Journal of Media and Cultural Studies*, Vol. 16 No 3 November 2002, p. 253.

19 Wheen, op. cit., 97.

20 David Tracy, *Dialogue with the Other: the Inter-religious Dialogue* (Louvain: Peters Press, 1990), p. 72.

21 Robert McKee, *Story. Substance, Structure, Style, and the Principles of Screenwriting* (London: Methuen, 1999), pp. 311–16.

22 Friedrich Nietzsche, *Daybreak. Thoughts on the Prejudices of Morality*, trans. R. J. Hollingdale (Cambridge: Cambridge University Press, 1986), p. 78.

23 Ibid.

24 Friedrich Nietzsche, *The Birth of Tragedy* and *The Genealogy of Morals*, trans. Francis Golffing (New York: Doubleday, 1956), pp. 25, 33, 81, 103.

25 Dylan Evans, *Emotion* (Oxford: Oxford University Press, 2001), pp. 79–80.

26 Wallace Stegner, *On the Teaching of Creative Writing* (New Hampshire: University Press of New England, 1980), p. 37.

27 Anita Brookner, issue 98 of 'The Art of Fiction', published online by *The Paris Review* http://www.theparisreview.org/interviews/2630/the-art-of-fiction-no–98-anita-brookner (accessed 12/08/2012).

28 See Sol Stein, *Solutions for Novelists. Secrets of a master editor* (London: Souvenir Press, 2000), p. 62.

29 Thomas Elsaesser, quoted by Elena del Río, *Deleuze and the Cinemas of Performance* (Edinburgh: Edinburgh University Press: 2008), p. 179.

30 Ibid.

31 Douglas Kellner, op. cit., p. 125.

32 See Sigmund Freud in Frank Tallis, *Hidden Minds. A History of the Unconscious* (New York: Helios Press, 2012), p. xiii.

33 Frank Tallis, *Hidden Minds. A History of the Unconscious* (New York: Helios Press, 2012), p. 60.

34 Susan Blackmore, *Consciousness* (Oxford: Oxford University Press, 2005), p. 67.

35 Elaine Showalter, 'The Grand Delusions', Key-note Lecture, Madness & Literature, 1st International Health Humanities Conference, The University of Nottingham, 7 August, 2010.

36 Alain de Botton, *The Architecture of Happiness* (London: Penguin, 2007), p. 106.

37 Gilles Deleuze, *Difference and Repetition*, trans. Paul Patton (London: Continuum, 2011), p. 321.

38 Natalie Goldberg, *Writing Down The Bones – Freeing the Writer Within* (Shambhala Books), p. 56.

39 Ibid., p. 57.

40 Ibid., p. 82–3.

41 Tallis, op. cit., p. 7.

42 Alfred Deikman, *The Observing Self: Mysticism and Psychotherapy* (Boston: Beacon Press, 1982), p. 94.

43 Warwick Mules, 'In Absence of the Human' in *Continuum. Journal of Media and Cultural Studies*, Vol. 16 No 3 November 2002, p. 268.

44 Terry Eagleton, *Trouble With Strangers. A Study of Ethics* (Oxford: Wiley-Blackwell, 2009), p. 239.

45 See Jason Lee, *Pervasive Perversions – Paedophilia and Child Sexual Abuse in Media/Culture* (London: Free Association Books, 2005).

46 Tallis, op. cit., p. 171.

47 Ibid.

48 Adriana Cavarero, *Horrorism. Naming Contemporary Violence*, trans. William McCuaig (New York: Columbia University Press, 2011), p. 53.

49 Norman K. Denzin, *The Cinematic Society. The Voyeur's Gaze* (London: Sage, 1995).

50 Geshe Kelsang Gyatso, *The New Meditation Handbook* (Ulverston: Tharpa Publications, 2003), p. 6.

51 Erich Fromm, *The Art of Loving* (London: Unwin Books, 1970), p. 57.

52 Goldberg, op. cit, p. 52.

53 Ibid., p. 53.

54 Lennard J. Davis, *Obsession. A History* (Chicago: University of Chicago Press, 2008), p. 106.

55 Ibid, p. 109.

56 Ibid.

57 Ibid., p. 113.

58 Tallis, op. cit., pp. 42–52.

59 Ibid., p. 117.

60 See Rollo Ahmed, *The Black Art* (London: Arrow Books, 1971).

61 Davis, op. cit, p. 127.

62 Rio, op. cit., p. 89.

63 Ibid., p. 189.

64 Gilles Deleuze, *Pure Immanence: Essays on A Life*, trans. Anne Boyman, (New York: Zone Books, 2001), p. 28.

65 Fromm, *To Have or To Be?*, op. cit., p. 128.

66 Aronson, op. cit., p. xv.

67 Clifford Coonan, 'Greenaway announces the death of cinema – and blames the report-control zapper', *The Independent*, 10 October 2007, http://www.independent.co.uk/news/world/asia/greenaway-announces-the-death-of-cinema--and-blames-the-remotecontrol-zapper--394546.html (accessed 23/08/2012).

68 See Jason Lee, *Pervasive Perversions* (London: Free Association Books, 2005).

69 See Jason Lee, *The Metaphysics of Mass Art*, Vol. II (New York: Mellen, 1999).

70 Christian Metz, *The Imaginary Signifier. Psychoanalysis and the Cinema*, trans. Celia Briton (Bloomington: Indiana University Press, 1977), p. 116.

71 Ibid., p. 66.

72 See Lee, *Metaphysics*, op. cit.

73 Goldberg, op. cit., p. 163.

74 *A Barthes Reader* (ed.) Susan Sontag (New York: Hill and Wang, 1982), p. 405.

75 Quoted by Amos Vogel, *Film as a Subversive Art* (New York: Random House, 1974), p. 5.

76 Robert Stam, Robert Burgoyne, and Sandy Flitterman-Lewis, *New Vocabularies in Film Semiotics. Structuralism, Post-Structuralism and Beyond* (London: Routledge, 1992), p. 144.

77 Doreen Carvajal, 'In Andalusia, on the Trail of Inherited Memories', *New York Times*, 21 August 2012, http://mobile.nytimes.com/2012/08/21/science/in-andalusia-searching-for-inherited-memories.xml (accessed 22/08/2012).

78 Stam et al., op cit., p. 147.

79 Ibid., p. 152.

80 See Michael Barnes, 'Persons – Objects or Observers? A Dialogue with Buddhism', *Person and Society in the Ignatian Exercises. The Way Supplement*, Spring 1993, no. 76, p. 105.

81 Mark Jancovich, 'Screen Theory', in *Approaches to Popular Film*, Joanne Hollows and Mark Jancovich (eds), (Manchester: Manchester University Press, 1995), p. 130.

82 Terry Eagleton, *The Meaning of Life* (Oxford: Oxford University Press, 2008), p. 97.

83 Ibid., p. 98.

84 Fromm, *To Have or To Be?*, op. cit., p. 109.

85 Henri Bergson, *Creative Evolution*, trans. Arthur Mitchell (New York: Dover, 1998), p. 89.

86 Jancovich, op. cit.

87 Rio, op. cit., p. 179.

88 Ibid.

89 *Holy Bible. New International Version* (Grand Rapids, Michigan: Zondervan, 1996), p. 822.

90 Ibid., p. 840.

91 David Wills and Peter Brunette, *Screen/Play. Derrida and Film Theory* (Princeton: Princeton University Press, 1989), p. 7.

92 Ibid., p. 6.

93 Ben Child, *The Guardian*, 'Batman film is liberal conspiracy, says rightwing DJ', Thursday 19 July 2012, p. 20.

94 *A Barthes Reader*, op. cit., p. vii.

95 Jancovich, op. cit., p. 139.

96 Alexander Stuart, 'Review of *The Wicker Man*', in *Films and Filming*, April 1974, Vol. 20, No. 7, p. 47.

97 Paul A Robinson, *The Freudian Left. Wilhelm Reich, Geza Roheím and Herbert Marcuse* (New York: Harper and Row, 1969), p. 5.

98 Ibid., p. 14.

99 Goldberg, op. cit., pp. 82–3.

100 Alain Badiou, *Infinite Thought. Truth and the Return to Philosophy*, trans. Oliver Feltham and Justin Clemens (London: Continuum, 2004), p. 83.

101 Robinson, op. cit., p. 16.

102 Ibid., p. 71.

103 Ibid., p. 72.

104 Ibid., p. 73.

105 See Jason Lee, *Shooting Panda's? Editing for Creative Writers* (Derby: Derby University Press, 2010).

Chapter 2

1 Amanda Boulter, *Writing Fiction – Creative and Critical Approaches* (Palgrave: London, 2007), p. 62.

2 Ibid., p. 68.

3 *Holy Bible*, op. cit., p. 833.

4 Aniela Jaffé, *From the Life and Work of C.G. Jung*, trans. R. F. C. Hull (New York: Harper and Row, 1970), p. 44.

5 I explain this in detail in *The Metaphysics of Mass Art*, Vol. II (New York: Mellen, 1999).

6 John Marks, *Gilles Deleuze, Vitalism and Multiplicity* (London: Pluto Press, 1998), p. 76.

7 Ibid., p. 107.

8 C. G. Jung, *Synchronicity. An Acausal Connecting Principle*, trans. R. F. C. Hull (Routledge and Kegan Paul: London, 1972), p. 107.

9 Tallis, op. cit., pp. 74–5.

10 Ibid., p. 77.

11 Ibid, p. 75.

12 Mark Edmundson, *The Death of Sigmund Freud. Fascism, Psychoanalysis and the Rise of Fundamentalism* (London: Bloomsbury, 2008), p. 64.

13 Tallis, op. cit., p. 6.

14 Ibid., pp. 12–13.

15 Edmundson, op. cit., p. 65.

16 Sigmund Freud, *Civilization and Its Discontents,* trans. David McLintock (London: Penguin, 2002), p. 106.

17 See Tallis, op. cit.

18 Freud quoted by Tallis, op. cit., p. 71.

19 Ibid., p. 15.

20 Amanda Boulter, op. cit., p. 71.

21 Jason Lee, *Celebrity, Ideology and American Culture* (New York: Cambria, 2010), pp. 179–90.

22 Jason Lee, *Seeing Galileo* (Canterbury: Gylphi, 2010), p. 56.

23 Neil Young, 'Look Out For My Love', from the album *Comes a Time,* 1978.

24 See Jason Lee, *Celebrity,* op. cit., pp. 233–40.

Chapter 3

1 Blackmore, op. cit., p. 69.

2 http://www.houd.info/unconscious.pdf (accessed 04/07/2012).

3 Charles Guignon, *On Being Authentic* (London: Routledge), p. 90.

4 Fromm, *To Have or To Be?,* op. cit., p. 111.

5 A. C. Bradley, p. 170.

6 Ibid., p. 191.

7 M. R. Ridley (ed.), *The Arden Shakespeare Othello* (London: Methuen, 1979), p. 1xi.

8 Jean Baudrillard, *The Transparency of Evil. Essays on Extreme Phenomenon,* trans. James Benedict (London: Verso, 1993), p. 89.

9 Ibid., p. 85.

10 Ibid., pp. 85–6.

11 Robert A. Segal, *Myth* (Oxford: Oxford University Press, 2004), p. 74.

12 Ibid., p. 83.

13 Ibid.

14 Ibid.

15 Ibid., p. 105.

16 Guignon, op. cit., p. 90.

17 Christopher Vogler, *The Writer's Journey* (London: Pan Books, 1993), p. 67.

18 See Jason Lee, *Pervasive Perversions,* op. cit.

19 Christopher Vogler, op. cit, p. 75.

20 Ibid., p. 35.

21 Ibid., p. 36.

22 Stephen Pfohl, *Death at the Parasite Cafe* (London: Macmillan, 1992), p. 182.

23 Ibid.

24 Ibid.

25 See Jason Lee, *The Metaphysics*, op. cit.

26 Eagleton, *The Trouble with Strangers*, op. cit., p. 307.

27 Wislawa Szymborska – 'Poetry: The Joy of Writing'. http://www.nobelprize.org/nobel_prizes/literature/laureates/1996/ szymborska-poems–5-e.html (accessed 23/10/2012).

28 Chris Jenks, *Transgression* (London: Routledge, 2002), p. 89.

29 Ibid., p. 90.

30 Fred Boting and Scott Wilson (eds), *The Bataille Reader* (London: Blackwell, 1997), p. 108.

31 Baudrillard, op. cit., p. 54.

32 Fromm, *To Have or To Be?*, op. cit., p. 101.

33 Keith Ansell-Pearson, 'Life Becoming Body: On the "Meaning" of Post Human Evolution', *Cultural Values*, Vol. 1 No. 2 1997, p. 223. Pearson argues against this strand in continental philosophy.

34 Anthony Stevens, *On Jung*, p. 195.

35 Don Richard Riso, *Personality Types. Using the Enneagram for Self-Discovery* (London: HarperCollins: 1998), p. 19.

36 Jerome Wagner, *The Enneagram Spectrum of Personality Styles* (Portland: Metamorphous Press, 1996), p. 1.

37 Ibid., p. 2.

38 Ibid., p. 13.

39 Ibid.

40 See Riso, op. cit.

41 Ibid., pp. 274–301.

42 Ibid., pp. 49–76.

43 Ibid., pp. 77–104.

44 Ibid., pp. 105–33.

45 Ibid., pp. 134–61.

46 Ibid., pp. 162–89.

47 Ibid., pp. 190–217.

48 Ibid., pp. 218–45.

49 Ibid., pp. 246–73.

50 Gilles Deleuze and Felix Guattari, *What is Philosophy?* (New York: Columbia University Press, 1994), p. 64.

51 Nietzsche, *Twilight of the Gods*, p. 95.

52 See Craig Batty and Zara Waldeback, *Writing for the Screen* (New York: Palgrave, 2008).

53 McKee, op. cit., p. 233.

54 Ibid., p. 243.

55 Charlie Moritz, *Scriptwriting for the Screen* (London: Routledge, 2008), p. 130.

56 Aronson, op. cit., pp. 57–8.

57 McKee, op. cit, p. 106.

Chapter 4

1 Aronson, op. cit., p. 448.

2 See Linda Anderson, *Creative writing: a Workbook with Readings* (Abingdon: Routledge, 2006).

3 Antonin Artaud, *The Theatre and its Double* (New York: Grove Press, 1958), p. 110.

4 Amos Vogel, *Film as a Subversive Art* (New York: Random House, 1974), p. 107.

Chapter 5

1 Syd Field, *Screenplay – The Foundations of Screenwriting* (New York: Dell, 1994), p. 115.

2 William Goldman, *Which Lie Did I Tell? More Adventures in the Screen Trade* (London: Bloomsbury, 2001), pp. 37–45.

3 Steven Maras, *Screenwriting. History, Theory and Practice* (London: Wallflower, 2009), p. 125.

4 Michel de Certeau, 'Reading as Poaching', in *The History of Reading*, (ed.) Shafquat Towheed, Rosalind Crone and Katie Halsey (London: Routledge, 2011), p. 133.

5 Ibid., p. 135.

6 Tanya Horeck and Tina Kendall (eds), *The New Extremism in Cinema – from France to Europe* (Edinburgh: Edinburgh University Press, 2011), p. 6.

7 Certeau, op. cit., p. 136.

8 Ibid., p. 137.

9 Stam et al., op. cit., p. 119.

10 Deleuze, *Cinema 2*, op. cit., p. 143.

11 The Book Review Show, BBC 2, 11 p.m., 24 August 2012.

12 Deleuze, *Cinema 2*, op. cit., p. 144.

13 Sally Potter, *Orlando* (London: Faber and Faber, 1994), p. ix.

14 Ibid.

15 Ibid., p. x.

16 Ibid., p. xi.

17 Frederic Jameson, *Signatures of the Visible* (London: Routledge, 1992), p. 90.

18 Kevin Conroy Scott, *Screenwriters' Master Class. Screenwriters Talk about their Greatest Movies* (London: Faber and Faber, 2005), p. 149.

19 Ibid., p. 150.

20 Ibid., p. 155.

21 Ibid., p. 158.

22 Ibid., p. 131.

23 Ibid., p. 133.

24 Ibid., p. 139.

25 Ibid., p. 144.

26 Ibid., p. 177.

27 Ibid., p. 178.

28 Ibid., p. 183.

29 Ibid., p. 186.

30 See Jason Lee (ed.), *Cultures of Addiction* (New York: Cambria, 2010).

31 Sandra W. Russ, 'Pretend Play, Emotional Processes, and Developing Narratives', in Scott Barry Kaufman and James C. Kaufman (eds), *The Psychology of Creative Writing* (Cambridge University Press: Cambridge, 2009), p. 251.

32 Ibid.

33 Ibid., p. 252.

34 Ibid, p. 254.

35 Ibid., p. 256.

36 Ibid., p. 257.

Chapter 6

1 See Lee, *Cultures*, op. cit.

2 Aronson, op. cit., p. 381.

3 Adorno, *The Culture Industry*, op. cit., p. 15.

4 Ibid., p. 18.

5 Claire Colebrook, *Gilles Deleuze* (London: Routledge, 2002), p. 46.

6 Ibid., p. 47.

7 Deleuze, *Cinema 2*, op. cit., p. 29.

8 Ibid., p. 86.

9 Ibid., p. 107.

10 Ibid.

11 Marks, op. cit., p. 132.

12 Walpola Sri Rahula, *What the Buddha Taught* (Bangkok: Haw Trai Foundation, 1995).

13 Ibid., p. 66.

14 Ibid.

15 Marks, op. cit., p. 150.

16 Ibid., p. 154.

17 Deleuze, *Cinema 2*, op. cit., p. 7.

18 Allister Mactaggart, *The Film Paintings of David Lynch – Challenging Film Theory* (Bristol: Intellect Books, 2010).

19 Wheen, op. cit., p. 97.

20 Virginia Woolf, *Orlando – a Biography* (London: Vintage, 1992), p. vii.

21 Wills and Brunette, op. cit., p. 163.

22 Ibid., p. 164.

23 Ibid., p. 9.

24 Ibid., p. 57.

25 Stegner, op. cit, p. 60.

26 Goldberg, op. cit., p. 189.

27 Ibid., p. 236.

28 Joel and Ethan Coen, Preface to *True Blood* (London: Faber and Faber, 1996), p. 6.

29 See B. F. Skinner, *Beyond Freedom and Dignity* (London: Penguin, 1988).

30 See Terry Eagleton, *Reason, Faith, and Revolution. Reflections on the God Debate* (New Haven: Yale University Press, 2009).

31 Quoted by John Gray, *Straw Dogs. Thoughts on Humans and Other Animals* (London: Granta Books, 2001), p. 191.

32 Thomas Pink, *Free Will* (Oxford: Oxford University Press, 2004), p. 53.

33 Ibid.

34 Lewis Mumford, *The Myth of the Machine* (New York: Harcourt, Brace & World, 1967), p. 286.

35 Ansell-Pearson, op. cit.

36 Ibid.

37 Jason Lee, *Celebrity, Pedophilia and Ideology in American Culture* (New York: Cambria, 2009), p. 3, with reference to, *Black Mass: Apocalyptic Religion and the Death of Utopia* (London: Penguin, 2007), by John Gray.

Select bibliography

Adorno, Theodor, *The Culture Industry* (London: Routledge, 1991).

Ahmed, Rollo, *The Black Art* (London: Arrow Books, 1971).

Anderson, Linda, *Creative Writing: a Workbook with Readings* (Abingdon: Routledge, 2006).

Ansell-Pearson, Keith, 'Life Becoming Body: On the "Meaning" of Post Human Evolution', *Cultural Values*, Vol. 1, No. 2, 1997, pp. 219–40.

Antonin, Artaud, *The Theatre and its Double* (New York: Grove Press, 1958).

Aronson, Linda, *The 21st Century Screenplay. A Comprehensive Guide to Writing Tomorrow's Films* (NSW, Australia: Allen and Unwin, 2010).

Axelrod, Mark, *Aspects of the Screenplay: Techniques of Screenwriting* (Portsmouth: Heinemann, 2001).

Backhouse, Halcyon (ed.), *The Cloud of Unknowing*, (London: Hodder and Stoughton, 1985).

Badiou, Alain, *Infinite Thought. Truth and the Return to Philosophy*, trans. Oliver Feltham and Justin Clemens (London: Continuum, 2004).

Barnes, Michael, 'Persons – Objects or Observers? A Dialogue with Buddhism', *Person and Society in the Ignatian Exercises. The Way Supplement*, Spring 1993, no. 76, pp. 98–108.

Batty, Craig and Zara Waldeback, *Writing for the Screen* (New York: Palgrave, 2008).

Baudrillard, Jean, *The Transparency of Evil. Essays on Extreme Phenomenon*, trans. James Benedict (London: Verso, 1993).

Beker, Marilyn, *The Screenwriter Activist. Writing Social Issue Movies* (New York: Routledge, 2013).

Bergson, Henri, *Creative Evolution*, trans. Arthur Mitchell (New York: Dover, 1998).

Bicat, Tony and Tony Macnabb, *Creative Screenwriting* (Marlborough: Crowood, 2002).

Blackmore, Susan, *Consciousness* (Oxford: Oxford University Press, 2005).

Boting, Fred and Scott Wilson (eds), *The Bataille Reader* (London: Blackwell, 1997).

de Botton, Alain, *The Architecture of Happiness* (London: Penguin, 2007).

Boulter, Amanda, *Writing Fiction – Creative and Critical Approaches* (Palgrave: London, 2007).

Bowden, Darsie, *Writing for Film: the Basics of Screenwriting* (New Jersey: Lawrence Erlbaum).

Bradley, A .C., *Shakespearean Tragedy* (London: Macmillan, 1985).

Brookner, Anita, issue 98 of 'The Art of Fiction', published online by *The Paris Review*, http://www.theparisreview.org/interviews/2630/the-art-of-fiction-no–98-anita-brookner (accessed 12 August 2012).

Brunette, Peter and David Wills, *Screen/Play. Derrida and Film Theory* (Princeton: Princeton University Press, 1989).

Campbell, Joseph, *The Hero With a Thousand Faces* (London: Fontana, 1993).

Carvajal, Doreen, 'In Andalusia, on the Trail of Inherited Memories', *New York Times*, 21/08/12, http://mobile.nytimes.com/2012/08/21/science/in-andalusia-searching-for-inherited-memories.xml (accessed 22 August 2012).

Caverero, Adriana, *Horrorism: Naming Contemporary Violence* (New York: Columbia University Press, 2011).

de Certeau, Michel, 'Reading as Poaching', in *The History of Reading* (ed.) Shafquat Towheed, Rosalind Crone and Katie Halsey (London: Routledge, 2011), pp. 130–9.

Chandler, Genevieve E. and Pat Schneider, 'Creation and Response: Wellspring to Evaluation' in Scott Barry Kaufman and James C. Kaufman (eds), *The Psychology of Creative Writing* (Cambridge: Cambridge University Press, 2009), pp. 316–31.

Child, Ben, *The Guardian*, 'Batman film is liberal conspiracy, says rightwing DJ', 19 July 2012, p. 20.

Coe, Jonathan, *The House of Sleep* (London: Viking, 1997).

Coen, Joel and Ethan Coen, *Blood Simple* (London: Faber and Faber, 1996).

Colebrook, Claire, *Gilles Deleuze* (London: Routledge, 2002).

Coonan, Clifford, 'Greenaway announces the death of cinema – and blames the report-control zapper, *The Independent*, 10/10/07, http://www.independent.co.uk/news/world/asia/greenaway-announces-the-death-of-cinema–and-blames-the-remotecontrol-zapper–394546.html (accessed 23 August 2012).

Davis, Lennard, *Obsession. A History* (Chicago: University of Chicago Press, 2008).

Deikman, Alfred, *The Observing Self: Mysticism and Psychotherapy* (Boston: Beacon Press, 1982).

Deleuze, Gilles, *Cinema 2. The Time-Image*, trans. Hugh Tomlinson and Robert Galeta (London: Continuum, 2011).

Denzin, Norman and Felix Guattari, *What is Philosophy?* (New York: Columbia University Press, 1994).

Denzin, Norman, *The Cinematic Society. The Voyeur's Gaze* (London: Sage, 1995).

—*Pure Immanence: Essays on A Life*, trans. Anne Boyman (New York: Zone Books, 2001).

—*Difference and Repetition*, trans. Paul Patton (London: Continuum, 2011).

Due, Reidar, *Deleuze* (Cambridge: Polity Press, 2007).

Eagleton, Terry, *The Meaning of Life* (Oxford: Oxford University Press, 2008).

—*Reason, Faith, and Revolution. Reflections on the God Debate* (New Haven: Yale University Press, 2009a).

—*Trouble With Strangers. A Study of Ethics* (Oxford: Wiley-Blackwell, 2009b).

Edgar-Hunt, Robert, *Screenwriting* (Lausane: AVA Academia, 2009).

Edmundson, Mark, *The Death of Sigmund Freud. Fascism, Psychoanalysis and the Rise of Fundamentalism* (London: Bloomsbury, 2008).

Evans, Dylan, *Emotion* (Oxford: Oxford University Press, 2001).

Felski, Rita, 'Context Stinks!', *New Literary History*, 2011, 42, pp. 573–91.

Field, Syd, *Screenplay. The Foundations of Screenwriting. A Step-by-Step Guide from Concept to Finished Script* (New York: Dell Publishing, 1994).

—*The Definitive Guide to Screenwriting* (London: Ebury, 2003).

Frensham, Ray, *Screenwriting* (London: Hodder and Stoughton, 2003).

—*Break into Screenwriting* (London: Teach Yourself, 2010).

Freud, Sigmund, *Civilization and Its Discontents*, trans. David McLintock (London: Penguin, 2002).

Fromm, Erich, *The Art of Loving* (London: Unwin Books, 1970).

—*To Have or To Be?* (London: Abacus, 1988).

Godard, Jean-Luc, *Alphaville*, trans. Peter Whitehead (London: Faber and Faber, 2000).

Goldberg, Natalie, *Writing Down The Bones – Freeing the Writer Within* (Shambhala Books).

Goldman, William, *Which Lie Did I Tell? More Adventures in the Screen Trade* (London: Bloomsbury, 2001).

Gray, John, *Black Mass: Apocalyptic Religion and the Death of Utopia* (London: Penguin, 2007).

—*Straw Dogs. Thoughts on Humans and Other Animals* (London: Granta Books, 2001).

Grove, Elliot, *Raindance Writers' Lab: Write and Sell the Hot Screenplay* (Oxford: Focal Press, 2001).

Guignon, Charles, *On Being Authentic* (London: Routledge, 2004).

Gyatso, Geshe Kelsang, *The New Meditation Handbook* (Ulverston: Tharpa Publications, 2003).

Hjort, Mette and Scott MacKenzie (eds), *Purity and Provocation. Dogme 95* (London: British Film Institute, 2003).

Hodges, Mike, *Get Carter* (Suffolk: ScreenPress Books, 1999).

Hollows, Joanne and Mark Jancovich (eds), *Approaches to Popular Film* (Manchester: Manchester University Press, 1995).

Holy Bible. New International Version (Grand Rapids, MI: Zondervan, 1996).

Horeck, Tanya and Tina Kendall (eds), *The New Extremism in Cinema – from France to Europe* (Edinburgh: Edinburgh University Press, 2011).

Jaffé, Aniela, *From the Life and Work of C.G. Jung*, trans. R. F. C. Hull (New York: Harper and Row, 1970).

Jameson, Frederic, *Signatures of the Visible* (London: Routledge, 1992).

Jancovich, Mark, 'Screen Theory', in Joanne Hollows and Mark Jancovich (eds), *Approaches to Popular Film* (Manchester: Manchester University Press, 1995), pp. 124–50.

Jenks, Chris, *Transgression* (London: Routledge, 2002).

Jung, C. G., *Synchronicity. An Acausal Connecting Principle*, trans. R. F. C. Hull (London: Routledge and Kegan Paul, 1972).

Kallas, Christina, *Creative Screenwriting: Understanding Emotional Structure* (Basingstoke: Palgrave, 2010).

Kaufman, Scott and James C. Kaufman (eds), *The Psychology of Creative Writing* (Cambridge: Cambridge University Press, 2009).

Kellner, Douglas, *Critical Theory, Marxism and Modernity* (Baltimore: Johns Hopkins University Press, 1992).

Leane, Elle and Ian Buchanan, 'What's Left of Theory?', *Continuum. Journal of Media and Cultural Studies*, Vol. 16, No 3, November 2002, pp. 253–8.

Lee, Jason, *The Metaphysics of Mass Art*, Vol. II (New York: Mellen, 1999).

—*Pervasive Perversions. Paedophilia and Child Sexual Abuse in Media/Culture* (London: Free Association Books, 2005).

—*Celebrity, Ideology and American Culture* (New York: Cambria, 2010a), pp. 179–90.

—*Seeing Galileo* (Canterbury: Gylphi, 2010b), p. 56.

—*Shooting Panda's? Editing for Creative Writers* (Derby: Derby University Press, 2010c).

—*Cultures of Addiction* (Cambria: New York, 2012).

Lehman, Ernest, *North by Northwest* (London: Faber and Faber, 1999).

Maitland, Sara, *A Book of Silence* (London: Granta, 2008).

Mantel, Hillary, *Beyond Black* (London: Fourth Estate, 2005).

Maras, Steve, *Screenwriting: History, Theory and Practice* (London: Wallflower, 2008).

Marks, John, *Gilles Deleuze, Vitalism and Multiplicity* (London: Pluto Press, 1998).

McGrath, Declan, *Screenwriting* (Switzerland: Mies, 2003).

McKee, Robert, *Story. Substance, Structure, Style, and the Principles of Screenwriting* (London: Methuen, 1999).

Metz, Christian, *The Imaginary Signifier. Psychoanalysis and the Cinema*, trans. Celia Briton (Bloomington: Indiana University Press, 1977).

Moritz, Charlie, *Scriptwriting for the Screen* (London: Routledge, 2008).

Mules, Warwick, 'In Absence of the Human' in *Continuum. Journal of Media and Cultural Studies*, Vol. 16, No 3, November 2002, pp. 259–71.

Mumford, Lewis, *The Myth of the Machine* (New York: Harcourt, Brace & World, 1967).

Nietzsche, Friedrich, *The Birth of Tragedy* and *The Genealogy of Morals*, trans. Francis Golffing (New York: Doubleday, 1956).

—*Twilight of the Gods* and *The Anti-Christ*, trans. R. J. Hollingdale (London: Penguin, 1968).

—*Daybreak. Thoughts on the Prejudices of Morality*, trans. R. J. Hollingdale (Cambridge: Cambridge University Press, 1986).

Parker, Philip, *The Art and Science of Screenwriting* (Exeter: Intellect, 1999).

Pfohl, Stephen, *Death at the Parasite Cafe. Social Science (fictions) and the Postmodern* (London: Macmillan, 1992).

Pink, Thomas, *Free Will* (Oxford: Oxford University Press, 2004).

Potter, Sally, *Orlando*, (London: Faber and Faber, 1994).

Proulx, Annie, Larry McMurtry and Diana Ossana, *Brokeback Mountain – Story to Screenplay* (London: HarperCollins, 2010).

Rahula, Walpola Sri, *What the Buddha Taught* (Bangkok: Haw Trai Foundation, 1995).

Ramachandran, V. S., *The Tell-Tale Brain. Unlocking the Mystery of Human Nature* (London: Windmill, 2012).

Ridley, M. R. (ed.), *The Arden Shakespeare Othello* (London: Methuen, 1979).

del Río, Elena, *Deleuze and the Cinemas of Performance. Powers of Affection* (Edinburgh: Edinburgh University Press, 2006).

Riso, Don Richard, *Personality Types. Using the Enneagram for Self-Discovery* (London: HarperCollins: 1998).

Robinson, Paul, *The Freudian Left. Wilhelm Reich, Geza Roheím and Herbert Marcuse* (New York: Harper and Row, 1969).

Russ, Sandra W., 'Pretend Play, Emotional Processes, and Developing Narratives', in Scott Barry Kaufman and James C. Kaufman (eds), *The Psychology of Creative Writing* (Cambridge: Cambridge University Press, 2009), pp. 247–63.

Said, Edward, *Culture and Imperialism* (London: Vintage, 1993).

Schrader, Paul, *Taxi Driver* (London: Faber and Faber, 1990).

Scott, Kevin Conroy, *Screenwriters' Master Class. Screenwriters Talk about their Greatest Movies* (London: Faber and Faber, 2005).

Segal, Robert, *Myth* (Oxford: Oxford University Press, 2004).

Selden, Raman, Peter Widdowson and Peter Brooker, *A Reader's Guide to Contemporary Literary Theory* (London: Prentice Hall, 1997).

Skinner, B. F., *Beyond Freedom and Dignity* (London: Penguin, 1988).

Sontag, Susan (ed.), *A Barthes Reader* (New York: Hill and Wang, 1982).

Stam, Robert, Robert Burgoyne and Sandy Flitterman-Lewis, *New Vocabularies in Film Semiotics.Structuralism, Post-Structuralism and Beyond* (London: Routledge, 1992).

Stegner, Wallace, *On the Teaching of Creative Writing* (New Hampshire: University Press of New England, 1980).

Stein, Sol, *Solutions for Novelists. Secrets of a Master Editor* (London: Souvenir Press, 2000).

Stevens, Anthony, *On Jung* (London: Penguin, 1990).

Stevenson, Jack, *Dogme Uncut. Lars von Trier, Thomas Vinterberg, and the Gang That Took on Hollywood* (Santa Monica, CA: Santa Monica Press, 2003).

Tallis, Frank, *Hidden Minds. A History of the Unconscious* (New York: Helios Press, 2012).

Tracy, David, *Dialogue with the Other: the Inter-religious Dialogue* (Louvain: Peters Press, 1990).

Vogel, Amos, *Film as a Subversive Art* (New York: Random House, 1974).

Vogel, Christopher, *The Writer's Journey. Mythic Structure for Storytellers and Screenwriters* (London: Pan Books, 1999).

Wagner, Jerome, *The Enneagram Spectrum of Personality Styles* (Portland: Metamorphous Press, 1996).

Wheen, Francis, *How Mumbo-Jumbo Conquered the World* (London: HarperCollins, 2004).

Wills, David and Peter Brunette, *Screen/Play. Derrida and Film Theory* (Princeton: Princeton University Press, 1989).

Woolf, Virginia, *Orlando – a Biography* (London: Vintage, 1992).

Woolley, Benjamin, *The Queen's Conjuror. The Life and Magic of Dr Dee* (Flamingo: London, 2002).

Index